Private Lives, Public Policy

100 YEARS OF STATE INTERVENTION IN THE FAMILY

by Jane Ursel

women's
PRESS

CANADIAN CATALOGUING IN PUBLICATION DATA
Ursel, Jane, 1948–

Private lives and public policy
Includes bibliographical references and index.
ISBN 0-88961-159-9

1. Family policy — Canada — History. 2. Social legislation — Canada —
History. 3. Social structure — Canada. 4. Patriarchy. I. Title.
HQ560.U77 1992   306.85′0971   C92-094131-1

Editors: Sue Findlay, Maureen FitzGerald
Copy editor: Ellen Quigley
Cover design: Sunday Harrison
Index: Beth McAuley
Cover photo ("Sisters"): Eleanor Gelmo
Cover photographs courtesy of Jane Ursel, Maureen FitzGerald and
Canadian Women's Movement Archives/Archives canadiennes du
mouvement des femmes.

For information address: Women's Press, Suite 233, 517 College Street,
Toronto, Ontario, Canada M6G 4A2.

This book was produced by the collective effort of Women's Press.
Women's Press gratefully acknowledges the financial support of the
Canada Council and the Ontario Arts Council.

Printed and bound in Canada
1 2 3 4 5 1996 1995 1994 1993 1992

To my parents
Angela and Charlie Ursel

Contents

PART 3

APPENDICES

List of Tables

Acknowledgements

This book was a very long time in the making and in the process I have benefited from institutional and individual support. The fact that I ever finished this study is due to the progressive politics of the Graduate Studies Department at McMaster University, that permits students who have experienced significant interruptions in their work to return, upon completion of their dissertation, to be reinstated as a student and to graduate. I did so after many years absence at the encouragement of Alf Hunter, who was at the time head of the Department of Sociology and with the willingness of Vivienne Walters, my advisor, to revisit a dissertation she had begun to supervise many years earlier. While there is much academic research and many government studies that identify differences in men's and women's career lines, few institutions seem prepared to accommodate these differences. I am extremely grateful for the support I received from McMaster University.

The other institution which made this book possible is Women's Press. Women's Press has become an important Canadian institution which has a long history of encouraging women's research and writing. Much of the inspiration for this study came from earlier publications of the press. I am particularly grateful to Sue Findlay and Maureen FitzGerald of Women's Press for their firm and sensitive editing and most importantly their generosity and support over the long haul.

Ideas are always the product of more than one mind and I am especially indebted to two colleagues at the University of Manitoba, Wayne Taylor and Steve Brickey, for sharing their ideas and responding to mine. They have been my most rigorous critics and my most enthusiastic supporters who have spent innumerable hours reading different drafts and discussing different ways to conceptualize the processes of change I was documenting. They have been the core of my intellectual community over the past decade as well as two of my closest friends. Other colleagues who have been an important source of support are Pat and Hugh Armstrong, Roberta Hamilton, Pam Smith and Raymond Currie.

Finally, I owe a special debt to several women who kept me sane during my years in government and encouraged me in this project. Dale McKenzie, Marlene Bertrand, Joan Eliesen, Elisabeth Wagner, Diane de Lucia and Roz Silversides — who were there to remind me that good women, good feminists work in government too!

Introduction

When we look at women's struggles today — the ones we've won (decriminalization of abortion, reform of family law) and the ones we continue to fight for (pay equity, daycare, affirmative action, to name a few) all have a common focus: the state. We fight to remove laws that discriminate against us and for laws that will protect us from the violence and discrimination in our society. Even when our struggles are located in the home (around issues of violence, custody or child support) or in the work place (around issues of harassment, pay scales or promotion) we invoke the state and the law to further our cause. We fight for policies that will provide more opportunity for ourselves and our children and increasingly we are fighting a rear-guard action against the dismantling of the welfare state. Women know, first hand, that when social services are cut the needs they met do not disappear. Cut backs in care for the elderly, daycare, social assistance or medicare translate directly and immediately into more work and responsibility for daughters, mothers, wives.

Women are increasingly vigilant of the changes in law and social policy that so dramatically and directly effect our every day life. Will the new "rape shield" law provide the protection women need from the engrained double standard and the normalization of violence in our culture? Will we be on trial if we report being raped or will the assailant? How will federal transfer payments and provincial social assistance enhance or inhibit our opportunities? Will we be able to get an education and raise our children as single mothers? Can we keep our jobs and our sanity and care for our elderly and/or disabled parents if home care and public health budgets are once again cut? These are the decisions women face every day and some of the many ways in which the state impacts upon our lives.

The centrality of the state to women's struggles and women's lives has given rise to an important debate among feminists concerning the patriarchal content and intent of the state. Is the state a power women can invoke to dismantle patriarchy or is it a tool of patriarchal interests? Given the variable outcomes of women's struggles to date, is it possible that the state is a contested terrain on which struggles for and against patriarchy are waged? If the state is in fact a contested terrain, how do women determine the issues on which state involvement would be helpful from those in which it would be harmful? Experience has taught women to be cautious about the state. Will we be in a better or worse situation if the state regulates reproductive technology, are we more or less protected if shelters for battered women are largely funded and hence largely dependent on the state? These are important strategic questions that require a better understanding of the nature and dynamic of patriarchy and its relation to the state.

It is increasingly recognized in feminist analysis that the operation of patriarchy today is substantially different than it was in the past and that one of the most significant differences is the extent to which the state has become involved. Some feminists now make a distinction between "familial patriarchy," which represents the experience of the past in which power and authority over women and children was largely exercised in the home, and "social patriarchy" typical of modern welfare states, in which support for and control over women and children increasingly resides in laws, institutions and the state. Ironically, at the very time women are organizing to fight the dismantling of the welfare state, we are also for the first time questioning its effect on the status of women.

Is the welfare state merely the benevolent face of social patriarchy? Some writers suggest that the welfare state simply represents the transition from private to public dependence for women (Hernes 1987). Others perceive a more complex and puzzling pattern. They identify social patriarchy as characterized by the state's dual and contradictory tendencies to structure women's collective subordination while championing individual rights to equality (Borchorst and Siim 1987). The puzzle of patriarchal dynamics and the strategic questions they give rise to today all point to the need for very specific evidence on the patriarchal content and intent of the state. This study is an attempt to contribute to that body of evidence.

The object of this study is to analyze the relationship between the institution structured by patriarchy (the family) and the institution that has become the terrain of struggle over patriarchy (the state). I document the dynamic and changing relationship between the family, the state and patriarchy through an analysis of changes in family, labour and welfare law over approximately a century of Canadian history. This project is both theoretical and historical. Theoretical because, although the consequences of patriarchy are well understood, the dynamics remain an enigma. It is known that patriarchy is universally present in written history, and it is known that its form and function differ at different points in time, however, it is not well known how these transformations occur, and contribute to patriarchy's overall persistence. I identify the need for greater clarity in theorizing reproduction is a precondition to specifying the dynamics of patriarchy and its relation to the state.

This study is historical because it documents the transformation from familial to social patriarchy associated with Canada's transition to a modern, industrialized nation. The study of a process of transformation is revealing in a number of ways. First, the transition from familial to social patriarchy is the process of increasing state involvement in the family and patriarchy — thus, a good starting point for identifying the patriarchal content of the state. Second, transitions are revealing because the often obscured relations between the family and the state become more observable when disruptions and realignments provoke escalated and more explicit patterns of state intervention. Finally, tracing the relationship of the state to the family over a hundred years gives us a sense of the trajectory of state intervention and hopefully a sense of the patriarchal intent of the state.

The Theory

Having described why the state is so compelling to women, my theoretical concerns focus on determining why women are so compelling to the state. The history of the state's increasing involvement in the family is also a history of the state's increasing involvement in women's lives. At the outset, I undertake to explain the state's growing and changing interest in women's bodies and women's work. My starting point is the structure of society. It seemed to me that the key to understanding the dynamic and changing forms of patriarchy lies not simply in understanding its subordinating effect on women, but in understanding what this effect achieves for the social system as a whole. It is the social system as a whole and not individual men in isolation that supports and perpetuates patriarchy. Turning my attention to the structural dynamics of a society, I focus on the most fundamental processes all societies must organize: the reproduction of its population and the production of resources to provide for that population. I explore the idea that the key to understanding the particular form and function of patriarchy at a given time lies in understanding the organization of and interaction between these two fundamental processes of production and reproduction.

Pursuing this train of thought permits identification of the family, in all its various historical formations, as the relations of reproduction. I define reproduction quite specifically as the production of human life which involves three processes: procreation, socialization and daily maintenance. I define patriarchy, in all its various historical formations, as the hierarchical structuring of reproductive relations, operative in most known societies as *the means of controlling reproduction*. This is achieved through a variety of systems of interpersonal and institutional divisions, foremost of which is the sexual division of labour, all of which have the effect of excluding women from the control of their bodies and their labour. I suggest that patriarchy is not a goal but a tool, and women's subordination is not an end but a means. The purpose of patriarchy is the control of reproduction.

Starting with the end result, the control of reproduction, the divergent and changing dynamics of patriarchy can be located in the divergent and changing systems of organizing reproduction. How reproduction is organized and why it changes over time is tied to its interaction with production, the other fundamental, irreducible necessity of human life. Each sphere has its own dynamic. The production of a car involves fundamentally different social relations than the production of human life. Each sphere has a distinct time frame. A production cycle can be daily, weekly or yearly, while a reproduction cycle is generational. However, the relation between the two spheres is co-determinative. A society cannot produce without human labour, it cannot reproduce its labour supply without the products of production. To specify the dynamics of patriarchy, within this co-determinative relation, I propose a theory of modes of reproduction, outlined in a description of communal, familial and social patriarchy, which coincide and interact with distinct modes of production. Just as class captures the fundamental character of productive relations in most recorded history, so patriarchy captures the fundamental character of reproductive relations in most known societies. Neither relation is inherent to the human condition, but rather a product of particular accommodations between the spheres of production and reproduction.

Given the identification of distinct modes of production and reproduction with distinct dynamics, the possibility of conflict or disjunctures between the two systems arises. This study documents how the organization of production around the wage-labour system comes into direct conflict with the organization of reproduction around the patriarchal system. The wage-labour system pays only for the labour it consumes, making no provision for the costs of reproducing a future labour supply or maintaining the dependants of the worker. This process, referred to as the commodification of labour, separates reproductive costs from productive costs, successfully producing profits for employers, while leaving the issue of reproduction unconsidered and unaddressed. Patriarchy is a particular form of organizing reproduction. Reproduction requires labour and income resources in order to function. Thus, the wage-labour system and the patriarchal system confront one another over the division of income and labour resources between the two spheres.

The relation of the state to the family is located in the context of this conflict between the interests of production and the requirements of reproduction. I identify the role of the state is as mediator, intervening in both spheres to co-ordinate the exchange of income and labour resources between them. However, state mediation is bound by its dual commitment to the wage-labour system and patriarchy, resulting in policies that simultaneously mediate and perpetuate the contradictory structures of production and reproduction. This dual allegiance implicates the state in a process of escalating and divergent intervention strategies, as policies that ameliorate the symptoms of conflict are, at best, an incomplete and inconsistent response to the underlying structural contradiction.

The Method

The application of structural analysis to the study of family-state relations directs attention to the macro-dynamics of production, reproduction and state restructuring. Utilizing an historical materialist methodology, my research strategy was to undertake a study broad enough to capture the three processes in transition and specific enough to attend to the particular issues of reproduction and patriarchy. As a result I selected an eighty-four-year time frame, three fields of legislative intervention (family, labour and welfare law) and three jurisdictions (Manitoba, Ontario and the federal government) in which to observe the changing dynamics between production, reproduction and the state. I am bold enough to claim coverage of a century in the title of this book, because I identify legislative processes leading up to the eighty-four years under review, as well as changing intervention strategies subsequent to the eighty-four-year period.

The time frame selected covers major processes of restructuring in all three entities. The eighty-four years encompasses the restructuring of production through the ascendency of the wage-labour system, the restructuring of reproduction through the development of social patriarchy and the restructuring of the state that was required to keep pace with the increasing necessity of intervention. The combination of a broad time frame and a specific focus on reproduction reveals two patterns of particular interest to the study of family-state dynamics. First, the ongoing tension between production and reproduction is reflected in a process of continual and successive displacement of the costs of reproduction away from production onto the family, then the municipality, then the province and, eventually, onto the nation state. This process identifies the material basis of the increasing dependence of the family on the state. Second, this process of displacement results in an increasing centralization of authority over and responsibility for the family within the state. This centralization of authority and support for reproduction captures the essence of the transition from familial to social patriarchy, identifying the material basis of the related development of social patriarchy and the welfare state. As the state evolves in its relation to women and children, as provider and patriarch, we better understand why it has become the focal point of struggle over reproductive and family-life issues.

In selecting legislative fields that reflect reproductive and productive dynamics, I identified family, labour and welfare law. These statutes are particularly revealing of state efforts to mediate production and reproduction because they serve to regulate flows of labour and resources within and between the two spheres. Thus, they are the best indicators of the pressures and tensions in the intersection of production and reproduction. Further, as primary state mechanisms for co-ordinating the two spheres, they clearly express the two tendencies of state intervention — support and regulation.

The selection of Ontario, Manitoba and the federal governments provides a multi-jurisdictional vantage point to consider the uneven and combined effects of development and reform in Canada. Given that each province was characterized by different levels and timing of development, and each jurisdiction was characterized by different administrative capacities, the most remarkable feature of the multi-jurisdictional review is the rapidity with which legislative interventions were diffused throughout the country. This discovery speaks to how fundamental and compelling the dynamics of production and reproduction are.

In analyzing the legislation, I divide the review into periods according to the changing manifestations of the contradiction between production and reproduction and the changing mediation strategies that developed over time. In determining the boundaries of each period, I identify key indicators of the interaction within and between the two spheres. Structural indicators are evidence of the source and severity of imbalance between production and reproduction that operate as the structural triggers to state intervention. They include: the state of the economy, labour supply as determined by birth rates and immigration rates, the gap between wages and reproductive costs, social and demographic factors affecting reproductive costs and the degree to which productive relations interrupt or are perceived to interrupt family reproductive patterns as indicated by women's employment rate. A second set of indicators are the conditions and directions of social struggle, specifically class struggle and women's struggle, which serve to translate the structural pressures into political pressure for state intervention. Finally, the degree of rationalization and centralization of the state is an important indicator of mediation potential, since the state capacity to intervene is determined by the structural capacities of the state system itself.

Dividing the time frame into periods helps to capture the complexity of the process of changing structural tensions and changing state interventions while maintaining a focus on the larger dynamic — state mediation of the restructuring of production and reproduction. Analysis of the shifting determinants of pressure and conflict between production and reproduction suggests that each period opens with a different manifest problem and that state activity within the period is designed to alleviate the particular problem. The first period (1884–1913) begins with growing evidence of a structural disorganization of reproduction and mounting public concern about the future of the family. The crisis is defined as the use of women and children in the labour force and the consequent disruptions of family dynamics. The state response was largely regulative and served to restrict the use of women and children in production (labour law) and enforce familial responsibility for support of its members (family law). The legislative and social discouragement of women's employment in combination with the legislative enforcement of men's role as providers created the support-service marriage structure, the male-breadwinner, female-home-maker division of labour. This marriage structure retained the primacy of women's reproductive role and preserved her position of dependency — both critical components for the control of reproduction. However, preserving these conditions of control within the wage-labour system transformed the head of household — the family "patriarch" — into a breadwinner, beginning the transition from familial to social patriarchy.

The success of the state's intervention strategy in the first period led to a different manifest problem in the second period (1914–39). The successful enactment of legislation that modified the use of labour in production and protected the family as the reproductive unit, without altering the fundamental dynamic of the wage-labour system, led to an income crisis for the family. By virtue of protecting the family's reproductive functions, the state limited the access of certain members (women and children) to employment. As a result, the number of employed and paid members of the family shrank as the number of dependent members grew. In response to the income crisis of the second period, state intervention involved the development of more systematic structures for the support of the family (welfare law), while extending the limitations on female and child labour (labour law) and elaborating on legislation to ensure familial support of its members (family law). The innovations of this period involved new welfare statutes, new tax laws and the development of provincial welfare departments as the state became increasingly involved in socializing the costs of reproduction. State intervention during this period occurred largely at the provincial level, as the state both regulated and underwrote the sexual division of labour and the support-service marriage structure.

In the third period (1940–68), the contradictions between production and reproduction manifested separately as an income shortage at the household level and a labour shortage at the production level. As a result, the central task of the state became one of realignment of income and labour flows between the two spheres and a restructuring of the state to accommodate the increasing demand to socialize the costs of reproduction. The consequences of this realignment were the modern welfare state, the absorption of women in the labour force and the erosion of the support-service marriage structure. In each period the state's efforts to co-ordinate the flows of income and labour between the two spheres resulted in the centralization within the state of support for, and authority over, reproduction. Thus, each period traces a major step in the transition from familial to social patriarchy.

Reading Options

This book was written with the understanding that different readers will have different interests. Thus, the theory, history and data sections can be read somewhat independently. In the first section I outline an historical materialist theory of reproduction. This was necessary for me in order to make sense of my research. However, for readers primarily interested in the historical section, it may not be particularly compelling. As a result, I have included a quick summary of my theoretical perspective in this introduction as a reasonable orientation for those who may choose to begin with Part 2.

The bulk of this book is the historical review in which I document the changing relation between the family and the state over a century of Canadian history. Part 2 begins with an historical backdrop to the events of the first period. I examine evidence of growing conflict between production and reproduction resulting from the introduction of the wage-labour system. I also examine the development of the Social Reform Movement that arose to protest the conditions of the family at the turn of the century and suggest that this movement was the architect of social patriarchy, the state its engineer. This is followed by reviews of legislative interventions in each of the three periods (1884–1913, 1914–39 and 1940–68). The third period is sub-divided because of the unique role of the state as manager of the Canadian economy during the Second World War. The first chronological sub-period covers the war years (1940–47), when the state was both manager and mediator. The latter deals with the post-war period (1948–68). In conclusion (Part 3), I consider some contemporary strategic issues that face feminists in light of the historic role of the state.

The appendices contain a discussion of the methodology of this project, as well as a chronological listing of enactments, amendments and repeals of family, labour and welfare statutes for the three periods and three jurisdictions under review. It is the metaphorical basement of this book, not only because it provides the empirical underpinnings of the analysis of each chapter, but more literally because it is the distillation of my years of research in the basements of law schools and archives in Manitoba and Ontario. It seemed a pity for these legislative chronologies not to be unearthed for those interested in research in this field.

PART 1

Towards a Theory
of Reproduction

Feminist theory has developed over the past two decades in an attempt to write women and reproduction into social analysis. Among feminists various theoretical strategies have been pursued, all of which revolve around the conceptualization of reproduction. Until recently two schools of thought, radical feminist and Marxist feminist, have tended to dominate structural theories of reproduction. The radical-feminist strategy[1] is to assert the primacy of reproduction in social relations to ensure its centrality in analysis and provide a clear focus on the continuity of patriarchal relations over time. However, their particular focus on the consequences of patriarchy to the exclusion of the processes of patriarchy results in little analytic capacity to address the issues of historical specificity and change. Conversely, the Marxist feminist[2] strategy asserts the primacy of production in social relations utilizing an historical materialist method to analyze specificity and change in patriarchal relations over time. However, their reliance on the "production is primary" principle frequently renders reproductive relations as passive and/or opaque.

Dual systems theory has evolved in response to the polarization of radical feminists and Marxist feminists on the issue of reproduction. It seeks to retain all of the insights and richness of the radical-feminist perspective, while at the same time incorporating the strengths of an historical materialist analysis. Proponents of this perspective back away from choosing whether it is class first or gender first that explains the dynamics of domination in our society. Instead, they identify reproduction and production as equally fundamental and interdependent social relations and posit "two systems" (Delphy 1984; Hartman 1979) or a "dual base" (O'Brien 1981; Eisenstein 1979) as the starting point of their analysis. I selected this model as my theoretical starting point because it appears to integrate the strengths of the two major schools of feminist structural analysis.

The works of M. O'Brien and Z. Eisenstein represent the most rigorous attempts to come to terms with the structure and dynamics of reproduction and patriarchy within a dual-systems model. As such their work was most influential in my attempts to theorize reproduction and specify patriarchy. Eisenstein and O'Brien begin with the premise that patriarchy is at one and the same time universal and historically specific and both identify its direction and dynamic in the struggle to control reproduction. I begin with O'Brien's assertion that reproduction has a dynamic of its own and her observation that specifying this dynamic becomes achievable when reproduction ceases to be derived from production. However, I rely most heavily on the work of Eisenstein when it comes to specifying the interaction between production and reproduction. She observes that the interests and dynamic of production and reproduction are not only separate and interdependent but are also often in conflict. From this observation she locates the connection between the state and patriarchy within the state's role as mediator of production and reproduction, which thereby maintains the system as a whole. Her work directed my attention to the interaction between the state, the family and patriarchy which became the focus for this study. Although I am particularly indebted to O'Brien and Eisenstein, in attempting to theorize the relationship between reproduction, production, patriarchy and the state, I have drawn on the works of a wide range of feminist theorists, historians and anthropologists of the past two decades.

Dual-Systems Model
and the Problem of Evidence

The assertion that production and reproduction are distinct but interdependent imperatives that constitute the base of society requires that the analyst using this framework be able to demonstrate the impact of each sphere on the other.

Evidence of the impact of production on reproduction is abundantly cited by Marxist scholars; thus, the real test of the co-determinative model is its ability to reveal the impact of reproduction on production. Arguments for the production determines model are enhanced by the immediacy of the impact of production on reproduction. For example, a major crisis in production like the Great Depression immediately reduces the supply of essential goods needed to sustain reproduction and, not surprisingly, results in declining marriage and fertility rates. Observers schooled in the production-determined model expect parallel evidence of the impact of reproduction. However, production and reproduction have dramatically different dynamics and completion times in terms of the product of their labour. A change in reproduction patterns will not be felt for fifteen or twenty years — the time required to transform a human infant into a productive labourer. While the short completion time of a productive process makes its impact on reproduction much easier to trace and therefore more evident, it is wrong to assume that reproduction does not exert an equally important (although time-delayed) impact upon production.

The delayed effect of reproduction makes its impact much less apparent because of the wide range of changes that can occur in twenty years and because of the large number of adaptations (e.g., immigration, emigration, guest workers, flight of capital, changing reproductive laws, etc.) that can be introduced in that time period to mitigate the effect. The impact of reproductive changes is nevertheless there, and its importance can be seen by the serious pursuit of adaptations to pre-empt any troublesome consequences produced by such changes. In fact, it is often the adaptations that serve as our only evidence of the impact of reproduction, since the very seriousness of labour supplies means that social systems cannot permit much margin of error in this regard.

The pursuit of evidence of the interdependence of the two spheres does not hinge on observations of short-term fluctuations in population or production, but rather seeks to explore the historic operation of patriarchy in widely divergent modes of production as a key to locating the subtle operation of the reproductive imperative.

Reconceptualizing Reproduction

To locate the subtle imperative of reproduction, it is essential to identify and specify the components and dynamics of this sphere. While there is a vast literature on the components and the dynamics of production[3] the most systematic analyses of reproduction are often found in anthropological literature.

Feminist anthropologist G. Rubin provides a first step in the identification of the components of reproduction with her concept of a sex-gender system as "…a set of arrangements by which the biological raw material of human sex and procreation is shaped by human, social intervention and satisfied in a conventional manner" (Rubin 1975, 165). In locating the components of the system she begins with C. Levi-Strauss's provocative observation that "…the sexual division of labour is nothing else than a devise to institute a reciprocal state of dependency between the sexes" (Levi-

Strauss 1971, 348). He reverses the usual understanding of the relation between gender and divisions of labour, arguing that sexual divisions of labour precede and create gender. People are engendered, he states, in order that marriage be guaranteed. From this perspective, sexual divisions of labour are seen not as some productive concession to biological differences, but rather a conscientious structuring of productive relations in the interests of the social organization of reproduction.

Rubin suggests that the necessity to engender in order to ensure marriage implies a radical questioning of all human sexual arrangements, in which no aspect of sexuality is taken for granted, including a predisposition to heterosexuality. She concludes that heterosexuality, the most fundamental prerequisite of procreation, is an instituted process. Based upon Levi-Strauss's deductions, Rubin identifies three critical components of reproduction that operate at the most general level: the sexual division of labour, gender and the structural enforcement/re-enforcement of heterosexuality.

The second feature, the dynamic of reproduction, is the process by which a society manages reproductive relations as well as co-ordinates the relation between production and reproduction. C. Meillassoux (1981) provides useful concepts for analyzing this dynamic. He argues that all societies must maintain a viable ratio of productive and unproductive members in the community. This ratio is achieved by regulating procreation rates so that each generation of productive adults produces and supports a sufficient number of children so as to ensure a future labour supply as adults age and become less productive. This ratio is in turn predicated on a ratio within the sphere of reproduction — the ratio of active reproducers to nonreproducers within the system. Thus, the regulation of procreation calls into play the operation of the sex-gender system, with its rules of marriage, sexual taboos and practices that operate to vary fertility rates according to the requirements of the society.

From this dynamic the intersection between the modes of production and reproduction can be located as an exchange of resources: labour resources, the product of reproductive relations, are exchanged for subsistence resources, the product of productive relations. Variation in resource allocation flows can alter the demographic composition which in turn can alter the productive capacity through changing current and future labour supplies. This approach effectively replaces the Marxist model in which production is said to determine reproduction with a model of co-determination. Any given economy or productive capacity (if we take that as our arbitrary starting point) is itself determined by the existing demographic composition (labour supply) of the community, which in turn is a product of prior interactions between the productive and reproductive modes. Conceived in this way, the relation between production and reproduction is cyclical or dialectical rather than linear or parallel.

At this abstract level it is possible to conceive of the organization of reproduction involving specific allocations of labour on the basis of age and sex and some restrictions of male and female sexual behaviour that does not, at least in theory, necessitate the subordination of women. However, the emergence of patriarchy as a means of organizing reproduction alters both the components and dynamic of the sex-gender system as outlined above. In addition to the sexual division of labour, gender and compulsory heterosexuality, female subordination now becomes a fundamental component of the system. The essential condition for the subordination of women within any patriarchal system is *control of women's access to the means of their livelihood*. By making women's access to subsistence contingent on entry into particular reproductive relations or by restricting their ability to be self-sufficient, women's labour, both productive and reproductive, becomes subject to comprehensive control. This control is the essence of patriarchy, its universal function and effect. The means of achieving control, however, varies according to the political and economic structure of the social system in question.

In order to specify the different types of patriarchy, to further our understanding of the interaction between production and reproduction, the concept of modes of reproduction is introduced. Three distinctive modes of organizing reproduction can be enumerated. These are (a) *communal patriarchy*, which corresponds with pre-class, kin-based social systems; (b) *familial patriarchy*, which corresponds with class-structured social systems characterized by decentralized processes of production; and (c) *social patriarchy*, which corresponds to advanced wage-labour systems. Although this study is primarily concerned with the transition from familial patriarchy to social patriarchy, it seems worthwhile to briefly outline all three systems in order to explicate the nature of the productive-reproductive dynamic.

Communal Patriarchy

The transition from simple male-female interdependency to hierarchical interdependency (female subordination) has provoked a lively debate among feminists concerning the origins of female oppression. Meillassoux's work provides an interesting alternative that avoids the usual biological/psychological differences of the sexes debate and concentrates on social responses to the reproductive imperative.

He locates the origins of women's subordination in the demographic problems peculiar to early, small social systems. He argues that the major demographic problem of small band communities was the necessity of ensuring an adequate ratio of productive and nonproductive members within the group at any given time — a ratio which could only be achieved by a fairly continuous pattern of procreation. However, sustained procreation in small demographic units is continually threatened by such accidents as morbidity, sterility, premature deaths, sex-ratio imbalances. Therefore, the reproduction and survival of the community depends on the political capacities of the communities to negotiate an adequate number of women at all times.

According to Meillassoux, the origins of women's subordination lie in their essential and irreplaceable function as reproducers, which motivates communities to impose the first sex-specific restraint — control over women's mobility. Effective, enforceable control over women's movement, however, presumes a generalized control over women.

When such a system coexists with communal divisions of goods and property, it does not necessarily imply overt oppression, but is clearly predicated upon female subordination. The very communal nature of communal patriarchy suggests that women's position is not necessarily characterized by a slavish subordination to or dependence on a particular spouse, for authority does not lie within a male spouse/father *per se*, but within the large male-dominated kinship network. Because authority relations between men and women are not atomized at the household level, because women's subordination is to the larger male kin network (including uncles, fathers, brothers, as well as husbands), this would tend to direct male dominance to the determination of the parameters of productive and reproductive work. Communal patriarchy could, at least in theory, allow women some degree of autonomy and maneuverability within the male-determined framework.

Thus the sex-gender system under communal patriarchy requires a generalized subordination of women but does not necessitate a particularized oppression of women by husbands/fathers. To have said this does not imply that such oppression will not occur, only that it is not essential to the operation of the sex-gender system in this form.[4]

Meillassoux provides us with an explanation of a gender-stratified system as a means of controlling reproduction, highlighting the operation of the reproductive imperative. The egalitarian principle of "those who do the work make the decisions" is replaced by a patriarchal system in which those who do the reproductive work (women) are excluded from major decision making that affects the work. That is the essence of patriarchy, its universal feature, its purpose and effect. At this stage it is predicated upon a centralization of authority out of the hands of all members of the community and into the hands of males as a class.

While this first form of alienation has a profound impact upon women, their bodies and their work, it does not result in a complete dichotomy between production and reproduction. At this stage (pre-class, gender stratified), male decision making occurs within a kin-based system which, while potentially less sensitive to the interests of women, is still confined to a structure (kinship) that links together production and reproduction. One could argue, however, that this first form of alienation facilitated the further separation of production and reproduction characteristic of class-stratified societies.

Reproduction and Class Formation

The processes of alienation and centralization first identified as dynamics of the sex-gender system under communal patriarchy are greatly augmented by the imposition of class stratification upon gender stratification. In "The Formation of the State and the Oppression of Women" (1977), V. Muller outlines the process of increasing centralization associated with class/state formation. She argues that *the* necessary pre-condition for the development of class stratification is the destruction of the unity of production and reproduction that is characteristic of kin-based societies.

Muller maintains that as long as the relations of production are circumscribed by the relations of reproduction, production is geared almost exclusively to consumption. This reflects the egalitarian nature of the distribution of goods and property in which the fundamental stimulus for production is need. Thus, in order for production to be geared to accumulation and exchange (a necessity for the development of a class society), its alienation from reproductive (kin) relations is essential.

The process of transition was gradual, it did not occur immediately through taking the productive functions away from the kin groups but rather was initiated by separating individuals from the productive-reproductive kin group.[5]

In pre-state societies reproduction was regulated and guaranteed by its unity with production, and family relations were structured and stabilized by their unity with the community. This direct relationship was destroyed with the development of state societies. The state was called upon to mediate this relationship, regulating reproduction through a series of laws and edicts in the interests of production. Muller's analysis suggests that state societies reverse the logic of the relationship between production and reproduction: in pre-state societies people produced to meet the needs of the reproductive kin-based group, whereas, in state societies the state regulates reproduction to meet the needs of production. Thus, in pre-state societies it was in the direct material interest of the individual and the kin group to reproduce. In state societies the material advantage of reproduction (the productive potential of the labour power produced) accrues increasingly to those who control production rather than to those who produce and reproduce.

Another consequence of the separation between production and reproduction was the distinction between the social (economic and political sphere) and the familial (reproductive sphere) and a resulting separation in the mechanisms of their organization. It is at this point that Eisenstein's distinction between familial and social patriarchy becomes relevant. In pre-state patriarchal or communal patriarchal societies this distinction does not apply because the family or kin system is the social system. Thus, what is a social mechanism of organization is also a familial mechanism; social and familial patriarchy are one and the same thing because of the unity of production and reproduction. Within the class societies, however, the distinction between social and familial patriarchy becomes much more relevant as the separation between the public/social and private/familial spheres begin to emerge. In fact, this distinction becomes the major criterion for distinguishing the two modes of reproduction operative in class societies.

Familial Patriarchy

The development of class/state societies predicated upon the destruction of the political power of the kinship system and the alienation of production from reproduction served to dismantle the existing kin-based mechanisms for co-ordination of the two spheres. The former system, in which males monopolize decision making (communal patriarchy), is replaced by a more centralized system in which the dominant class has the monopoly on critical decision making. Communal male social authority is reduced to individual male household authority. Thus, communal patriarchy gives way to "familial patriarchy" — a system characterized by the decentralization of male dominance which is subject to and reinforced by the centralized political and economic authority of the dominant class. Patriarchy is maintained as the mechanism of organizing reproduction, but transformed by the separation of the productive and reproductive spheres and the dominance of the former over the latter. The necessity of controlling reproduction within these divisions and making it responsive to class interests results in a division of patriarchy's operation into two spheres, the social and the familial. Social patriarchy is manifest in the laws of marriage, property and inheritance, which preserve male dominance within a class system. Social patriarchy in this system is clearly essential, but also clearly secondary in that the locus of power of patriarchy within this mode is the family. Hence the identification of this mode as familial patriarchy. Eisenstein (1980) uses the term "feudal patriarchy" to refer to the same system.

Familial patriarchy presupposes a decentralized process of production because male control of essential resources is the material basis of his authority/power. Women's subordination, therefore, becomes particularized. The destruction of communal distribution of goods now makes women dependent upon their husbands/fathers whose control of resources, while limited by their class location, is greater than women's due to patriarchal property and inheritance laws.

The destruction of the old kinship form of social organization called for a restructuring of the social system to provide order and ensure the interests and privileges of the dominant class. This was achieved through the formation of the state, the legal system and the military, which structured and enforced the parameters within which production could occur. If reproduction were a mere function of production, the rules controlling production should be sufficient to control and manipulate reproduction. The control of productive capacity and the distribution of surplus indirectly controls reproduction, for the quantity of goods available for consumption has an important if indirect impact upon reproduction. Such a dynamic is, however, a very rough mechanism of co-ordination, which usually tends only to become operative in crises of imbalance, (e.g., population declines due to starvation). Thus, the state and/or religion is called upon to forestall such crises by instituting laws that directly effect reproductive relations through the codification of marriage, divorce and inheritance systems, which conform to the particular mode of production of a period. Such rules and restrictions operate to co-ordinate production and reproduction to provide for adequate replacements of labour but restrict population density in order to preserve desirable levels of surplus extraction.

Although state mediation provides a much more finely tuned mechanism for co-ordinating the two spheres, it is limited in the realm of enforcement. While it is possible to legislate sanctions against deviations from the patriarchal norm, for example, adultery or illegitimacy, it is much more difficult to legislate procreation or enforce marriage (although authorities have on occasion attempted to do so through the imposition of punitive taxes on eligible unmarried males [Homans 1941, 188]). The structure of familial patriarchy, however, provides much more effective incentives for marriage and procreation.

Control of production translates into control of reproduction through the operation of familial patriarchy. This is effected through the pattern of subordination and dependency familial patriarchy creates and its fit within the class hierarchy. Through this system a woman is dependent upon a man, husband/father, for access to crucial survival (productive) resources, ensuring male control over her body and her labour. The man, however, is dependent upon the dominant class or its representatives for access to these basic productive resources. Failure to comply with policies on production or reproduction at any level in the authority hierarchy carries the threat of loss of access to basic resources required for one's livelihood. In this way major social policy decisions can be translated into compelling structural imperatives at the individual household level.

In a class society in which the family operated as the productive unit, legislation controlling reproduction is barely distinguishable from legislation controlling production. Thus, it appears that the control of production is the only system operative. For example, G.C. Homans's (1941) study of the shift in inheritance laws from partible inheritance to impartible-joint-family inheritance to primogeniture are discussed primarily as laws controlling production. They are understood to reflect an interest in controlling population density to prevent the reduction of arable land to tiny plots sufficient only to sustain peasants. Such laws have been analyzed in terms of their effect, which is obviously to enhance the productive interests of the dominant class. However, an analysis of the cause reveals the uneasy balance in existence between production and reproduction and the necessity of continually monitoring that balance. The changes in inheritance laws were introduced specifically to restore an exchange of resources between production and reproduction that reflected the interests of the dominant class, an exchange upset by the dynamics of reproductive relations.

The characteristic feature of familial patriarchy is its pronatalist dynamic. This results from the nature of the interaction between class and patriarchy that creates a logical relation between productivity and procreation at the household level. The dynamic of familial patriarchy operates in the following way: the family is the productive unit and the patriarch is the head of this unit. The family has a vested interest in increasing its productivity because this will improve its life style. However, the class system ensures that the head of household has limited control over resources necessary to increase production. Control over resources (land) is out of the hands of the patriarch; it is determined by the dominant class. Technological innovation in peasant societies is limited and also usually out of the control of the head of household. The only resource the patriarch can control, which can enhance productivity, is labour power. In labour-intensive peasant societies more children may well translate into greater productivity. Because this is the only resource men can control, there develops a logical relation between productivity and procreation at the household level. Thus, in societies in which the family is the productive unit, the dynamic of familial patriarchy is towards the maximization of procreation.

Over time this dynamic clearly leads to problems of population density. However, these problems do not interrupt the pro-natalist dynamic either at the household level or at the societal level. At the household level the patriarch will still have a sufficient vested interest in procreation even under a system of diminishing returns. First, because it is the only possible resource he can control, even when the strategy is a "long shot," it is better than no strategy at all. Second, even when the costs equal or out-balance the pay off, in terms of production, the patriarch's interest in procreation is not upset because the patriarchal family structure ensures that the costs associated with the failing strategy are borne, not by the patriarch, but by the women and children. Patriarchal laws of marriage, inheritance and property ensure that the holdings will not be diminished to the point of mere subsistence, and when population density does pose a potential threat to surplus extraction, the surplus population can simply be discarded, or pushed off the land. Thus, the privileges of class and gender are preserved by laws (the operation of social patriarchy) which guarantee that any immediate negative consequences from an imbalance in production and reproduction do not fall upon male land holders or the dominant class.

Familial patriarchy is ideally suited to the needs of class societies in which the production process is decentralized and labour intensive. This system can accomplish the one thing neither the state nor the dominant class can — to guarantee a constant and predictable rate of reproduction. The problems that result from the pro-natalist character of familial patriarchy can be much more easily controlled by legislation than can the initial problem of promoting procreation. A study of the evolution of marriage and inheritance laws in European feudal society provide evidence of the effectiveness of legislation in modifying or containing the dynamic of familial patriarchy when population density does become an issue.

Homans's (1941) classic study of everyday life in feudal England clearly indicates how changes in property laws over time were a response to the need to co-ordinate productive-reproductive capacities in the interests of the dominant class. Partible inheritance is associated with the period of expansion in which increasing population could be put to use to cultivate expanding land holdings. In this phase, there was no need to curb the pro-natalist dynamic of familial patriarchy. The next phase, in which expansion of property was limited, was characterized by impartible, joint family inheritance. This served to keep land holding intact, but permitted an increasing density of population on the land. The final phase, in which population density became a potential threat to surplus extraction, was marked by the rule of primogeniture, which insured that only one productive-procreative unit could stay on the land. This effectively handled the problem of population density in two ways. First and most commonly the surplus population, the disinherited children, were forced off the land and into armies, monasteries, nascent towns and commercial centres, providing a variety of cheap labour functions at no obligation to the feudal lord. Second, custom and law permitted the disinherited offspring to stay on the land by renouncing their right to a family.

These customs, laws of marriage, property and inheritance, have typically been analyzed as examples of how rules of production control if not determine reproductive dynamics, and this of course is correct when one concentrates upon effects. However, the question ignored is cause — the cause of the problem of population density develops from the dynamic of patriarchy, an entrenched pro-natalist dynamic that can only be effectively curbed by threat of barring access to basic productive resources (land). By broadening our analytic focus and clarifying the actual process of familial patriarchy, it becomes evident that reproductive relations do have an active rather than just reactive dynamic and that this dynamic influences rules of production and property as much as it is effected by those rules.

In summary, the minimization of conflict between production and reproduction in the familial mode of reproduction was achieved through a finely co-ordinated system of centralized and decentralized authority. While control of production necessitated the centralization of authority over land in the hands of the dominant class, the control of reproduction required a decentralized system of authority over women in the hands of the household patriarch. These dual levels of authority were structurally complementary because of the amenability of the resource (land) to centralization in conjunction with the decentralized nature of the productive process. The authority and interest of the patriarch did not compete with those of the dominant class precisely because the material conditions of this household authority (access to land) were based upon his submission to class authority. This symbiotic relationship between class and patriarchy was possible as long as the productive process was decentralized, and the family operated as a productive unit.

The Wage-Labour System and Familial Patriarchy

In Europe, familial patriarchy remained a viable system throughout the transition from the feudal mode of production to the early commercial stages of capitalism. This was a result of the decentralized nature of production, which maintained the family's function as a productive unit for the bulk of the population. Although a class of propertyless wage labourers evolved during this period, the definitive dissociation of family formation from control of productive resources did not emerge until the massive proletarianization of the population occurred with the rise of industrial capitalism.

Industrial capitalism, characterized by the centralization of the process of production, led to the predominance of the wage-labour system. Wages now replaced productive property as the economic basis of the family. The family no longer had productive resources other than the labour power embodied in each member. This seriously undercut the material basis of the patriarchal family, for the control of productive resources was the basis of the patriarch's authority. The husband/father's ability to control the labour power of his family was lost to those who now controlled access to productive resources, that is, employers. Furthermore, the husband/father's ability to reap reward from the control of his family's labour power was lost because the gain from their productivity was largely skimmed off by the employers who left them with a wage seldom sufficient to cover their own maintenance costs. Finally, the husband/father's interest in controlling that labour power could and often did come into conflict with employers who were interested in unfettered access to the cheapest labour possible. Thus, not only could the male worker not reap sufficient benefit from the labour of his wife and children, but he confronted women and children in the work place as direct competition and a serious threat to his own wages and job security.

In short the dynamic of industrial capitalism, the centralization of production, upset the delicate balance between centralized and decentralized authority that had permitted the complementary co-existence between class and patriarchy. Class interests were now structurally incompatible with patriarchal interests.

While destructive of patriarchal authority, the wage-labour system did not in any way liberate women and children from the yoke of male authority, it simply centralized it in the hands of the employers. However, the wage-labour system did definitively destroy the pro-natalist dynamic of patriarchy, although this effect took some time to manifest itself. For it was decreasingly in the interests of the male wage earner to encourage procreation when he was no longer in a position to control or benefit from the labour power of his children and when he was increasingly forced to bear the costs of the dependency period of those children. This effect was operative even in the period of minimal dependency due to the extensive use of child labour. John Foster's (1974) study of wage earners in nineteenth-century England indicates a direct correlation between the presence and number of children in the home and the impoverishment of the family.

One of the early effects of a more widespread dissociation of family formation from control of productive resources was the deregulation of reproductive relations. "The importance of economic foundations for a marriage continued but when wages replaced inherited property couples became more independent of familial constraint" (Tilly and Scott 1978, 96). Thus, the availability of wage labour for both men and women when combined with favourable sex ratios[6] led to increasing marriage rates and often declining age at marriage. Throughout the period 1750–1850 most of Europe manifested higher marriage rates, higher birth rates and higher illegitimacy rates. Although this burst of fertility seems to contradict our claim that the wage-labour system discourages high birth rates, it is important to note: first, this effect was relatively short lived and tended to be limited to the early phase of the expansion of wage labour; second, it resulted more from the breakdown of the old system of controlling family formation than from any structural encouragement for procreation; third, evidence of the incompatibility between the wage-labour system and high birth rates developed in the growing problems of neglected and abandoned children, infanticide and abortion (see McLaren 1978a, 1978b; Gordon 1977; Fryer 1965).

By the mid- to late-nineteenth century, however, most industrialized countries were experiencing a steady decline in birth rates, and the Malthusian specter of overpopulation was replaced by a more fearful possibility, "race suicide." The increasing demand for and evidence of the practice of birth control and abortion (see McLaren 1978a, 1978b; Gordon 1977; Fryer 1965) in addition to the growing problem of abandoned children were all cited as evidence of race suicide, a term coined by social reformers to express their concern with the declining quantity and quality of the population. Although the population was not declining as a result of the declining mortality rate, evidence that women were rejecting their sacred calling, motherhood, added fuel to the growing concern that the family was in serious disarray.

The growing evidence of the structural incompatibilities

of class and patriarchy gave rise to a remarkable consensus among diverse social groups over the need to save the family. This historically unprecedented consensus, which encompassed feminists, church groups, labour, women's organizations, farmers organizations and some far-sighted industrialists attests to how fundamental patriarchy was to the ideology and organization of the social system.[7] Beneath the moralizing Victorian rhetoric on the sanctity of motherhood, the home and the innocence of children, an understanding began to emerge that the wage-labour system in its unmediated, unregulated form was destructive of the family as they knew it (familial patriarchy).

State response to the growing evidence of family disorganization and pressure from reform-minded groups was remarkably similar in most industrialized countries. The prohibition of child labour and the selective protection of female labour served as a first step in modifying the dynamic of productive relations that had become most devastating to family life (Lewis 1986; Strong-Boag 1981). These reforms provided a legal recognition of the significance of children as the future labour force and prevented the wholesale exploitation of child labour, which used up much of their potential contribution as mature labourers and reproducers. It also forced a legal recognition of the value of women's reproductive role and protected women as active or potential reproducers from being completely consumed in the productive process. Such legislation provided minimal structural protection/support for the reproductive process by holding back the dynamic of production that led to the indiscriminate consumption of all labour power. These reforms were consciously fought for and justified in terms of the indispensability of the patriarchal family (Wilson 1977; Seccombe 1986a).

In addition to the above attempts to regulate production there was also a concerted effort to regulate reproduction through the introduction of a series of repressive laws designed to reinforce the relation between sexuality and procreation. Abortion laws in England, Canada and the United States, which were largely a nineteenth-century phenomenon,[8] were strengthened and made more punitive at the turn of the century (McLaren 1978a, 1978b; L. Gordon 1977). Laws requiring, under penalty of criminal prosecution, the presence of an attendant at all births and the registering of all births, including still born, were aimed at reducing the incidence of infanticide (McLaren 1978a; L. Gordon 1977). And finally, the recommendation, advertising or selling of birth- control devices or information became a criminal offence. These laws provided important legislative weight to the pro-family, pro-natalist sentiments of the crusading reform movement.

While the state has always played a role in regulating reproduction, through marriage and inheritance laws, this early legislation indicated a new level of involvement on the part of the state in support of the patriarchal family. But, why did the state become implicated in the preservation of patriarchy? The answer lies in the role of the state as the guardian of the overall integrity of the social system. The introduction of the wage-labour system and the destruction of the family as the productive unit brought to the fore a nascent contradiction within all class systems — the contradiction between the short-term interests of the dominant class in the extraction of surplus and the long-term interests of the dominant class and society as a whole in the reproduction of the conditions for this extraction, that is, the reproduction of labour. The heightening of this contradiction demanded a more active role on the part of the state in mediating the demands of production with the necessity of reproduction.Thus, this early legislation not only marked the beginning of a new era of state intervention (in productive and reproductive relations), but was also the first step in the reorganization of the patriarchal system.

Social Patriarchy

As a result of the destruction of the decentralized base of patriarchal authority (household production) and the subsequent deregulation of reproductive relations, the state was pressured to assume many of the supportive and regulative functions previously confined to the family. Consequently, there was a shift in the locus of power from familial to social patriarchy. Unlike previous transitions in which one form of patriarchy replaced another, familial patriarchy remained an essential component, although the material basis of power was centralized in the state (hence, the identification of this mode as social patriarchy). As some of the patriarchal relations of the family are undermined by social and economic developments, the state, through the system of social patriarchy, attempts to reinforce familial patriarchy. This is demonstrated by the peculiar paradox of our time: the liberalization of family law, the emergence of women's and children's rights, while appearing to be the end of patriarchy, are, in fact, a manifestation of the growth of social patriarchy. The process that led to the ascendancy of social patriarchy and the dependency of familial patriarchy is rooted in the incompatibility of the current mode of production, specifically the wage-labour system, with the reproductive system and the role of the state in mediating the two spheres.

The modification of employment practices that were most destructive to family life established a precedent of state intervention on behalf of reproduction without in any way altering the tenuous economic basis of the family — the wage. The working-class struggle for a "living wage," understood in terms of maintaining the independence and viability of their families, confronted and was defeated by the fundamental logic of the wage-labour system. The wage-labour system is individual and contractual responding only to the market value of the labour power embodied in a particular individual disregarding all consideration of reproductive needs, such as, size of family, or number of dependants. Therein lies the flexibility, economy, efficiency of the wage-labour system over previous productive relations. It is precisely the characteristics that make the system so unresponsive to the reproductive needs of the population that also make it so effective as a system of extracting surplus. The operation of this system is, therefore, non-negotiable in terms of the interests of the dominant class.

Confronting the unwavering resistance of employers to absorb the costs of reproduction, the labour and reform movements over time directed their demands to the state. The struggle for a family wage has given way in the twentieth century to the struggle for the "social wage," the social wage being nothing other than a state-organized system for socializing the costs of reproduction, commonly referred to as the welfare state. The welfare role of the state arises directly from the necessity to compensate for the erosion of the material base of the family. Thus, the socialization of reproduction became a corollary of the socialization of production.

The material basis of patriarchy has always been male control of resources essential to the maintenance of the family. What distinguishes social from familial patriarchy is the increasing centralization of that control — access to essential resources is now controlled by the employer on the one hand and the state on the other. Thus, the individual patriarch is no longer the central force in the maintenance of control over reproduction. The employer's interest in the maintenance of patriarchy is a distant second to their interest in the extraction of surplus; when the two conflict it is a foregone conclusion that the interests of surplus extraction predominate. As a result, the state stands alone as the only entity that has both an interest in preserving patriarchy and the material resources to do so.

It is important to note that social patriarchy is not confined to the state, its legislation or welfare services. It is broadly manifest in institutions quite removed from state control, for example, media, the arts, and religion. While the ideological support of patriarchy is critical in these institutions and should not be underestimated, we must distinguish between the operations of social patriarchy that reinforce and those that provide concrete material restrictions to women's options and concrete material support for the patriarchal family. It is in this sense that the operations of social patriarchy within the state are singled out for particular analysis.

The political economic thrust of social patriarchy is two-fold: first, it functions to maintain the patriarchal family structure by compensating for the male head's loss of control over resources, that is, socializing the costs of reproduction, the social wage; second, it serves to maintain women's generally subordinate status, controlling her options to mothering and motherhood through the institutionalization of her political-economic dependence. The former function reflects the supportive or benevolent face of the welfare state; the later function reveals its coercive or repressive side.

While it is true that the state is uniquely characterized by having both an interest in preserving patriarchy and the material resources to do so, its support of the patriarchal family is not nearly as unambiguous as such a statement might imply. The interaction between social and familial patriarchy mirrors the more fundamental contradiction between production and reproduction. Thus social patriarchy, which operates as a support system for familial patriarchy, can and often does undercut the authority of familial patriarchy.

The harmony that characterized the interaction between familial and social patriarchy in the previous mode was based upon the symbiotic relation between centralized and decentralized authority. With the destruction of that relation and the increasing move toward centralization, the interaction between social and familial patriarchy becomes much more problematic. Social patriarchy is by definition directly shaped by both class concerns and patriarchal concerns, interests that are contradictory within the wage-labour system. Social patriarchy as manifest in the state moves inexorably toward centralization of control, while familial patriarchy is based upon the decentralized authority of the individual head of household. Thus, the dynamic of social patriarchy is at odds with the institution it is designed to support. This has raised the question among some theorists as to whether social patriarchy is the alternative to rather than the corollary of familial patriarchy.[9]

Social Patriarchy, Corollary or Alternative?

In attempting to assess how critical familial patriarchy is to the social patriarchal mode of reproduction, I found it helpful to reconsider the three processes of reproduction — procreation, socialization and daily maintenance — to distinguish the areas in which the state has direct control and those areas dependent upon the mediation of familial patriarchy. In the case of daily maintenance, the welfare activities of the state have clearly supplanted a number of traditional familial responsibilities with regard to support of the non-productive members, for example, pensions, unemployment insurance and welfare to name a few. In the area of socialization, the institution of compulsory education is a direct takeover of important familial functions. However, there are areas in which the state is unable to supplant family functions and must settle for indirect forms of intervention, forms that rely upon the operation of familial patriarchy.

Procreation, the primary process of reproduction, can be encouraged through pro-natalist legislation, can be supplemented by immigration, but it cannot, it appears, be legislated. The recent history of declining birth rates in the face of repressive reproductive laws criminalizing birth control and abortion, suggest there are some levels of control that the state cannot penetrate. A fundamental reproductive problem in wage-labour societies is to ensure adequate levels of procreation, because it is a system in which the reproducers bear most of the material costs (as well as social and psychological costs) but receive little if any material benefit from producing the new generation of labour. An intense emotional and ideological motivation to reproduce, appears to be necessary to overcome obvious material disincentives to reproduction. Such intensely personal motivations to have children seem to be best generated within the intense emotional environment of the patriarchal family. Similarly, there does not appear to be a viable substitute for the patriarchal family, which creates the critical milieu in which the sex-gender system reproduces itself as an apparently natural and inevitable process.[10] The location of the psycho-sexual socialization of each new generation within the biological-procreative unit obscures the process of learning/repression involved in the reproduction of gender, sexual divisions of labour and heterosexuality and presents it as a biologically determined maturation process.

The family has become an essential albatross of the state, indispensable but grossly expensive and decreasingly effective. Because there does not seem to be a viable alternative to the patriarchal family for the fulfilment of the above functions critical to the maintenance of the sex-gender system, it is maintained through state support and regulation. Evidence of the staggering expense to the state of socializing the costs of reproduction is appearing in all industrialized nations. The 1985 report of the Organization for Economic Co-operation and Development (OECD) indicates that the pattern of escalating social expenditures is a characteristic feature of all of its twenty participating nations: "Social expenditure has been the fastest growing component of total public expenditure, its share in the OECD area increasing from 47 1/2 per cent in 1960 to over 58 1/2 per cent by 1981" (OECD 1985, 18). Further, the report indicated that in 1981 five countries (Germany, Belgium, Denmark, the Netherlands and Sweden) spent over 30 percent of their Gross Domestic Product (GNP) on social programs. In the United Kingdom, Canada and the United States, the proportion of GNP expended on social programs was 24%, 22% and 21% respectively. In dollar terms, in Canada in 1976 this amounted to $24,883,000,000.00 expended by all levels of government on social security expenditures alone (this does not include education expenditures) (Leacy 1983, Series C599).

At the same time that expenditures are mounting, evidence of the declining ability of the family to perform the patriarchal functions it is uniquely designed to perform is equally abundant, although perhaps less systematically documented. An examination of the patriarchal family's ability to deliver the goods — reproduce the sex-gender system as an apparently natural process and ensure steady and adequate levels of procreation — reveals an institution clearly on the defensive. The centralization of the productive process, which dissociates family formation from control of productive resources, also separates marriage and heterosexual bonding from economic survival. Although patriarchal custom and laws struggle to minimize this fact through the perpetuation of a generalized subordination of women, the existence of employment for women and individual access to welfare creates real alternatives to marriage as a form of survival. At the very minimum, the existence of alternatives puts real constraints upon the patriarch's exercise of power.

The increasing integration of women into the labour force brings into sharp relief the contradiction between the ideology and the reality of the family. Paternalism, the ideology of the patriarchal family, holds out the promise of security for the price of freedom. Utilitarian individualism, the ideology of the market place, holds out the promise of freedom at the expense of security. Women's experience of the contradictions of both systems increasingly reveals the bankruptcy of the systems' claims. As a wage worker, in a patriarchal society women are not free from sexual discrimination; as a home maker in a class society, women are not guaranteed economic security. The contradiction between market ideology and patriarchal ideology and their necessary but uneasy coexistence severely undermines the family's ability to ideologically reproduce the sex-gender system, for every patriarchal adage, its promise or its threat, coexists with its negation in the market place.

The dissociation between marriage and economic survival erodes male-female economic interdependency, eroding one of the most fundamental mechanisms of the sex-gender system — the material imperative to heterosexuality. The strength and persistence of patriarchy has been ensured by structuring its operation into the very processes of survival. The equation of marriage, and heterosexuality, with economic survival has always been the best guarantor of the observance of patriarchal rules. It ensured that the pursuit of whatever options might be conceivable, non marriage, or homosexuality, would relegate the person to a perpetually marginal position in society. It ensured that the price of non-traditional choice would be high and that the exercise of choice in sexual-reproductive behaviour could appear only as deviance.

The removal of the material imperative to heterosexuality serves to materially normalize the exercise of choice in these areas, that is, to make it possible to stay within the mainstream of the economy regardless of such choices. Intense ideological reinforcement of heterosexuality attempts to reverse this trend, attempts to restrict employment options on the basis of sexual preference, attempts to ghettoize, in order to reassert the homosexual's marginality, their easy identification as deviant. However, the dissociation of these measures from any material imperative makes their motives transparent, their legitimacy questionable; such tactics are more readily identifiable as repression. Homophobia emerges as a peculiarly modern phenomenon, an hysteria grown out of the absence of the material necessity of heterosexuality. The removal of the material imperative has already evidenced the growth of a strong gay liberation movement, and for the first time, sexual preference has become a major political issue. The virulence of the traditionalist's response may well be a good measure of their lack of confidence in the system's ability to ensure/enforce heterosexuality.

The above observations suggest that the ability of familial patriarchy to reproduce the sex-gender system is complicated by the increase in countervailing pressures in society today. However, the decreasing effectiveness of the system does not logically lead to its dispensability, especially in the absence of a viable alternative. I suggest that increasing state intervention and regulation is an attempt to mitigate some of these countervailing pressures and thus is, in intent if not always in effect, a program to support familial patriarchy rather than replace it.

Last, to argue that the patriarchal family is indispensable as a mechanism for organizing and controlling reproduction one must address the apparent anomaly of societal indifference to consistently declining birth rates in industrialized nations. While declining birth rates were the source of great alarm in the early twentieth century resulting in pro-natalist legislation and restrictions on women's employment, the continuance of this pattern no longer seems to provoke much concern.

It is easier to argue that the patriarchal family is indispensable, that production and reproduction are co-determinative when there is some concrete evidence of the reproductive imperative exerting pressure upon the productive process. The turn of the century provides such evidence. Popular sentiment, social policy and legislation explicitly acknowledged the existence of an imbalance between production and reproduction manifest as a labour-supply problem and linked directly to the declining birth rate. Today the anti-natalist dynamic of the wage-labour system is, if anything, more pronounced and pervasive, yet there is no similar evidence of pro-natalist sentiments or policies. One might reasonably argue, in fact, that much of current sentiment and policy exacerbates the existing anti-natalist dynamic. What has happened to the reproductive imperative, the necessity of co-ordinating production and reproduction?

The Political Economy of Reproduction

While it is clear that modern industrialized societies are not without their problems, reproductive concerns — declining birth rates, labour supply — do not appear to be among them.[11] In the face of current economic problems, unemployment, inflation, the fiscal crisis of the state, the focus is on production, and the significance of the reproductive imperative, the necessity of co-ordinating production and reproduction, fades. However, in spite of appearances, reproductive issues are central to the current problems of industrialized nations. While state intervention and the global organization of production has altered the manifest effect of imbalance between production and reproduction, it has not and cannot alter the fundamental necessity of co-ordinating the two spheres. Many of the "economic" problems afflicting the modern welfare state are a direct, if obscured, result of the growing separation between production and reproduction and the consequent imbalance this creates.

An imbalance between production and reproduction resulting from declining birth rates provokes concern when it is manifest as a labour-supply problem precisely because its impact upon production is so immediate. Labour shortages are experienced as a concrete threat to productive interests, forcing a temporary conciliation between the short-term interests in the extraction of surplus and the long-term interests in reproducing the conditions for that extraction. Concessions to long-term interests (reproduction) are most likely to occur when reproductive patterns pose a direct threat to short-term interests, extraction of surplus. Today reproductive patterns in industrialized countries do not pose such a threat, the answer to why this is the case lies in an examination of the changing relation between capital, labour and the state.

The class struggle between capital and labour expresses the fundamental contradiction between production and reproduction: the contradiction between the short-term interests of the dominant class in the extraction of surplus and the long-term interests of the dominant class and society as a whole in the reproduction of the conditions for this extraction, the reproduction of labour. In the interests of short-term extraction of surplus, capital moves towards complete dissociation from the costs and concerns of reproducing its labour supply, that is, the commodification of labour. Labour, on the other hand, resists in any way they can this commodification process, which is a direct threat to their standard of living. Unionization and political pressure for progressive labour legislation and the social wage have been their most effective tactics in counteracting the commodification process.

The welfare state developed as a means of mediating and temporarily resolving this fundamental contradiction. The welfare state is an attempt to meet demands for better living conditions in a manner that leaves capital relatively unfettered by such costs and concerns. This has been achieved largely by taxing the private wage (Russel 1984) to create a social wage thereby socializing the costs of reproduction. The long-term effect, however, was to raise the costs of labour as the standards of reproduction and maintenance rose with increasing state support. Although the state has always shown reluctance to visit these costs upon capital, eventually capital experiences them indirectly through taxation or more commonly through increased wage demands. Because revenue for socializing reproductive costs is generated from production, sooner or later the owners of production will feel the costs of an increased standard of living of its population.

The high cost of labour in industrialized countries has a negative effect upon profit margins and eventually drives capital to seek alternatives. Thus, the problem of labour for capital becomes one of cost not supply. The issue of supply is easily resolved by the mobility of capital and the mobility of labour. The pursuit of cheap labour has taken the form (in various countries) of immigration, guest workers and/or flight of capital. In advanced industrialized countries that have access to these options, indigenous birth rates are irrelevant to labour supply. For industrialized countries that do not have access to these alternative labour supplies, for example, in the recent past Eastern European countries, declining birth rates were experienced as labour shortages and provoked a variety of pro-natalist social policies. In these countries the problem of co-ordinating production and reproduction was immediate, evident and contained within particular national boundaries.

For capitalist countries, however, characterized by multinational corporations and their global organization of production, employers have solved their problems of labour supply. The preferred option now appears to be flight of capital to the most abundant and cheapest sources of labour. This leads to a kind of global division of reproductive labour. Women in North America and Western Europe, who operate within a social patriarchal mode of reproduction, produce low-quantity, high-cost, highly skilled, educated labour, and Third World women operating within a familial patriarchal mode of reproduction produce high-quantity, low-cost, unskilled, uneducated labour.

In addition to pursuing external sources of cheap labour capital also has a variety of strategies for undercutting indigenous labour costs: capital intensification, maximum use of less expensive indigenous labour (e.g., women), use of part-time labour and union busting. All of these strategies designed to reduce the wages of labour reveal the relentless dynamic of capital towards the commodification of labour. The essence of this process is the dissociation of the short-term interests in extraction of surplus (production) from the long-term interests of reproducing the conditions for this extraction, reproduction of labour. While this dynamic is not new, nor are the demographic consequences of declining birth rates, the political economic consequences today are quite different than they were at the turn of the century.

At the turn of the century the imbalance between production and reproduction manifested as a labour shortage and had a direct impact upon production; hence, the conciliation between short- and long-term interests was realized through the development of the welfare state. Today, the very existence of the welfare state in conjunction with the global organization of capital serves to insulate capital from the consequences of the imbalance between production and reproduction. Capital's mobility permits it to pursue labour wherever it is cheap and convenient, while the welfare apparatus assumes responsibility for underwriting the ongoing reproduction and maintenance of the population at home. Thus, capital is structurally freer from the costs and considerations of reproduction than it has ever been before. While the consequences of this process of dissociation are of little or no immediate concern to capital, they are problematic for the society.

The increasing separation between production and reproduction is the source of some fundamental economic and demographic problems for welfare-state nations. First, the continued anti-natalist dynamic of the wage-labour system is producing a seriously skewed population structure in these nations. Increased longevity in the presence of declining birth rates results eventually in problematic dependency ratios, an increasing proportion of the population that is not productive. Second, capital's pursuit of cheap external labour serves to slough off expensive indigenous labour transforming productive members of the population into dependants through unemployment. Furthermore, the very strategies that capital pursues to avoid or cut labour costs serve to erode the economic base upon which the state can generate revenue to support this growing burden of dependants.

Resources for financing the welfare state are inevitably generated from production. The dominant form of revenue generation is through personal income tax. Thus, employer strategies that serve to erode the wage serve ultimately to erode the revenue base of the welfare state. In addition, increasing unemployment is experienced not only as an added dependency burden but also as a loss of revenue (loss of taxable income). Finally, flight of capital in pursuit of cheap labour means not only loss of jobs but also loss of productive capacity as it is exported to other nations. It is a direct erosion of the productive base upon which the state is dependent for financing its welfare costs. Under these conditions the growth of dependency expenditures becomes overwhelming.

Capital's voracious, short-sighted pursuit of surplus extraction inevitably erodes the economic base for reproduction, first on a familial scale, now on a national scale. The problem is not simply demographic, although it takes that form, nor is it simply fiscal, although it is experienced that way as well. The problem is the separation of production from reproduction carried to its logical conclusion in modern industrial societies. As the guarantor of the overall integrity of the social system, the state has been forced over time to assume increasing responsibility for the long-term interests of society, that is, the reproduction and maintenance of the population, at the same time that it actively supports the strategies of capital that undermine those interests. It is this contradictory location of the state mediating the fundamentally incompatible interests of production and reproduction that explains its complex relation to the patriarchal family.

The purpose of controlling reproduction in class societies is to ensure that reproduction operates in the interests of production. While there are numerous historical examples where manipulation involves programs of increasing the birth rate there are also examples where the best interests of production are served by curtailing reproduction. Our current situation is a case in point. Channeling women's labour into production in preference to reproduction best meets the interests of capital in advanced industrialized societies. The fact that this process occurs without the apparent active intervention of the state does not imply that manipulation or control — patriarchy — is expendable.

Because of the anti-natalist dynamic of the wage-labour system, the increasing allotment of female labour to production over reproduction will occur without obvious intervention on the part of the state. The visibility of state intervention seems to be related to attempts to modify the existing reproductive dynamic. State intervention, in the familial patriarchal mode, only becomes obvious when there is need to curtail its pro-natalist dynamic. Within the social patriarchal mode, state intervention only becomes apparent when the state must modify the anti-natalist dynamic. In both cases the periods of apparent nonintervention presume the active functioning of the particular patriarchal mode.

In advanced industrial nations the clear predominance of short-term interests over long-term interests operates to funnel women's labour into the productive sphere, minimizing the social significance of reproduction. Because this takes the form of the increasing proletarianization of women, patriarchy appears to be significant only as a system in service of immediate surplus extraction, women as cheap labour. This interpretation characteristic of traditional Marxist analysis, focusses exclusively upon the immediate and most apparent economic implication of patriarchy. However, by missing the significance of reproductive factors (which are admittedly obscure at this time), they have great difficulty explaining the contradictory relation between patriarchy and production.

The interests of the dominant class are as dependent upon patriarchy for preserving its long-term interests (reproduction of labour), as they are on the mechanisms of class for enforcing their immediate interests (surplus extraction). Patriarchy operates in the service of production by providing a system for the maximum manipulation of fifty percent of the population, the critical fifty percent who service production's short-term (wage labour) and long-term (reproductive labour) needs. The global division of reproductive labour masks the fact that production is still dependent upon pro-natalist patriarchal operations. The industrialized-nonindustrialized dichotomy separates in time and place the dual potential of patriarchy — the manipulation of women's labour in production and/or reproduction. In the Third World patriarchy primarily serves production through meeting its long-term labour supply needs. In North America and Western Europe, patriarchy's most evident service to production takes the form of meeting immediate surplus extraction needs — women as cheap labour.

Although patriarchal operations in industrialized and capital-intensive countries appear primarily in the service of short-term economic interests, these operations do not express the whole nor even the most important aspects of patriarchy. Patriarchy's fundamental function in class societies, ensuring the continued organization of reproduction in the interests of production, links it inextricably to the long-term needs of the system, which are in contradiction to the short-term (surplus extraction) needs. In this context patriarchy comes into conflict with production, and also in this context patriarchy is most fundamentally indispensable to the social system as a whole.

Familial and Social Patriarchy: The Essential Components of Modern Reproductive Relations

An exclusive focus on the consequences (economic advantage) of women's historically subordinate status obscures the historic process and costs involved in maintaining that subordination. Taking women's subordination as problematic (requiring continued social engineering) rather than biologically or historically given permits us to understand the current contradiction between patriarchy and production. The very conditions, subordination and dependence, that make women a particularly exploitable sector of the labour force have been secured by a history of state support/maintenance of familial patriarchy. Whether this is or is not a necessary structural prerequisite for women's subordination is not nearly as important as the fact that it has been treated as such. The patriarchal family is the established institutional base for the physical and ideological reproduction of the sex-gender system, critical to women's subordination-exploitation, not to mention the generation-regeneration of labour. The family is an institution that continually generates demands for long-term reproduction and maintenance resources (an anathema to the commodification of labour).

Our recent history suggests a link between the control of reproduction, the subordination of women and the patriarchal family. Since all three factors are operative today, it seems premature to be announcing the death of the patriarchal family. The transition of the locus of power from the patriarch to the patriarchal state can be understood as an adaptation for the preservation of familial patriarchy rather than proof of its demise. In the face of the centralizing dynamic of production and its erosion of the material basis of the family, the economic support of the welfare state becomes critical to sustaining a decentralized process of reproduction. While the decentralized character of familial patriarchy often comes into conflict with the organization and interests of production, it also services production through the privatization of the costs of reproduction in addition to the perpetuation of the sex-gender system.

Ironically, the state sustains the institution (family) that serves to privatize much of the costs of reproduction through the selective socialization of some of the costs of reproduction. Even the most generous estimates of a welfare state's expenditures on reproduction suggest that individual families absorb the bulk of the costs. Ian Gough (1979) estimates that the British welfare state absorbs thirty percent of the reproductive costs of its population.

The economic advantages to the state and the dominant class of privatized child rearing becomes evident when we compare the costs of child rearing with the costs of caring for the elderly. It is instructive to note that within government documents the elderly dependant category is always calculated as two and half times more expensive to the state than the youthful dependant category (Foot 1982, 1446A). While I don't question these calculations as a real reflection of social costs, it is important to ask why the elderly are socially more expensive. If no distinction is made between social and familial costs, I doubt that the care of totally dependent infants and young children would be any less than the costs of care for the elderly. The difference is that patriarchy provides the free labour services of women in the care of children, and the family provides the structure within which this occurs. Familial patriarchy legitimates the fact that the primary costs of generationally reproducing the labour force should lie within the family. Although the state has been pressed to provide more support for young families within the last thirty years, the per capita costs of supporting the young is far below the per capita costs of supporting the old, as revealed in the government's own calculations. But even though the cost of the care of the elderly is more socialized than the cost of the care of the young, this does not imply that the state absorbs all or most of the costs of the elderly. The family and women's unpaid labour remains a critical resource in the provision of care for its senior members or, for that matter, its disabled members as well. The amount of women's unpaid labour necessary to support seniors and the disabled is well documented in J. Finch's and D. Groves's work, *A Labour of Love: Women, Work and Caring* (1983). At the same time that the patriarchal family is a cost to the state, as part and parcel of the state's growing responsibility for maintaining the population as a whole, it also operates privately to absorb a large share of the costs of reproduction.

If one concedes that industrial societies, like all other societies, are not exempt from the concerns of co-ordinating production and reproduction, then it must be acknowledged that the control of reproduction continues to be essential to the maintenance of social stability. The patriarchal family, as unstable as it is, keeps the costs of generational reproduction largely private, has historically maintained women as a particularly exploitable category of labour in the home and in the labour force and still serves as the primary institution for the physical and ideological reproduction of the sex-gender system. In the light of such operations I suggest that familial patriarchy remains a critical mechanism for controlling reproduction and, hence, an essential institution in advanced industrialized societies. Having argued for the continuing significance of familial patriarchy, however, I hasten to add that its increasing structural dependency upon the state implies that a complete analysis of the dynamic of patriarchy in industrial societies is dependent upon an analysis of the interaction between its social and familial forms and how they reflect the interaction between production and reproduction.

The ascendance of a generalized system of subordination (social patriarchy) over a particularized system (familial patriarchy) serves to forestall the contradiction between production and reproduction through political (welfare state) and geographic (flight of capital) displacement of long-term reproductive interests. However, the contradictions remain and reappear, although perhaps in altered form, testifying to the fact that reproduction cannot be endlessly manipulated in the interests of production without creating serious consequences, consequences that ultimately impede the productive process itself. Thus, in spite of the apparent effective subordination of reproduction to production, the fundamental co-determinative nature of their interaction is reflected in the continued necessity of engineering this subordination and the obvious imperfection, incompleteness and inconsistency of this process. The problems involved in this process of engineering are evident in the ever-changing pattern of social policies and their frequently undesirable consequences.

From Theory to History

In the subsequent chapters I will apply the above elaboration of the dual-systems model to an analysis of state intervention in production and reproduction in Canada. The problems of evidence — the generational time frame of reproduction in contrast to the immediacy of the impact of production — require a "long view" to identify the subtle effects of the reproductive imperative on production. As a result I will examine the dynamic relation between production, reproduction and the state over approximately one hundred years of Canadian history. I will trace the processes of intervention (their successes and their limitations) through an analysis of changing patterns of legislation. As an introduction to the "empirical" section of this study, I begin with a brief history of the initial impact of industrialization on the family and the process whereby Canadians organized to lobby for state intervention.

PART 2

Historical Background: The Impact of Industrialization in Canada

Canada in the mid-nineteenth century was experiencing major structural changes in population, economy and state that were contributing to our country's rapid and uneven transition from a frontier society to an industrial society. This transition was characterized by a continuous spin off of destitute dependants in the great migration from old country to new, rural to urban and job to job. Mass migrations in the past were always accompanied by a certain amount of disruption and dislocation of reproductive relations. However, the collision between the new economic order and the old patriarchal family threatened to transform these temporary problems into a chronic, concentrated (urban) condition of industrialism. Fearful of the impact of industrialism on the family and the Canadian way of life, a Social Reform Movement arose to document, define and publicize the root of this social problem — and to call upon the state to "save the family." Given their vision and their effectiveness in constructing a new social order, I identify the Social Reform Movement as the architects of social patriarchy — the state its engineer.

Between 1851 and 1891 the population of Canada doubled from 2.4 million to 4.8 million (Foot 1982). The growth was a product of both natural increase and immigration. Immigration rates were particularly high in the decade 1881 to 1891 in which over nine hundred thousand immigrants came to Canada (Canada Immigration statistics 1979). Population growth provided a labour supply essential to the process of industrialization, and as Canada became more populated, new political structures emerged. The creation of the Canadian state in 1867 and the subsequent development of the national policy in 1879 instituted protectionist tariffs to support Canadian industry (G. Kealey 1980). With a substantial labour supply and more secure markets, the process of industrialization accelerated as did the spread of the wage-labour system.

These changes were ambiguous for workers. While productivity and demand for labour increased, it was associated with deskilling and increased competition (Palmer 1979; G. Kealey 1980). The effect of the wage-labour system — the commodification of labour — meant declining bargaining power for individual workers with the consequence that a single wage was increasingly insufficient to support a family. In 1871 women and children made up 42% of the industrial work force in Montreal (Ames 1972) and 34% in Toronto (G. Kealey 1980). The employment of women and children was not uncommon in smaller industrial towns as well. In Paris, Ontario, where the primary industry was knitting mills, 59% of the employees in the mills in 1883 were women (Parr 1990).

The spread of the wage-labour system seriously restricted the labour and income available to reproduction. Low wages limited the flow of income into the family, driving women and children into the work force to support the family. However, the employment of women and children in production for long hours eroded the labour available for reproduction and household work. This resource squeeze, limited income-limited labour, made it very costly for working-class and low-income Canadians to reproduce.

Wage Labour and Reproduction

One of the first indicators of a lack of fit between the old family structure and the new industrial society was the declining birth rate that became evident in Ontario in the 1880s. The Registrar General of Ontario reported with grave concern that the province's birth rate had dropped 17% in one decade from 23.1 in 1883 to 19.2 in 1894 (*Registrar General's Report for the Province of Ontario, 1895* [*R.G.R ... Ontario, 1895*] Sessional Papers 30: 2). This trend gave rise to great concern and speculation that "neomalthusianism" (the Victorian euphemism for birth control) was becoming a wide spread practice in Ontario. "...it is apparent that some cause or causes are operant to produce a decline of births so serious, in a still sparsely settled Province, as to call for the attention of all interested in the moral, social and economic welfare of the people" (*R.G.R. ... Ontario, 1896* Sessional Papers 30: 2)·*

Concern with the declining birth rate was exacerbated by evidence that the Ontario rate seemed to be lower than those of other industrializing countries. In 1895 the Registrar General of Ontario called attention to the fact that Ontario's birth rate not only fell far below that of England, Wales and Scotland, but that it was also lower than the rates in France and Massachusetts, jurisdictions with acknowledged birth-rate problems (*R.G.R. ... Ontario, 1895* Sessional Papers 30: 2)· Table 1, taken from the Registrar General's report, documents Ontario's low birth rate relative to the other jurisdictions.

While the data indicated a decline in legitimate birth rates, illegitimate birth rates were showing an increase, in 1874 the ratio was 6.9 or one in every 144 live births, by 1884 the ratio was 14.4 or one in every 69 live births, and by 1900 it was 1 in every 55 live births (*R.G.R. ... Ontario, 1888* Sessional Papers 3: 11; and *1901* Sessional Papers 9: 33). These statistics were particularly alarming because, although the Registrar General complained throughout the 1800s that births tended to be underreported, the most underreported births were the

---

All abbreviated references are listed in full in the bibliography.

Table 1
Birth Rates per 1,000 Population for Selected Jurisdictions

England and Wales	Scotland	France	Massachusetts	Ontario
1883..33.5	1883..32.8	1882..24.8	1881..24.73	1884..23.1
1884..33.6	1884..33.7	1883..24.8	1883..25.17	1885..23.5
1885..32.9	1885..32.7	1884..24.8	1884..25.45	1886..22.0
1886..32.8	1886..32.9	1885..24.2	1885..25.12	1887..21.7
1887..31.9	1887..31.7	1886..23.9	1886..25.37	1888..21.8
1888..31.2	1888..31.3	1887..23.5	1887..25.80	1889..22.6
1889..31.1	1889..30.9	1888..23.1	1888..25.89	1890..22.0
1890..30.2	1890..30.4	1889..23.0	1889..26.19	1891..21.1
1891..31.4	1891..31.2	1890..21.8	1890..25.81	1892..19.7
1892..30.5	1892..30.8	1891..22.6	1891.. —	1893..19.8
1893..30.8	1893..31.0	1892..22.1	1892.. —	1894..19.2

SOURCE: *R. G. R. … Ontario, 1895* Sessional Papers 30: 2

illegitimate ones. Thus, there was the growing concern that the relation between marriage and procreation was breaking down: married people were having fewer children and apparently taking direct measures to prevent conception, while the rate of illegitimate births was rising.

As concern about birth rates increased, attention also turned to infant mortality. Throughout the first period, infant and child mortality accounted for a very high percentage of total deaths. From 1876 to 1902 infant mortality (children dying under one year of age) accounted for 20–25% of all deaths; when the child-mortality rate was included (children dying under five years of age), children accounted for 25–30% of all deaths. Furthermore, given the continued trend toward urbanization, it was upsetting to discover that urban mortality rates were often twice as high as rural mortality rates. The report of the Ontario Registrar General in 1905 states that child mortality in urban areas was 5.2 per thousand population while the rate in the rural areas was 3.4 per thousand population. Infant mortality rates revealed the same pattern: 4.1 per thousand population in the urban districts and 2.6 for the rural (*R.G.R. ... Ontario, 1905* Sessional Papers 9: 3). Discussion of this phenomenon began to take up an increasing portion of the annual report, and in 1910 the Registrar General was moved to report on the "modern slaughter of the innocents, which has been going on with very little abatement for many years" (*R.G.R. ... Ontario, 1910* Sessional Papers Pt. 4, 19).[1]

The above vital statistics indicate that patterns of procreation were changing, that the ability of parents to care for their children was also changing and that these changes were most pronounced in urban industrial areas. Other evidence of a disruption of reproductive relations associated with urbanization and industrialization comes from the records of charitable agencies and institutions. Their task was to provide for the disinherited, those individuals who were not in a position to be self-supporting and did not have relatives on which they could make claims for support. Splane's (1965) study of early social-welfare programs provide us with some indication of the magnitude of this problem. He points out that in the twenty-year period between 1870 and 1890 the number of houses of refuge in Ontario increased eight-fold while the number of orphanages doubled and their inmates tripled. Similarly, the rapid urbanization of Winnipeg in the late 1800s, brought on by the great influx of immigrants to western Canada, was associated with an increase of orphanages, foundling homes and homes for unwed mothers (*R.I.P.I. ... Manitoba, 1890–1899* Sessional Papers).

The cast-offs of a disorganized familial system and an insecure wage-labour system congregated in the urban areas putting great strain on municipal and private charitable facilities. Not surprisingly, women and children were the most frequent victims of this social upheaval. Table 2 combines the figures on orphanage and refuge inmates to get the total number of institutionalized destitute in Ontario, for selected years at the turn of the century. Throughout those years women and children consistently accounted for 78% or more of the population.

The increase in the number of foundling homes during this period is a further indication of the breakdown of reproductive relations, for they were specifically designed to take care of abandoned and illegitimate children. Such homes frequently came to public attention because they were characteristically plagued with high infant mortality rates. The death rate rose in the Infant Home in Toronto throughout the 1880s exceeding 50% in 1889 (Splane 1965, 242). In 1883 the Ontario Inspector of Charitable Institutions reported without comment the sombre record of 199 deaths in a year in which there had been

Table 2

Total Number of Institutionalized Destitute, Women and Children as a
Percentage of Total Residents in Ontario, Selected Years 1884–1912

Year	Orphanage Inmates	House of Refuge Inmates	Refuge* Inmates	Total	Women and Child as % of Total
1884	3,407	1,042	911	5,359	83%
1888	3,452	1,376	986	5,814	83%
1892	3,742	1,775	1,477	6,994	78%
1897	4,222	3,020	1,456	8,698	83%
1904	4,562	3,305	1,823	9,690	81%
1908	4,718	8,876	2,071	10,665	80%
1912	4,998	3,886	2,169	11,053	80%

*The two sets of data under House of Refuge come from two reporting districts in Ontario.

SOURCE: *Reports of the Inspector of Charitable Institutions for the Province of Ontario, 1884* Sessional Papers 19, *1888* Sessional Papers 40, *1892* Sessional Papers 6, *1897* Sessional Papers 35, *1904* Sessional Papers 40, *1908* Sessional Papers 43, *1912* Sessional Papers 24

224 admissions in the Bethlehem Home for the Friendless in Ottawa. The problem was two-fold: abandoned children usually entered the home in poor physical condition, and the inability to provide breast milk made matters worse.

At a somewhat later date this problem became manifest in Manitoba as well. In 1897 the St. Boniface Orphanage reported an increase in abandoned children as an explanation of the higher than usual death rate (*Report for the Inspector of Public Institutions. Department of Public Works for the Province of Manitoba [R.I.P.I. ... Manitoba], 1897* Sessional Papers: 75). In 1903 the St. Boniface Infant's Home reported 72 deaths among 105 admitted. Most deaths were attributed to the fact that the infants had been abandoned and suffered from exposure. Between 1897 and 1905 the number of maternity hospitals and orphanages expanded to accommodate the increased number of illegitimate and foundling infants (*R.I.P.I. ... Manitoba, 1905* Sessional Papers: 14). While we cannot conclude that the rate of abandonment was rising any faster than the increase in the population (there is no base line upon which to make such estimates), this evidence does suggest that illegitimacy and abandonment was becoming an increasingly public problem.

As the disruption of reproductive relations became public in visibility, costs and consequences, a national reaction emerged and was articulated by the Social Reform Movement. This was a broadly based, diverse and influential movement, which undertook to document, define and publicize the social problems of the day. It created the dominant discourse in turn-of-the-century Canada, and reproduction was the central issue in its campaign.

Social Reform Movement

The social reform movements characteristic of industrializing countries at the turn of the century provide an interesting study in contrasts and similarities. The Canadian Social Reform Movement was no exception. While remarkably homogeneous in its leading members, drawing largely from the Anglo-Saxon Protestant middle classes (Bacchi 1978, 460), it was remarkably diverse in the issues pursued and the alliances formed. Historians of the Social Reform Movement frequently comment on the diverse alliances forged during this period, which saw the Trades and Labour Council working with the National Council of Women on the issues of protective legislation, or the United Grain Growers meeting with the Women's Christian Temperance Union to support women's suffrage. In the face of the diversity of groups and their unpredictable alliances, historians have searched for a common thread to make sense of them as a movement. Some historians[2] have suggested that certain ideologies (social purity, moral reform, racial regeneration) provided the temporary meeting grounds for unlikely alliances and the "moral cement" that gave cohesiveness to the otherwise disassociated groups.

I would suggest that their common ground was material rather than ideological, and the unifying factor within these diverse organizations was a commitment to stabilizing reproductive relations. The shared patriarchal heritage of the members and allies of the Social Reform Movement provided the common meeting ground and is reflected in the pro-family, pro-natalist, pro-patriarchal thrust of their diverse activities. This commonality of interest was expressed in a diversity of organizations because of the differences in class, region, and sex of the participants. Thus businessmen, farmers and feminists alike were all concerned with the disruption of family life that resulted from the extension of the wage-labour system, rapid population growth and urbanization. While divided by their specific circumstances in life, they were united in their conviction that a stabilized (patriarchal) family was not only the key to a stable society but also a critical component to achieving their own needs and interests. In short the social reformers were the architects of social patriarchy.

The concept of the social reformers as the architects of social patriarchy provides a somewhat different focus in interpreting and understanding their activities. It highlights the reproductive concerns underlying the wide range of activities and organizations contained within the movement, and it provides an explanation of the location, the rise and the demise of the movement. Most social historians are in agreement that the rise of the reform movement was a direct response to the social problems that became increasingly manifest in urban industrializing areas. While there is consensus on the reasons for the reform movement's urban origins and growing strength at the turn of the century, there is some confusion in the literature over the causes of its demise shortly after the First World War. Carol Bacchi (1976) attributes the eclipse of the reform movement to "inner inconsistencies and eventual disillusionment," which is similar to Richard Hofstadter's (1955) account of the demise of the American reform movement. I would suggest that the purpose of the reform movement was to push the state into a more active interventionist role specifically to protect reproductive relations. By the end of the first period (1884–1913) a comprehensive legislative framework was in place for the development of social patriarchy. Thus, the demise of the movement is not particularly mysterious, given that they had largely achieved what they were after by the end of the period.

The social reformers by virtue of the intersection of their class and patriarchal interests were well situated to come up with reform policies that were sufficient both to the task (stabilizing the patriarchal family) and to the political possibilities of the time. In spite of the remarkable diversity of the issues they addressed, they did, to a significant degree, speak with one voice on the issue of the family. Their consistently pro-family, pro-natalist, pro-patriarchal thrust meant that they were seldom working at cross purposes. Their diversity did not result in competing or contradictory policies with regard to the family. Perhaps the most important factor in explaining the influence and success of the reform movement and its policies is the lack of opposition. There was not one significant counter-movement. Their policies are the best historical case, literally and figuratively, of a "Motherhood Issue."

Naming the Problem

The reformers, by virtue of their middle-class position, had a profound vested interest in the new economic order. It was not to be seen as the fundamental source of the problem. While their class location ensured that they benefited from the economic system as a whole, they received no specific advantage from the more exploitative practices of the time, and furthermore, they feared and sometimes suffered the consequences of such excesses. Disease and crime, the products of poverty and overcrowding, could not necessarily be confined to the poor and added an element of self-interest to their altruistic pursuit of reform.

Blocked by class interest from a systemic critique, their focus turned to the symptoms of the contradiction between patriarchy and the wage-labour system. On the one hand, their patriarchal heritage had taught that the family was sacrosanct, women's "divinely ordained" function was maternal and the only rightful purpose of sexuality was procreation within the married state. On the other hand, the increase of women in the labour force (21.4% between 1891 and 1901),[3] created considerable anxiety about the changing role of women, and the data on declining legitimate birth rates and rising illegitimate birth rates seemed to confirm their worst suspicions. In addition, the higher birth rate among French-Canadian women and the increasing flow of non-English immigrants upset their ethnic sensibilities and interests. The reformers' commitment to an English-dominated Canada added an immediate political relevance to their pro-natalist patriarchal agenda.

Their focus on the family seems almost structurally inevitable, as well as politically opportune. Their perspective furnished them with a politically neutral (non-inflammatory) explanation of social problems — family disorganization — that emphasized the commonality of interest in reproductive relations across class and regional divisions, rather than drawing attention to the differences behind those interests.

An abundance of evidence exists, from the writings of the reformers themselves and the historians of the movement, which suggest that the reformers did have a shared patriarchal conception of the family. Studies of three of the major women's reform organizations of the time, the National Council of Women (NCW), the Young Women's Christian Association (YWCA) and the Women's Christian Temperance Union (WCTU), indicates that their self-professed purpose was the promotion of social reforms that would strengthen the family (see Mitchinson 1977). Underlying the diversity of issues addressed by these women, be it race suicide, prostitution, prohibition or women's employment, the common denominator was reproduction, defense of a patriarchal sexual code and the promotion of motherhood. As enthusiastic proponents of the patriarchal family, they justified their own involvement in extra-familial organizations as mothering on a national scale.

The National Council of Women became strong advocates

of government regulation of women's employment. Their concerns were explicitly reproductive: "...our duty to the race demands that we should govern the conditions of this woman's work so that in late years she may have the chance of becoming the mother of a sound generation" (Klein and Roberts 1974, 231). The YWCA's shift in focus from fallen women to working women in the 1880s and 1890s reflects the common assumption of the time that participation in the work force would lead to a decline in women's morals (Mitchinson 1977, 373). The WCTU's promotion of prohibition and later women's suffrage had its ultimate purpose in the protection of the family.

The women reformers, however, were not the only ones concerned with motherhood. If anything, their male counterparts frequently outdid them in their concern with protecting and if necessary enforcing women's "natural" procreative role. The church and the medical profession, bastions of male authority, were particularly outspoken on this issue. The clergy, invoking the will of God, and doctors, citing the "evidence" of medical science, added weighty voices to the defence of motherhood and the cry for the regeneration of the race. Apart from invoking different authority, the approach of the clergy and the medical profession was remarkably similar. They both attacked the practices of birth control and abortion as immoral, unhealthy and disastrous in its consequences for individuals and society.

The educational reformers of the mid and late nineteenth century saw schools as agents of social reformation and social discipline (Graham 1974, 171). For example, the Free Kindergarten begun in Manitoba in 1892 had as their motto emblazoned on their annual reports, "Give me the child and the state shall have the man." The early educators emphasized the importance of moral education, and their vision of the appropriate moral code was synonymous with the reform movement's ideal.

Finally, journalists played a particularly important role within the ranks of the reform movement in publicizing the problems identified and the solutions proposed by the movement. In Toronto, John Robertson of the *Telegram*, John Cameron (the editor of the *Globe*), as well as J.J. Kelso, Goldwin Smith and suffragette Flora MacDonald Denison were active social reformers and prolific publicizers of the cause. In Manitoba, J.S. Woodsworth, clergyman, reformer, author and later politician, wrote prolifically in church magazines and Winnipeg newspapers on the social problems of the time. Similarly, author and suffragette Nellie McClung continually kept the issues alive in the Winnipeg press. Their writings all reveal a fundamental concern for family stability and a patriarchal vision of motherhood.

The organizational and professional composition of the reform movement provided a comprehensive coverage of Canadian opinion makers and disseminators with broad institutional access to the Canadian population (schools, churches and newspapers, to name a few). Consequently, their definition of the problem and its resolution extended beyond the immediate boundaries of their organizations or their geographic location. The reformers' focus upon the family permitted alliances with rural organizations that had little else in common with the urban groups. Farmers' fear of rural depopulation and their anti-urban sentiments found particular focus in the defence of the family, the productive unit of agrarian life (Bacchi 1978, 100). The family-centred orientation of rural organizations such as the Women's Institute and the United Grain Growers allied them to urban reform causes on a number of occasions, specifically women's suffrage, temperance and support for domestic science in the schools.

The connections between reformers and government were close. The government frequently recruited from the reform movement to staff the various commissions and inquiries conducted during this period, and reformers were an important source of testimony in the hearings as well (Splane 1965, 55). The Women's Institute, a rural women's organization, initiated and funded by the Department of Agriculture in Ontario and later Manitoba, provided a major avenue for urban reform ideas on hygiene, child-rearing and family living to filter into the rural areas. Another example of the connection between government and reformers is the National Council of Women, which was founded by Lady Aberdeen, the wife of the Governor General. Its executive was largely composed of the wives and daughters of successful businessmen and politicians, and its informal connections with government were close[4] (Trofimankoff and Prentice 1977). Although the reform movement is not reducible to the Canadian political or economic elite, it was nevertheless characterized by significant involvement and integration of the elite into their organization.

The final factor in explaining the success of the reform movement is the absence of opposition. This is rather remarkable given the magnitude of the changes being advocated — the general thrust towards greater government intervention in production and reproduction. There are three groups at the time that could be identified as having interests potentially in opposition to those of the reformers. Business and labour had for very different reasons some objective class interests that were contrary to the particular forms of intervention in production advocated by the reformers. Women, on the other hand, had objective interests that were contrary to a number of interventions in reproduction supported by the reformers. The fact that these objective differences did not lead to a sustained opposition is important to understanding the influence of the reform movement, as well as to revealing the significance of reproduction to all three groups.

Business, Labour and Patriarchy

Business and labour were the central protagonists in the development of the wage-labour system and the consequent restructuring of society. As the central forces in the evolution of the new industrial order, their co-operation, support or at the minimum non-interference with the reform movement is critical to understanding the development of social patriarchy in Canada. In addition to sharing the roles of central protagonists, business and labour also shared a marked ambivalence towards the patriarchal thrust of the reform movement. Patriarchy both served and contradicted their interests. Thus, although there is evidence within both groups of resisting certain aspects of reform, their shared patriarchal heritage and their conflicting interests were sufficient, not only to inhibit any effective resistance to the reform movement, but also to provide some strong and outspoken allies.

In the short term, employers could both gain and lose from patriarchal tradition. On the negative side, familial patriarchal laws and custom inhibited the progress of the individual contract, which was critical to the spread of the wage-labour system, as well as inhibiting the full scale integration of women into the labour force. Thus, we see enthusiastic reports in the *Monetary Times* of the advantages of the Married Women's Property Act (15 June 1883) and equally enthusiastic reports of the benefits to all of women's integration in the labour force. "Faithful working and weary waiting have at last shown some result in demonstrating the fitness of the weaker and the daintier part of the human family for self-help and self-support" (5 April 1881). However, in the same article, patriarchal tradition is invoked to assert the legitimacy (as well as the advantage) of women receiving lower wages than men.

Certain ideological and structural aspects of patriarchy were clearly advantageous to the business perspective. Patriarchal assumptions about women's worth and women's place (in the home under the care of husband or father) justified their lower wage scale. It was assumed that women were never self-supporting, in the real sense, but were helpful in subsidizing the family's income. When the reality of single women on their own became too obvious to be ignored, we find that the Canadian Manufacturer's Association came to the aid of the YWCA, whose mandate was to create a home away from home for the working woman. This response is typical of the interaction of business with the Social Reform Movement. Their interest in procuring cheap housing for their workers, "to keep the cost of living low so that manufacturers could keep wages down" (Bliss 1974, 71), neatly coincided with women reformers' concern for providing a highly controlled environment to preserve the virtue and domesticity of Canadian womanhood (Mitchinson 1977, 368).

In addition to these short-term interests of business, we also find evidence of concern over the long-term process of reproducing and socializing the future labour force. Labour supply was always of central concern to employers of this period, and while immigration was clearly their preferred method of increasing supply (Pentland 1981), this method was not without serious problems that many businessmen could not ignore. For political and economic reasons, the business community shared with the reform community a vested interest in the dominance of the Anglo-Saxon population in Canada (McLaren 1978a; Artibise 1975). Consequently, they were particularly susceptible to the social reformers' dire predictions of "race suicide," especially after the 1890s when the flow of immigrants began to reduce British predominance, not only in the West, but in Ontario as well. This translated into enthusiastic support of pro-natalist policies, which, within a wage-labour system, comes into conflict with the interests of integrating women in the labour force.

Encouraging English-Canadian women to produce English-Canadian children was, however, only half the problem. The socialization of the new generation of labour (especially new Canadians) was a matter of concern to many forward-looking members of the business community. Businessmen were exposed to the social problems of the time through their membership on boards of charitable institutions, Children's Aid Societies and Industrial Schools (G. Kealey 1973; Splane 1965; Bliss 1974). Over and over again the problems of crime, undisciplined labour and a rebellious citizenry were explained in terms of poor family, lack of adequate education and improper socialization (Splane 1965; Sutherland 1976). The most popular conception of a properly run home assumed the presence of a full-time mother-homemaker dedicated to the careful supervision of her children (Sutherland 1976). Concerns with the quantity and quality of the future generation of labour came into direct contradiction with the interests of maximal exploitation of women's and children's labour. Therefore, business did not present a united front to oppose the factory acts, which greatly inhibited the employment of women and children. In fact, both the *Monetary Times* and the Canadian Manufacturers' Association came out in favour of such reforms (Bliss 1974, 67).

Labour's[5] position on the "woman question" was as contradictory as that of business. While the low salaries of individual male workers necessitated the employment of their wives and children, male wage earners as a group confronted women and children in the labour force as a direct threat to their job security and their wages. While they were unambiguously critical of child labour and could find numerous allies within the reform movement on this issue, the matter of women's employment was much more complex. Male unionists were torn between their new working-class ideology, which held out the promise of strength and protection through solidarity, and the old patriarchal ideology, which had in the past delivered male privilege and familial order. The physical separation of work and family life served to perpetuate the co-existence of these mutually contradictory commitments. Furthermore, working-class struggles to secure their position in the labour force frequently brought them into alliances with the reform movement, which reinforced and legitimated their patriarchal commitments. As a result of this ambiguity, labour's response to women's employment fluctuated between exclusion, protection and unionization (White 1980).

A series of articles and editorials in *The Voice*, a Winnipeg labour paper, reveals labour's ambivalence to women's employment. The event that provoked the series was the first strike of women workers in Winnipeg in 1899. The debate that ensued was over the position of male unionists — should they support these striking women? After several articles and editorials, *The Voice* finally came out with a qualified if not begrudging support. They concluded,

A serious problem frequently confronts us relative to the employment of women. Doubtless they (women) could have saved themselves many trials and tribulations did some of them see the folly of entering establishments where men should rightfully be holding the same position. 'Tis true that woman has put man in a serious position by such action, but when we consider the condition they were placed in and their desire to earn a living which was upright in order to protect themselves morally, we can well — and rightfully do we — accept their explanation. (*The Voice*, 24 Feb. 1899)

Perhaps the best publicized women's strike during this period was at Bell Telephone in 1907. Four hundred non-unionized women operators, protesting poor conditions, low wages and an increase in working hours went out on strike. The threatened strike attracted so much public attention and support that the mayor of Toronto called in W.L.M. King to attempt to forestall it. When King was unable to prevent the strike, the controversy resulted in the formation of a Royal Commission to investigate the matter. During this time, the women attempted to unionize, twice passing resolutions to affiliate with the International Brotherhood of Electrical Workers (IBEW), which had claimed jurisdiction over telephone operators. According to J. Sangster, however, the IBEW had developed a strong tradition of inequality based on the belief that women made poor union members. "The electricians claimed that unskilled operators might make foolish decisions on craft matters which they did not understand. There was also a strong apprehension about 'petticoat rule': the large number of operators, it was feared, would come to control the union" (Sangster 1978).

Consequently, the union did not help to organize the telephone operators, abandoning the struggle to reformers who translated the strike from a labour issue to a motherhood issue. The press and the commission were most sympathetic to the women, but their sympathies were for protecting these women as future mothers rather than workers. The women's demands for unionization and higher wages were lost in the subsequent inquiry, which focussed upon medical-maternal matters. Medical evidence to the commission stated: "...they turn out badly in their domestic relations. They breakdown nervously and have nervous children, and it is a loss to the community....The effects moreover upon posterity occasioned by the undermining of the female constitution cannot receive too serious consideration" (*Labour Gazette*, Oct. 1907: 397–99).

While labour's position on women's employment fluctuated throughout this period, they were most likely to receive support from the reformers for protectionist policies, and they most frequently settled on this strategy. Labour's relative weakness in relation to employers encouraged their alliances with the middle-class reformers; however, this resulted in a pattern of short-term patriarchal solutions, with protectionist and exclusionist policies predominating. If these strategies do represent compromises it is important to note that these compromises were greatly facilitated by the labour movement's longstanding prejudices about womanhood.

Women and Patriarchy

The last group identified as having possible interests in contradiction to the reformers' patriarchal blueprint were women, especially the organized group of feminists associated with the suffrage movement. Much has been written about the early women's movement, not only in Canada, but also in England and the United States, documenting the gradual transformation of the early women's movement from an overtly antipatriarchal stance to a maternal feminist position.[6] The maternal feminists represented a modern defence of patriarchy by advocating a more prominent position for women in society on the grounds of their special qualities as nurturers and moral guardians.

In spite of the similarities in the ethnic and class background of reformers and early feminists, their response to the changing productive and reproductive relations brought on by industrialization were quite different. In contrast to the reformers' focus on family and motherhood, the early feminists focussed on women and advocated equal opportunity and equal treatment of the sexes. The equal rights strategy failed precisely because it was not a "motherhood issue" literally or figuratively. The problem with the feminist strategy was three-fold. First, their focus on women rather than the family failed to address a predominant concern of the period, the declining birth rate. Not only did they bypass this issue but their strategy, which opposed the concept of a woman's sphere, was popularly perceived of as a program that would only exacerbate the problem. In a rabidly pronatalist period, such a position was bound to provoke opposition. Second, while reformers were able to invoke patriarchal tradition to support their cause, the early feminist strategy flew in the face of all patriarchal tradition. Consequently, important institutional sources of support for the reformers were equally important institutional sources of opposition for the feminists. Third, the equal-rights strategy served to alienate business, labour and professionals alike. Labour organizations and professions, dominated by males, resisted the unwelcome category of competition. Business was united against the equal-rights strategy because it would erode the unique value of women to employers — the cheapness and malleability of the labour supply — all of which presupposed patriarchal family structures and tradition.

The social reformers had all the political advantages the early feminists lacked. They could invoke patriarchal tradition, could ally themselves with labour, business and professionals in a way that promised a more concrete set of resolutions to distressing social problems and in a manner that would elevate women's status (granted, within narrowly prescribed roles). With reformers increasingly promoting women's suffrage as a means to their ends, the suffrage movement was engulfed by the reform movement. The early feminists, founders of the suffrage movement, were confronted with a simple choice: accept their absorption in the reform movement and the consequent social legitimacy, powerful allies and a reasonable expectation of success in a shorter period of time, or opt out. Not surprisingly the majority stayed in, leaving behind a splinter group too small and isolated to carry on any effective resistance to the patriarchal blueprint of the social reformers.[7]

In the subsequent chapters I will examine the extent to which state intervention conformed to the social reformers' vision of the good society. I will further explore the connection between the Social Reform Movement and social policy, while I note the transformation from private philanthropist to public servant as the personnel and policies of the movement became integrated into new state regulatory agencies.

PERIOD I:
1884–1913

In 1884 Ontario passed the Factories Act; this has been long recognized as an historic moment in industrial relations in Canada since this act became the model for most early labour legislation in the English-speaking provinces. It was also an historic moment in reproductive relations. With the exception of some earlier legislation in the area of the family, 1884 marks the onset of a flurry of legislative activity in the areas of labour, family and welfare law, which, when examined as a whole, reveals a remarkable pattern of state intervention into the processes of reproduction and production.

The pressures for state intervention result from the growing imbalance between production and reproduction. This imbalance exists as a potential in all class systems, but becomes most manifest and problematic in a wage-labour system, because it separates the short-term interests of production, profit, from the long-term interests of society as a whole in the reproduction of the population. Historically, the contradiction between production and reproduction is manifest in different forms under different material conditions. In this period it is manifest as a serious disruption of reproductive relations. Empirically, state intervention is observable in legislative and policy changes that attempt to achieve some accommodation between the two spheres. I identify the goal of state intervention as accommodation because the state, to date, has shown no inclination to fundamentally restructure production to better meet the needs of reproduction. Thus, state intervention is best understood as an attempt to reduce the extreme consequences of imbalance, to ameliorate the most troublesome symptoms of the contradiction.

Accommodation in this period took the form of a legislatively sanctioned separation of productive and reproductive roles. Following the blueprint provided by the social reformers, "saving the family" became synonymous with keeping women in the home. The result was the legislatively engineered "support-service" family structure — the male-breadwinner, female-homemaker family ideal. This accommodation, which would be sustained throughout the first two periods, involved both a reformation of the wage-labour system and a transformation of patriarchy.

State intervention typically involves three processes. First, state-commissioned inquiries serve to translate broad-based demands into specific recommendations upon which the state could act; second, specific legislation is passed; and third, regulatory agencies are developed to enforce the provisions of legislation. The latter element is clearly as critical as the legislation itself. Although the reform of the wage-labour system and the transformation of patriarchy are structurally and historically interconnected, these processes are manifest in different inquiries, legislation and agencies. The wage-labour system was reformed by labour laws that increasingly limited the use of child and female labour in the productive sphere. The old patriarchal system was transformed through family and welfare legislation. Both of these processes were critical in realigning the patriarchal order with the new economic system. The analysis follows the same trajectory as actual state intervention — inquiries, legislation and regulatory agencies.

The Reformation of the Wage-Labour System

According to H. Clare Pentland (1981), the state in Canada has a long history of mediation in the labour process that significantly predates industrialization or the Factories Act. The significance of the Factories Act does not, therefore, lie in the fact of intervention, but rather in the nature of intervention. Prior to 1884 state interventions in the labour process were primarily designed to repress and police labour in the interests of employers (Pentland 1981).

An examination of labour legislation before 1884 indicates that there were only a few statutes on the books in Manitoba and Ontario, such as the Master and Servant Act and the Apprentices and Minors Act, that contained any clauses protecting workers' interests and or rights. Such laws provided minimal protection and the absence of any system of enforcement and/or regulation suggests minimal commitment on the part of the state to the protective intentions of these acts. On the other hand, the criminal code of Canada treated unions as criminal combinations in restraint of trade until 1872; unregistered unions were criminal until 1889. The General Railway Act (SC 1868 c.68) set fines of four hundred dollars or five-year jail terms for strikes, and the Militia Act (SC 1868) provided troops to local governments to police labour.

In the 1880s, however, a change in the character of state mediation began to emerge. Canadian historians point out that the late-nineteenth and early twentieth century was a period of growing labour organization and resistance (G. Kealey 1980; Pentland 1968; Palmer 1979). One indication that this was putting pressure, not only on employers, but also on the state is the number of federal royal commissions dealing with labour disputes — twenty-one in the thirty-year period. Under such pressure the state could no longer politically afford the public role of employers' henchman. It became increasingly necessary to make some concessions to labour. As a result, the degree of legislative activity in the area of labour accelerated dramatically after 1884. Ontario introduced nine new labour laws in the ten-year period between 1884 and 1894. While the amount of legislation marks a substantial break with the past, the most important difference lay in the content of the legislation, which for the first time set out to regulate conditions of work and employment (e.g., the Factories and Mines Acts of 1884 and 1890), as well as to provide some legal recourse to workers abused by the system (e.g., Wages Act 1885 and Workmen's Compensation Act 1886).

This new mediating role of the state, derived from its mandate to co-ordinate the competing demands production and reproduction, is best understood as an attempt to modify two of the most troublesome aspects of the wage-labour system; first, the relentless drive towards the commodification of labour and, second, the indiscriminate consumption of labour regardless of age or sex. These tendencies not only provoked great struggle on the part of labour, but were also particularly problematic in their effect on reproductive relations. Employers dissociated their short-term profit interests from their long-term interests in reproducing the labour force. In the nineteenth century, the result was wage levels set so low that they barely ensured the daily maintenance of the worker themselves, much less their generational reproduction. As well, no compensation beyond the actual labour time was available. Thus, the Workmen's Compensation Act of 1886, limited as it was, introduced an important restriction of the commodification process. It extended the obligation of the employer beyond the actual labour time paid for, by providing compensation to workers injured under certain circumstances. This legislation is a good example of the intricate balancing act of the state mediating productive and reproductive pressures by locating a point of consensus between the polarities of employer-employee interests. On the one hand, the act was a major piece of protective legislation that guaranteed the right of workers and their families to make claims upon their employers in case of accidents in the work place; on the other hand, the act also served to protect employers by institutionalizing a limited degree of liability.

The Factories, Shops and Mines Acts of 1884, 1888 and 1890 are examples of attempts to modify the second aspect of the dynamic of the wage-labour system, the indiscriminate consumption of labour power. The increasing scale of female and child employment in industrial areas raised a dual spectre: on the one hand the exhaustion and/or abuse of female workers implied the depletion of societies' reproducers; on the other hand the exhaustion and/or abuse of child labour implied the depletion of future labour resources. The more benevolent aspects of these acts, therefore, served to limit the use of labour and to improve the health and safety conditions under which labour worked.[1]

But the indiscriminate use of labour presented another kind of problem — one that threatened the interests of patriarchy. There was no built in assurances that the employment of women would respect certain patriarchal necessities — the maintenance of women's subordinate status relative to men. Patriarchal tradition and perhaps the physical conditions of work during the early industrial period resulted in a clear sexual division in the labour force, with women concentrated in light industry and men concentrated in heavy industry. However, with the advent of machino-facture, there was no mechanism within the wage-labour system itself that would ensure the perpetuation of such a division. Employers in their short-sighted pursuit of profit could well extend the use of cheap female labour to other, previously male, occupations. If the pursuit of profit was a stronger motive than the perpetuation of patriarchy, this could seriously disrupt the sexual segmentation of the labour force. Since the appeal of the wage-labour system lay precisely in its ability to facilitate the short-term extraction of surplus, regardless of reproductive considerations (including a disregard for patriarchal traditions that do not directly enhance the surplus extraction process), then it is not unreasonable to assume that the unmeditated dynamic of the wage-labour system could reduce distinctions between male and female labour.

Not only could the extensive integration of women in the labour force threaten the patriarchal premise of female subordination, and conflict with the long-term process of generational reproduction, but it would also erode women's special appeal to employers as a cheap reserve of labour. Women's status as a cheap reserve is dependent upon their marginalization. If they became an integral part of the labour force, this particular characteristic would be lost. Labour legislation in this period played a crucial role in perpetuating the sexual division of labour, maintaining the primacy of women's reproductive role and reinforcing patriarchal structures by restricting women's productive role.

Commissions and Inquiries

In the seventeen years from Confederation to 1884, there were thirty-one Royal Commissions in Canada, only one of which — an inquiry into labour laws in Massachusetts — dealt with the concerns of labour. However, the growth of the labour-reform movement in the 1880s exerted increasing pressure on the federal and provincial governments of central Canada. Although bills to regulate factories were introduced at nearly every session of the federal parliament during the 1880s, no legislation was enacted (G. Kealey 1973, ix). The Macdonald government resisted legislation on the grounds of constitutional jurisdiction, but did initiate a series of investigations in an attempt to placate labour reformers. Indeed, between 1884 and 1913 there were no less than twenty-one federal royal commissions concerning labour and industrial disputes. Ontario, the most industrialized province, followed suit; there was a royal commission in 1910 on the question of workmen's compensation, and three special committee reports, one concerning female labour in 1900, one concerning child labour in 1907 and a report on underground work in Ontario mines in 1912. There were no official government inquiries in Manitoba at this time.

Two consistent themes emerged from the federal and provincial inquiries. First, there was a growing conviction that the state must play an active mediating role in employer-employee relations. Second, there was strong consensus that female labour is different from male labour and, therefore, must be subject to special protections and restrictions. The commissioners' vision of the role of the state is illustrated in their routine recommendations that the state regulate hours and conditions of work through the initiation and enforcement of factory acts. Recognizing the importance of expanding the state's role in this area, the Royal Commission on Labour and Capital 1889 (Labour Commission) advocated the institution of a Labour Bureau, which would continually monitor labour conditions across Canada. An act establishing the Labour Bureau was passed in 1890, although it did not become operative till 1900. It is interesting to note that although the Labour Commission was divided according to the members' class sympathies, there was a general consensus on two points — the need to expand the mediating role of the state and the need to regulate and restrict the role of women in the work place.

Inquiries that addressed the issue of female labour had

several features in common. First, it was agreed that adult women workers be separated from adult male workers and that they be included with children in recommendations on hours and conditions of work. Second, special attention was paid to the impact of employment on women's health, and finally, there was a unique concern with the impact of employment on the morals of female workers.

The commissioners' special concern for women's health reflects the common assumption during this period (actively fostered by the medical profession) that women's reproductive capacity made them physically vulnerable, and that if women were to be employed, then the work environment must take this into consideration. As the Labour Commission noted: "...medical testimony proves conclusively that girls, when approaching womanhood cannot be employed at severe or long-continued work with out a serious danger to their health, and the evil effects may follow them throughout their lives" (G. Kealey 1973, 22). Thus "girls," unlike "boys," were perceived to become more vulnerable with age rather than less. The report of the commissioners on the dispute between Bell Telephone and its operators contained some unusual recommendations that can only be understood in terms of reproductive considerations. In addition to the usual issues of hours of work, age at employment and conciliation, they recommended the appointment of a commission of medical experts, regular health examinations and better seats for this largely female workforce.

The concern for morals tended to focus on two issues, the intermingling of the sexes on the job and the importance of separate sanitary facilities. While it was recognized that sex-segregated work places would be impractical, recommendations stressed the importance of minimizing and controlling the contact between the sexes on the shop floor. The Labour Commission recommended the provision of separate lavatories and the employment of female factory inspectors and shop floor supervisors as the primary means of achieving this separation.

This approach to female labour suggests that the very first steps taken by the state to mediate in the productive process, not only reflected a nineteenth-century patriarchal model of womanhood, but also through its recommendations served to ensure that this model with its procreative assumptions would not be abandoned in the face of a major economic transformation. These underlying reproductive considerations are also evident in the legislation that served to institutionalize the special status of women workers recommended by the commissions.

Legislation

The manifest concern of the early factory legislation was the improvement of the conditions of labour. However, beneath this manifest goal, there was a more fundamental and determinative concern — the co-ordination of the productive-reproductive needs of society. Labour legislation directly addressed the intersection of production and reproduction through laws that determined the special conditions of female and child labour and distinguished it from the conditions of male labour. It is possible to assess the extent to which these laws spoke to the presumed interests of women as reproducers, the self-expressed interests of women as workers and the existing sexual segmentation of the labour market as a means of illustrating the latent goals and concerns guiding state intervention.

Ontario's labour statutes precede and are the model for Manitoba legislation. For example, the Workmen's Compensation Act (1886) and the Shops Act (1888), introduced first in Ontario in 1886, were replicated almost word for word in the drafting of the Manitoba legislation. Differences in the economic development of the two provinces explain the differences in the schedule of legislation.

Although Manitoba's Factories Act contained the same basic clauses as the Ontario legislation, it was applied more stringently. For example, in Ontario in 1900 the legislation defined a child legally as any one under fourteen, where as in Manitoba legislation stipulated sixteen as the cut-off age. The two provinces also diverged in terms of coverage of factories. Initially, in Ontario the legal definition of a factory was any establishment employing twenty persons or more and involved in the manufacturing of goods with machines. By 1897 the definition was revised to cover establishments employing five persons or more. In Manitoba the initial act applied to all establishments employing two persons or more. The Manitoba act was revised in 1904 loosening up the restrictions and bringing them more in line with Ontario. It also lowered the legal age to fourteen for boys and fifteen for girls and applied the act to those establishments employing five persons or more. Inspite of these differences, the laws that established a legal distinction between male and female labour were present in both provinces, and Ontario statutes are consistent with and in most cases anticipatory of Manitoba legislation. (See table A2.1. Protective Labour Legislation in Ontario and Manitoba, Period I.)

The Factories, Shops and Mines Acts initiated legal distinctions between male and female/child labour. These three laws are important because they institutionalized the patriarchal conventions upon which these distinctions were derived and set the parameters for subsequent legislation, which expanded upon and perpetuated such conventions. Also, the acts encompassed a broad range of occupational fields, covering all of the manufacturing and mechanical sector (Factories Act), much of the commercial sector (Shops Act) and an important component of the primary sector (Mines Act). Throughout the first period, these three laws were subject to frequent amendments and consolidations that introduced ever more distinctions between male and female/child labour. It is important to note that these amendments were cumulative. Indeed, by 1912 these three acts contained twenty-three major distinguishing clauses that enumerated and entrenched the legal distinctions between male and female/child labour. (See table A2.2. Ontario Legislation: Changes in the Regulation of Female and Child Wage Labour, Period I.)

A number of social historians have observed that the above legislation had more to do with women as reproducers than as workers (Klein and Roberts 1974). As architects of this legislation, reformers and commissioners clearly had a one-dimensional definition of womanhood — woman as mother. In this sense, the legislation can be understood as a form of legal recognition of the value of women's reproductive role, since it protected women, as active or potential reproducers, from being totally consumed in the productive process. The legislation introduced limitations on the hours that women could work, the places in which they could work and the quality of the work environment. Such a focus highlights the protective, benevolent character of these acts and were included in the factory inspectors' reports of improvements in the safety, health and sanitary conditions for female labour.

The frame of reference for this legislation was the presumed needs of women as reproducers. I use the term "presumed" advisedly because it was not working women themselves who defined these needs. In fact, there is some evidence that the working women did not share the patriarchal model of womanhood assumed in this legislation. Given the general antinatalist dynamic of the wage-labour system, the legislators option was to circumscribe women's productive role in deference to the requirements of reproduction. However, the increasing demand for birth control and abortion and the declining birth rate suggest that women had another accommodation in mind. Furthermore, on the occasions when women workers' demands have been recorded, their concerns — better wages, better hours and unionization — were not much different than those of men (Klein and Roberts 1974).

The omissions in the legislation are as telling as the acts themselves. The number of women workers excluded from these statutes is striking. The single largest category of employed women, domestics, were excluded from any protective legislation (Leslie 1974). Similarly, women working in their homes doing piece work or women working in small establishments were also exempt since the Factories Act initially applied to places employing twenty persons or more. It appears that, the closer work approximated women's traditional role, the less likely it was that legislators would see the necessity for state regulation, regardless of how exploitive the conditions of labour were.

The most significant omission, however, was the legislation's failure to address the most compelling problem for women workers — the wage disparity between men and women. While it is true that the issue of wage scales did not enter into any legislation during this period, it is important to note that, in making the case that women were a special category of labour subject to special concerns and in need of special protection, a rationale existed for intervention on wage disparities. Of all the "special needs" of women workers, the wage discrepancy was clearly the most fundamental.

Evidence available from the Ontario Bureau of Industries and the *Labour Gazette* indicates that throughout the first period it was nearly impossible for a female factory worker

Table 3
Earnings and Budget Position of Female Workers in Ontario, 1889

	Women Over 16 Years of Age without Dependants	Women Over 16 Yearsof Age with Dependants
Average number of dependants	0	2.10
Average number of hrs./week worked	54.03	58.20
Average number of days/yr. worked	259.33	265.43
Average wages/yr. from occupation	216.71	246.37
Extra earnings aside from regular occupation	0	23.05
Earnings of dependants	0	16.48
Total earnings/yr.	216.71	285.90
Total cost of living/yr.	214.28	300.13
Surplus/Deficit (-)	2.43	-14.23

SOURCES: *Annual Report of the Bureau of Industries for the Province of Ontario, Pt. 4, 1889* Sessional Papers 22.7: 43,49; Rotenberg (1974).

to make a living wage. The wage and cost of living figures for female factory workers in Toronto in 1889 clearly illustrates this problem (see table 3). Female workers without dependants made a tiny surplus over subsistence costs. This subsistence was achieved only if she maintained a fifty-four-hour work week, presumably never missing work due to illness or accidents and never having additional medical or other expenditures beyond the most basic food, clothes and shelter costs. In the case of women with dependants, the table indicates that, even when these women worked five hours more per week and six days more per year than women without dependants, their wages failed to meet the most basic costs of survival.

A report in the *Labour Gazette* twenty-four years later indicates that the situation of women workers had not substantially changed. C.M. Derrick of McGill University reports that the average wage of female factory workers in Canada in 1913 was $261/year or $5/week (1913: 1373). The living wage at that time was considered to be $390/year or $7.50/week.

Further evidence of the pervasive practice and serious consequences of low wages for female workers was provided by the Social Survey Commission, which was established in 1913 to investigate the problem of prostitution in Toronto. The commission argued that women's inability to make a living wage was a major factor in contributing to prostitution and recommended the passage of a minimum-wage law. Despite the fact that female factory workers were among the most protected workers under the legislation of the time, this protection did nothing to alleviate the primary economic problem they faced. By 1914, one third of employed women were working in factories in Ontario, yet their ability to earn a living wage was no better than before the passing of the Factories Act (*Report of the Royal Commission on Unemployment* 1914, 59).

Labour Bureaucracies

One indication of the seriousness with which the Canadian state pursued its new mediating role was the establishment of government agencies, which, in the case of labour, had two functions. First, labour bureaus both at the federal and provincial levels operated as ongoing commissions or inquiries, compiling labour statistics, as well as reports from labour representatives on current issues of concern or controversy. Second, the factory inspectorate, at the provincial level, monitored employers' compliance with state regulations, informed employers of violations and fined or prosecuted offenders when necessary.

However, the state was reluctant to assume its new monitoring role as in most cases there was a significant time lag between the passage of the legislation and the emergence of a fully operational agency. At the federal level, there was a ten-year time lag between the establishment of a labour bureau in 1890 and its actual operation in 1900. In Ontario a labour bureau was established in the Department of Agriculture in 1882 but did not operate as such until 1900 when it was relocated in the Department of Public Works. The Ontario Factories Act passed in 1884 called for the inspection of factories; however, the first inspector was not hired until 1887, and in 1890 there were only three inspectors for the whole province. These numbers increased only gradually; in 1895 the first female inspector was hired, and in 1904 a second woman was added. By 1909 there were nine inspectors including two women for the province. Once hired, however, the factory inspectors in Ontario were diligent in their duties, and from 1888 onward the Ontario Sessional Papers contained detailed annual reports on factory conditions throughout the province.

Manitoba's enforcement of the Factories Act was much less systematic than Ontario's. The first reference to the existence of an inspector appears in the Manitoba Sessional Papers in 1902, buried in a paragraph in the Public Works report. Manitoba had only one inspector on staff until 1913 to monitor all factories within the province. Only two reports on factory conditions appeared in the Manitoba Sessional Papers in the first period. In the 1912 report the inspector indicates that the biggest area of complaints of abuse was in the shops of Manitoba, an area over which he had no authority to inspect, and apparently no one else was responsible for enforcing the Shops Act in the province.

Factory inspector's reports are a good indicator of the philosophy and practice of government intervention in the sphere of production. The Ontario reports reflected and amplified the same patriarchal assumptions and concerns articulated by the commissioners and legislators. The rationale for protective legislation and the necessity for enforcing it is eloquently argued by one factory inspector:

> When I tell you that today we have in this province, women working in the foundries, machine shops, and breweries, some of the weaker sex, and not a few of their champions will be surprised. I do not mention this as meaning to say that labour for women and children is degrading, but rather to show ample reason why they should be protected ... the effect of propagation by the present race and the degeneration of future generations. (*Reports of the Inspectors of Factories for the Province of Ontario* [*R.I.F. ... Ontario*], 1905 Sessional Papers 37: 21)

The inspectors' perception of their role reflected the dominant reform philosophy of the time, which maintained that government regulation was designed to protect employers who wanted to initiate reform as much as it was to protect workers. As one inspector put it, "Factory laws are for the mutual benefit and protection of both manufacturing and labouring classes" (*R.I.F. ... Ontario*, 1908 Sessional Papers 49: 58). The aspiration to serve both employer and employee by definition limited the concerns of inspection to work-environment issues rather than wage issues. Concern with the health and morals of the working woman translated into detailed reports on lunch-room facilities, seats for women, communal drinking pails and, above all, the provision of separate, modest and clean lavatories.

The inspectors' preoccupation with sanitation was reinforced, if not determined, by the limitations imposed on them by the legislation. The labour laws did not interfere with the central nexus of employer-employee relations — the wage. The legislation ignored the issue of exploitative wage rates in the case of female and child labour. It also failed to legislate on well-documented abuses of the wage system, such as the manipulation of apprenticeship/training periods and excessive fining for errors or lateness, which frequently left women and children with next to no wage by the end of the week. Even when the legislation permitted and the inspectors addressed serious issues of exploitation, the limits of their authority made it clear they were no match for the industrialists when a serious conflict of interest occurred. For example, in the 1908 inspectors' report there was a lengthy discussion of how the employment of children in mica factories in the Ottawa area violated the existing labour laws. The inspector reported that when he confronted the employers with these violations they stated that if the inspector attempted to enforce the law they would simply relocate to Quebec where restrictions were not so severe or establish a putting-out system (production in the household). Indeed when pressed to comply with the law, the employers carried out their threat to relocate with impunity.

The final stage of state activity, the development of regulatory agencies, is consistent in process and perspective with the preceding stages. All levels of intervention are characterized by a sustained, if somewhat reluctant, increase in the mediation role of the state generally and a consistent commitment to a specific pattern of perception and protection of women as reproducers.

Transformation of Patriarchy

The accommodation of reproduction to production in this period took the form of a socially and legislatively sanctioned sexual division of labour — the support-service marriage structure. Labour legislation contributed to this model by restricting women's role in production to ensure her specialization in reproduction. It was, however, equally necessary to legislate the "support" component of this family structure. This involved the legislative transformation of the "patriarch" into a breadwinner. This transformation constituted the first step in the transition from familial to social patriarchy. It involved more than just enforcing men's responsibility to provide for their family; it also involved a new role for the state. As the authority of the individual patriarch over women and children declined, it did not just disappear. It was centralized in the state, and with its new authoritative role, the state was also called upon to provide support in the absence of the breadwinner.

Analytically, the transition from familial to social patriarchy can be broken down into three component processes: first, the erosion of the patriarch's legal authority over women and children, revealed in a shift in the legislation from father/husband's rights to father/husband's responsibilities; second, the increasing assumption of the patriarch's traditional authority by the state; and, third, the provision of resources to subsidize the familial unit of reproduction. This transition process can be traced in two areas of state activity: family law and welfare law.

Two specific aspects of family legislation — laws determining the disposition of children and laws determining the disposition of property within a marriage and upon its dissolution — are most revealing of the actual content of family relations, particularly power relations. Correspondingly, two features of welfare legislation — the extension of state authority over the care and disposition of children and the growth of welfare resources to meet the needs of certain categories of dependants — show the process of increasing state intervention, which transformed the patriarchal family in order to save it.

Family Law

During the nineteenth century in Canada there was no clearly defined category of family law; in fact, family law is itself quite recent, dating from the mid-twentieth century. As a result, early laws regulating family relations were dispersed over a variety of property laws, estate statutes and illegitimacy and guardianship acts. This results in a number of differences in the development of family legislation relative to the other legislation under review in this book. First, during this period no inquiries or commissions specifically addressed family law. Second, no regulatory agencies developed to enforce the legislation. The existing court system continued to handle cases concerning disposition of property or children in an adversarial rather than a regulatory system. Finally, family law, unlike labour or welfare legislation, was marked by a high degree of legislative activity prior to 1884.

The first step in the transition from familial to social patriarchy — the erosion of the patriarch's legal authority over women — was the Married Women's Property Act introduced in Ontario in 1859. Prior to this change, marital property law was based on the common-law concept of "legal unity," whereby women's married identity was submerged in that of her husband's. Thus, all property upon marriage belonged to the husband.

The Married Women's Property Act (MWPA) and subsequent amendments gradually extended to married women the same property rights as single women, thus abrogating the common law concept of "legal unity" (see table A2.3. Disposition of Marital Property in Ontario and Manitoba,

Period I). A consequence of the act was the elimination of the common-law practice of curtsey, included in a number of property laws, which had ensured a husband's claim on his wife's property. The complement of curtsey was "dower," which ensured a wife's claim upon a portion of her husband's property, if he died without a will, and prohibited a husband from willing all his property away from his wife. Interestingly enough, the dower law was not abolished with the introduction of the MWPA. Thus curtsey, which reflected a patriarchal right, was abolished while dower, which reflected a patriarchal responsibility, was maintained.

In keeping with this new emphasis upon male responsibility, Ontario (1888) and Manitoba (1900) introduced legislation that made husbands liable for support of wives and children in cases of desertion or separation. However, these acts while significantly reordering the balance between rights and responsibilities contained some unambiguously patriarchal clauses, the adultery clause being the most significant. A woman lost all right to sue for an order for protection, for maintenance by her husband or to claim her children if she was found at any time to have committed adultery without her husband's collusion. Thus, regardless of how brutal her husband, how long the separation or desertion or how legitimate her claim to her children, all would be lost if she did not maintain a chaste existence. Since marriage laws essentially contracted a woman's sexuality to her husband, regardless of the dramatic changes in property rights for married women, this fundamental premise of patriarchy was left untouched. Given the inaccessibility of divorce at this time,[2] a husband in effect maintained a life-time ownership of his wife's sexuality, and this feature was preserved in the new property laws. Thus, although a husband may have lost access to his wife's sexuality through legal separation, he never lost control in law over her capacity to reproduce.

An interesting exception to the extension of married women's property rights was the abolition of dower in Manitoba and the other western provinces in 1885. Dower had not become a part of statute law in Manitoba, but dower rights were included in estate law and property law until 1885. The explanation for this anomaly appears to lie in the transformation of the land-registry system in western Canada. In this period of rapid settlement and development in Manitoba, land speculators were lobbying the government to adopt a new registry system referred to as the Torrens system. The virtue of this system was that it guaranteed uncontestable ownership of property upon issue of land titles. This was particularly important in view of the complex and cloudy nature of land claims in western Canada.[3] The new system required the government registry department to settle all claims before issue of title. Thus, anticipating and following the adoption of the Torrens system, a whole series of legislative amendments occurred to clarify and often eliminate claims based upon old laws and agreements. Native Canadians, Metis and women, through the abolition of the dower, seem to have been the major victims of the "streamlining" process.[4]

Twenty-five to thirty years after the establishment of the Torrens system, most provinces re-established dower rights, not only in the common-law practice, but in the legislation of Dower Acts. This move was in response to pressure from a number of women's groups including the National Council of Women. This case provides an interesting example of the interaction between economic and reproductive interests. While the general pattern towards extending and protecting married women's property rights was clearly established during the first period, the history of dower in western Canada shows how the power of economic interests determine the parameters within which the transformation of patriarchy occurs.

The general erosion of the patriarch's legal supremacy in property law was repeated in the area of child custody (see table A2.4. Legislation of Parental Custody Rights and Responsibilities in Ontario and Manitoba, Period I). Under British common law, children belonged solely to the father, who was the only family member endowed with legal personhood. Thus, women had no legal claim to their children within a marriage or in cases of separation, desertion or divorce. Even in widowhood, if the husband chose to will custody to an adult other than the mother, women had no legally recognized recourse. The first legal recognition of a mother's claim to her children appeared in Ontario in 1855 and considerably later in 1878 in Manitoba. Through the Infants Act and the MWPA, the right of the mother's claim to custody and guardianship became extended.

Although the legislative changes introduced are significant, it is important to note that, throughout the first period, fathers were assumed to be the rightful custodian, and mothers' custody rights were granted under particular circumstances, (i.e., the "tender years" concept, cruelty or desertion). Thus, while this era witnessed the establishment of equity of property rights, within a marriage there was no concept of equity of parental rights. Furthermore, all custody rights extended to mothers were subject to the same adultery clause that limited the rights of married women in property law — a clause that never applied to men.

As men's rights over their children were being eroded, their responsibilities were being extended. This pattern is particularly clear in the Illegitimacy Acts of the first period. In Upper Canada prior to 1859, a father of an illegitimate child could be ordered to pay restitution to the mother's guardians on the assumption of loss of service during time of pregnancy and birth. In 1859 the act was amended, significantly changing the legal basis of restitution from one of lost services to one of responsibility for one's progeny. In Manitoba this transition did not occur until 1912, when the Illegitimacy Act was introduced. The entrenchment of a mother's right to sue for support simultaneously served to recognize the mother as a legal person in her own right, rather than as a ward, and to legislate a father's economic responsibility regardless of marital status.

The crisis in familial patriarchy brought on by the wage-labour system was a product of the male head of household's loss of control over the resources necessary to sustain his family. This translated into a declining ability of men in general to support their dependants and a consequent decline in their authority. The end product of this development was the transformation of married men's status from *patriarch* to *breadwinner*. This transition should make clear that the bottom line of patriarchy is *not* male privilege *per se*, but control of reproduction through control of women. The above legislation suggests that traditional male privileges were dispensed with when they got in the way of controlling reproduction[5]. The reforms in family law were necessary for such a transition and reveal a consistent goal — to maintain and enforce, where necessary, the privatization of the costs of reproduction. This was accomplished by four major pieces of legislation that described male responsibility and removed legal encumbrances that had prevented women from assuming the responsibility in the absence of a functioning breadwinner (see table A2.5. Ontario Family Legislation, Period I: Reductions in Patriarchal Authority over Family Property and Guardianship and Increased Responsibility for Maintenance). The overall pattern that emerges is, as predicted, an extension of women's rights and an extension of men's responsibilities.

Family law reform was a necessary but not sufficient step

toward accommodating patriarchy to the new economic order. The declining ability of men to support their dependants, the declining benefits to men for assuming such responsibilities and the limited earning power of women meant that there were many cases in which the norm of privatizing reproductive costs could not be enforced. Thus, a necessary corollary of the revisions in family law was the development of welfare legislation that attempted to fill the gap created by declining male authority and a growing number of destitute dependents.

Welfare

In response to the resource and authority crises of the family, state welfare intervention in the late-nineteenth century was characterized by increasing levels of authority over the family and an increase in the provision of resources to certain categories of dependants. A review of the extension of state authority over the care and disposition of children in Ontario and Manitoba illustrates this process. Typically, analyses of state welfare activity focus on the provision of resources and emphasize the apparently benevolent character of such intervention. The relation between the provision of resources and authority has not previously been as systematically addressed. However, the assumption of greater authority over the family by the state is an integral and critical feature in the transition from familial to social patriarchy.

Control of reproduction has always been achieved by making submission to particular reproductive policies a first order condition of access to necessary resources. Although control of women is a consistent and universal feature of this process, the mechanism of control can vary dramatically from one society to the next, with men as a class having authority over women as a class (communal patriarchy), individual males having authority over individual females (familial patriarchy) or the state having control over the reproductive unit (social patriarchy).

The rapid substitution of state authority for the waning authority of the patriarch suggests a continued commitment to the control of reproduction. While such control was most blatant in the revision of the criminal code in 1892, in which birth control was criminalized and penalties for abortion increased (SC 1892 c.29), the operation of the regulatory clauses in welfare law illustrates the more subtle and pervasive character of this control. An enumeration of conditions of family life meriting the extension of state authority over children gives us a fairly good indication of the model of family life the state was committed to supporting/enforcing. This model, when considered in conjunction with the limitations imposed by labour and family law, suggests a clear and conscious state commitment to patriarchy, albeit in a revised and modernized form.

Commissions and Inquiries

State welfare intervention involved inquiries, legislation and the creation of regulatory agencies. While there were no specific "welfare commissions" during this period, many inquiries, especially those dealing with labour, crime and health, made reference to and occasionally recommended welfare programs or policies. These inquiries questioned the prevailing assumption that parents had the best interests of their children at heart and suggested that parent's ideas of the child's best interest could be seriously at odds with the state's idea.

In the past, the only explicit indications of the state's interest in the protection of children were the laws prohibiting infanticide or severe physical abuse. What commissioners and reformers alike came to advocate was the need for a series of laws to specify the necessary conditions for child well-being. Child welfare legislation was to be, not merely a list of crimes to be punished, but a series of positive conditions to be required of families, concerning the health, education and behaviour of the child and the legal, economic and moral condition of the parents. The reordering of familial authority between parents and the state was supported by the emergence of a new concept "children's rights." Indeed, Kelso, the long time social reformer appointed as the first Superintendent of Neglected Children for the province of Ontario, began his first report in 1894 with a quote from Bernardo:

> Are parental rights to be regarded as sacred when parental duties have not been neglected but outraged, and when the parents have done all in their power to make the life of the child while with them bitter and degraded! Has a child no rights? Are all the rights parental? (*Report of the Superintendent of Neglected Children for the Province of Ontario* [R.S.N.C. ... *Ontario*], *1894* Sessional Papers 47: 13)

Richard Splane's analysis of social welfare in Ontario identifies the 1890 Royal Commission on the Prison and Reformatory System as the most important inquiry in advancing public knowledge and official action in regard to child welfare. As he points out, the terms of reference of the commission were sufficiently broad to cover much of the contemporary field of social welfare: "Child welfare, was in fact, directly involved in each of the first three of the seven matters referred to the commission for investigation: Those relating to the causes of crime, the improvement of the industrial schools and the rescue of destitute children from criminal careers" (Splane 1965, 268).

The recommendations made by the commission advocated a much more active role for the state in the regulation of domestic life. The recommendations were particularly important because by and large they were implemented by 1913, suggesting a high degree of responsiveness on the part of the state. Included in the report was the recommendation that "an association...be formed having local boards in every important center of the Province who shall take upon themselves the important but delicate duty of looking after and caring for these (improperly cared for) children" (R.S.N.C. ... Ontario, 1891 Sessional Papers 18: 18). This was realized the same year with the founding of the Children's Aid Society. Furthermore, the commissioners recommended that the province defray "the actual expenses incurred" by proposing a voluntary association. They made a strong recommendation in favour of expanding the number of industrial schools and suggested they be included under the provisions of the Charity Aid Act, thus qualifying the schools for much more extensive state support. Also emphasized was the importance of school attendance, and measures were recommended for its "vigorous enforcement." As preventative measures, the commissioners recommended municipal curfews and supervised municipal playgrounds and gymnasia. Finally, in the area of corrections, they recommended the separate trial and detention of children. This issue was a central concern for prison reformers and was eventually realized in the introduction of the Juvenile Delinquency Act in the Criminal Code of Canada in 1908.

While no other inquiry seems to have been as wide-ranging in its approach to and recommendations for child welfare as the 1890 commission, subsequent inquiries stressed the continued necessity for state intervention. The Special Report on Immigrant Children in 1898, prepared by the Superintendent of Neglected Children, applauded the Child Immigrant Act but advocated further regulation and monitoring of immigrant children (*R.S.N.C. ... Ontario, 1898* Sessional Papers 60). The Special Committee appointed to report on the condition of the feeble minded called for greater government attention to separating and institutionalizing the "feeble minded," reflecting in this proposal a popular eugenic concern about preventing the deterioration of the race. Finally, the Special Committee on Infant Mortality and the Royal Commission on Milk (both in 1909) called for greater government initiative and activity in ensuring the physical and social welfare of children.

Helen MacMurchy, who was the director of the Special Committee on Infant Mortality, identified a number of social factors contributing to the problem of infant deaths. Women's employment was seen as particularly troublesome to the well being of young children. In response to this problem MacMurchy suggested, but did not formally recommend, several possible solutions. First, recognizing the link between women's employment and men's wages, she stressed the importance of a family wage. "... any man who does useful and necessary work ... should be paid enough to allow him to marry and support a family." Addressing the cases of women forced, through economic need, to return to work immediately after the birth of a child, MacMurchy stated, "It should not be allowed to happen. The mother should have a pension, if necessary, to take care of the family" (*Special Report on Infant Mortality, Ontario, 1910* Sessional Papers 9: 8). As a general measure to improve the quality of child care, she recommended a state-sponsored education campaign including health and nutrition pamphlets and visits to mothers and families by employees of the Public Health Department.

Despite the differences in terms of reference, the above inquiries share with the labour inquiries of the period a consensus on the necessity of increasing government intervention and regulation. The commissioners' and reformers' conviction that many people could not or would not be good parents paved the way for the state and its regulatory agencies to assume increasing authority and control over women and children in the family and justified increasing intervention on the grounds that the state was the best and most impartial judge of a child's well being. However, these inquiries differed from the labour inquiries in that their recommendations for intervention were implemented much more promptly through the enactment of the necessary legislation and the creation of the necessary agencies. This indicates the importance the state put on regulating women's lives at the point of reproduction.

Welfare Legislation

Prior to 1887 Manitoba and Ontario welfare law consisted of two statutes, the Apprentices artd Minors Act and the Charity Aid Act. Both acts dealt with the problem of care and support for the destitute. The Apprentices and Minors Act provided for the indenture of children who were orphaned or abandoned. The Charity Aid Acts established provincial support for hospitals and institutes for the destitute and the Ontario Charity Aid Act provided a formula for funding.

The year 1887 marks the onset of systematic welfare activity in Manitoba and Ontario (see table A2.6. Welfare Legislation in Ontario and Manitoba, Period I). The goals of the new legislation were threefold: first, the extension of support to public welfare institutions; second, increased government regulation of public welfare institutions; and, third, the increased regulation of children's environment and behaviour both within public institutions and in private families. Four statues, the Industrial Schools Act, the Infants Protection Act, the Child Protection Act and the Child Immigration Act, present in Manitoba and Ontario, formed the legislative framework for the child-welfare system in the two provinces. As in the case of labour law, Manitoba statutes followed Ontario legislation a number of years later and were very closely modeled on them.

The legislation of this period reveals increasing government intervention in and regulation of family life through increasing state authority over the disposition of children.[6] Indicators of increasing state authority over children include the specification of conditions for apprehension of children (including familial status, acts of children and acts of parents), the proliferation of agents of state authority and the growth of institutions or agencies for the apprehension of children.

The amendment of the Industrial Schools Act in Ontario in 1887 removed industrial schools from the authority of school boards and empowered charitable institutions to develop and supervise such schools. Board members of charitable institutions took on their new responsibility with enthusiasm, and the first industrial school was opened in Toronto in 1887. With the establishment of such institutions, provisions of the Industrial Schools Act that permitted state apprehension of children were now enforceable. These conditions were very important because they were the precursors of all later welfare clauses that provided for apprehension of children:

A child apparently under the age of fourteen years could be apprehended:
(1) Who is found begging or receiving alms, or being in any street or public place for the purpose of begging or receiving alms;
(2) Who is found wandering, and not having any home or settled place of abode or proper guardianship or not having any lawful occupation or business, or visible

means of subsistence;

(3) Who is found destitute, either being an orphan or having a surviving parent who is undergoing penal servitude or imprisonment;

(4) Whose parent, step-parent or guardian represents to the police magistrate that he is unable to control the child, and that he desires the child to be sent to an industrial school under this Act;

(5) Who, by reason of the neglect, drunkenness or other vices of parents, is suffered to be growing up without salutary parental control and education, or in circumstances exposing him to lead an idle and dissolute life. (SO 1874 c.29, sec. 4: 219)

In the same year as the amendment to the Industrial Schools Act, an Act for the Protection of Infant Children was passed, which provided for state regulation of maternity boarding houses, usually private homes that would take in destitute pregnant women. This act is particularly important because it reflected the first attempt by the state to regulate adoption procedures. The 1897 amendment to this act required that the Children's Aid Society (CAS) supervise and determine the adoption of all children under one year of age from private maternity homes. A 1912 amendment extended CAS's authority over adoption by including all children under three born in these homes. Although a specific adoption law did not appear until 1922, the state was, through this and other acts, slowly expanding its authority over adoption procedures.

In 1888 the Child Protection Act provided for state apprehension and custody of children under sixteen years of age judged ill-treated, neglected or delinquent and the prosecution of parents found guilty of neglect or abuse. In 1893 an amendment established the office of Superintendent of Neglected Children in the direct employ of the provincial government. This amendment also empowered the CAS, as the major regulatory agency, to inspect homes, apprehend children and place them in institutions or foster homes. Interestingly, neither this act nor the Industrial Schools Act, which were the major legislative devices for removing children from the custody of their parents, undermined the tradition of private responsibility for the costs of reproduction. Indeed, both acts contained clauses permitting the state to sue the parents for support of their children while in government institutions. Thus, although parents lost legal rights to their children, they were still held responsible for their maintenance.

In 1897 the Child Immigration Act was finally passed after years of controversy among social reformers concerning the impact of these children upon Canadian society (Sutherland 1976, 33). While these children had initially been welcomed as an inexpensive source of labour, growing concern about the quality of a child's environment, the purity of the race, and the rising demands on public welfare funds led to a more critical view of child immigrants. Some commentators argued that they were of "inferior stock," that filled the jails and poor houses, leading Canadian children astray. Other critics pointed out that the conditions to which these children were subjected in Canada were often neglectful or abusive. These concerns, in conjunction with organized labour's objection to the importing of cheap child labour, led the government to tighten control over the admission of child immigrants and to monitor their activities carefully during their first few years in Canada.

The above acts and amendments provided the legal apparatus for extending state control over children and the family. The acts were cumulative, adding more conditions for the apprehension of children, more agents to apprehend and supervise them and more institutions into which the state channeled their wards. A quick before and after comparison makes the point quite clearly. Prior to 1887 *one* law (The Apprentices and Minors Act) under *one* condition (a child without legal guardian) empowered *three* agents (charitable institutions, mayors or magistrates) to provide for children in *one* way (apprenticeship). By 1913 legislation had resulted in a proliferation of conditions under which the state could assume wardship, an expansion of institutions and programs for the disposition of such wards and the growth of regulatory agents to supervise and regulate public and private institutions of child care.

As of 1913 the welfare statutes had legislated *twelve* different conditions for state custody (in addition to the one original condition of a child without a legal guardian). These conditions referred to parents' or children's behaviour that was deemed unacceptable. Parents found to have committed the following acts could lose legal custody of their children: commitment of a child to a government-regulated institution; abandonment; neglect; immoral conduct; ill treatment or abuse of a child; permitting or encouraging a child to violate curfew, begging, vagrancy and labour laws. Children found to have committed the following acts, or in the following circumstances, would become state wards: begging or vagrancy; petty crime; children reported by parents or guardians as uncontrollable; any child under fourteen years of age whose actions resulted in their being brought before the court; institutionalized immigrant children; children expelled from school for vicious or immoral acts.

At the same time, the number of regulatory agents or agencies empowered to apprehend children also increased, from the original three (mayors, magistrates and charitable societies) to *eight* different government or charitable agencies. Finally, the number of agencies or institutions for the disposition of state wards similarly increased from the one provision of apprenticeship to *seven* different provisions: ranging from institutionalization, to adoption or to deportation in the case of immigrant children (see table A2.7. Ontario Welfare Legislation, Criteria for Apprehension of Children and Extension of State Authority over Children, Period I).

In summary, the welfare legislation affecting the disposition of children reveals two main points: the acts during the period 1887–1913 were clearly more regulative than supportive; the usual solution to a "bad" home environment was removal of the child and, frequently, prosecution of the parent. Also, it became increasingly evident that in order to enforce such legislation a comprehensive regulatory network had to be developed. The CAS assumed that responsibility and acquired a unique status as a quasi-state agency, empowered and financed by the state yet operating as a private agency run by its own board.

Welfare Bureaucracy

With the passing of the Child Protection Act, the state had committed itself to a new and more comprehensive child welfare program, without providing for any additional agents or agencies to administer the new program. Before long it became evident that enforcement of the Child Protection Act and other welfare statutes required some regulatory agency to administer the program.

The CAS, founded in Toronto in 1891 by the influential reformer J.J. Kelso, became identified with a broad range of "child-saving" programs. Its rapid spread throughout the province and its inexpensive operation (based largely on volunteer work) recommended the CAS as an ideal mechanism to administer the new child welfare program. In 1893 the Ontario Child Protection Act was amended to establish the position of the superintendent of neglected children and to empower the CAS with the right to apprehend children, inspect private homes upon complaint and supervise adoption. The legal power and the financial support accorded to the CAS by these amendments established it as the first welfare bureaucracy in the province and provided a model that would be adopted, not only in Manitoba, but in most of the other English-speaking provinces.

The use of a private agency to meet welfare needs was not surprising given that most welfare agencies, such as orphanages and refuges in this era, were run by private boards and largely funded by private contributions. What was unusual about the CAS was that it was legally empowered to enforce aspects of welfare law, specifically the apprehension of children. Further, unlike many other agencies incorporated into the state, it has retained its private status and experienced minimal government regulation. With the decentralized CAS reporting to the superintendent of neglected children, the government could now launch its new policy of monitoring childcare, not only in public institutions, but also in private homes.

The assumption of power by the CAS was not always smooth, as a case in Manitoba illustrates. The Child Protection Act was passed in Manitoba in 1898, and a CAS was founded in Winnipeg the same year. One year later, however, a major controversy erupted over the conduct of the CAS, brought to the attention of the Lieutenant Governor of the province by William Scott of the Winnipeg Labour Party. Scott was representing the case of a Winnipeg mother who had entrusted her children to the care of the CAS while she was ill, with the understanding that it was temporary care. When she was better she went to reclaim her children only to discover that the CAS had placed her children for adoption. This was most unexpected because in Manitoba and Ontario it was common practice at the time for parents to put their children in orphanages or other institutions during a time of ill health or other family crises and reclaim them when the problem was over. It was the investigation into this case ordered by the Lieutenant Governor that resulted in the Children's Aid Society Act in 1900.[7] The act provided a clearer statement of the authority of the CAS and more specific procedures for the apprehension of children including the requirement of a signed document from the parents releasing custody of their children in the absence of a court order.

The expansion of the CAS was rapid in comparison to the growth of the state-employed inspectors of public institutions. Between July 1893 and December 1895, the superintendent of neglected children in Ontario helped no less than twenty-nine societies to organize. As the number of societies expanded, the number of children under their care also increased. By 1897 the CAS in Ontario were placing two hundred children or more a year. The numbers increased steadily, and annual placement rose to six hundred in the period from 1910 to 1913. More important perhaps than the numbers were the type of children coming under the care of the CAS. From their earliest records it is clear that the majority of children were not orphans or abandoned, but were apprehended by the CAS from undesirable homes. A sample of wards' backgrounds in 1902 revealed that out of 200 only 63 had been abandoned or orphaned, while 112 had been apprehended because of "immoral homes, pauperism, lack of control." The remainder of the sample had been apprehended because of parental neglect, abuse or drunkenness (*R.S.N.C. ... Ontario, 1902* Sessional Papers 43). More detailed reports in 1912 and 1913 revealed that over 70% of CAS wards were apprehended from undesirable homes, with cruelty or neglect accounting for only 9% of the apprehensions in 1913 and 20% in 1912.

The shift from parental rights to parental responsibilities evident in the family legislation was more rigorously enforced in the welfare legislation. While family law limited itself to enforcing a parent's economic responsibility to children, the CAS, through various clauses in the Child Protection Act, took on the task of enforcing parents' moral responsibility. The Superintendent of Neglected Children's 1911 annual report contained an important paper entitled "Parental Responsibility" written by C.S. Pedley of the Woodstock CAS. Pedley began with the assertion, "Parental affection is an instinct, ...but parental responsibility is something different" (*R.S.N.C. ... Ontario, 1911* Sessional Papers 26: 101). Because even some affectionate and well-meaning parents may fail in their responsibility, it was the task of the CAS to correct the situation; as Pedley put it "...in the very act of taking their children from them we do something to bring their responsibility home to them." While he spoke of the advantage of returning children to their parents on probation, Pedley emphasized that there are cases where this should not be done:

> But if the natural parents are too far below average, so that the State steps in and takes charge of the children, it is not a question of interference, and an invasion of parental right — it is just the resumption of a trust out of the hands of trustees who have failed to make good. (*R.S.N.C. ... Ontario, 1911* Sessional Papers 26: 101-02)

The Superintendent's report in 1913 indicates just how frequently parents were found to be "too far below the average." While 72% of their wards that year were apprehended from undesirable homes, only 17% were returned to their parents on probation. From the beginning, officers of the CAS proved to be vigorous and enthusiastic moral entrepreneurs. There is, however, evidence of resistance by parents to their "child-saving" program, prompting an amendment to the Child Protection Act in 1890 that made it a criminal offence for a parent or any person to attempt to induce a child to run away from an institution or home to which they had been committed under the authority of the Child Protection Act.

While controversy has surrounded the CAS since its beginning, there is no doubt that in its work, philosophy and unique relation to the state it epitomized, perhaps as no other single organization did, the great transformation that characterized this period. CAS policies reflected a remarkable integration of the two imperatives of social patriarchy: the privatization of reproductive costs on the one hand, and increasing the authority of the state over the family on the other. Its policy of de-institutionalization, its aggressive interpretation of the breadwinners' responsibility, its commitment to keeping mothers in the home — all under increasing scrutiny of the state — are the perfect blueprint for social patriarchy. Even its organizational structure anticipated the great transition from private philanthropist to public health-and-welfare bureaucracies and the professionalization of social work in the twentieth century. By the end of the first period, the CAS had changed from a diverse group of "child savers" to a powerful regulatory agency enforcing welfare statutes at the behest of the state.

Welfare Expenditures

The state's move to fill the authority and resource gaps created by the demise of familial patriarchy was not without expense. Although welfare institutions relied most heavily on private donations during the first period, there was a growing demand for state welfare expenditures. The demand for government welfare occasioned by the disruption of reproductive relations and the rising number of destitute was first felt at the municipal level. By 1913 Ontario municipalities were spending $0.81 per capita on welfare, while the province expended $0.55 per capita. In that same year Manitoba municipalities were spending $2.38 per capita on welfare, while the province spent $0.90 per capita. The high expenditures in Manitoba were the result of population growth, which saw the western provinces urbanizing at a rate six times faster than central Canada (*Dominion-Provincial Commission Report*, 1937, Ch. 2, 85). The costs of welfare were unequally distributed among the three levels of government throughout the first period. For example, the *Dominion-Provincial Commission Report* (1937) indicates that in 1913 the welfare expenditures of all municipalities in Canada amounted to $5.8 million; in that same year all provincial welfare expenditures equalled $4.3 million, and federal welfare expenditures were $2.6 million.

Despite the fact that the federal and provincial governments were less burdened than the municipalities, their welfare budgets at the end of the first period represented a substantial growth from the beginning of the period. The provincial increase from $657 thousand in 1874 to $4.3 million constituted a 550% increase, while federal growth from $213 thousand to $2.6 million in the same time period marked a 1,120% increase in expenditure (see table 4).

Although the burden was unequally distributed, the overall pattern indicates a consistent increase in welfare costs to all levels of government. It is important to remember, however, that an accounting of government expenditures provides only the most conservative estimates of the social costs of the contradiction between production and reproduction. Throughout the first period, private charity and volunteer philanthropy played a significant role in absorbing these

Table 4

Provincial-Dominion Welfare Expenditures
for Selected Years (All of Canada) (In Dollars)

Year	Provincial Total	Dominion Total	Dominion Expenditures as % of Provincial Expenditure
1874	657,000	213,000	32%
1896	1,472,000	946,000	64%
1913	4,343,000	2,617,000	60%

SOURCE: *Dominion-Provincial Commission Report* 1937, Ch. 2, 63, 82.

costs. Despite the heavy welfare burden borne by private charities and local governments, the growth of provincial and federal budgets in this period was a harbinger of the expanding role the state would play in supporting the Canadian family.

Summary

The primary manifestation of the contradiction between production and reproduction during early industrialization in Canada was a disorganization of reproductive relations. This in turn led to an expanding role for the state in reorganizing and stabilizing those relations. The resolution of this contradiction involved a reorganization of the wage-labour system and a transformation of patriarchy. Evidence of the reorganization of the wage-labour system comes from the early labour laws, particularly the legislation that distinguished between male and female labour. This legislation was both supportive and regulatory in terms of reproduction. Its supportive thrust is revealed in the discriminatory clauses that protected reproducers (women) and future labour (children) from being completely exhausted in the production process. These same clauses also regulated the character of reproductive relations in that legislation reinforced the distinction between male and female labour and, thus, operated to preserve and solidify the existing sexual segmentation of the labour market. The outcome of this was, in most cases, to maintain women in an economically dependent position compared to men and, hence, to preserve the fundamental component of patriarchy — female subordination.

While the state intervened in the production process to accommodate certain patriarchal necessities, it was at the same time involved in restructuring patriarchy to fit the new economic system. Through substantive reforms in family law, the state dismantled the old patriarchal system and transformed patriarchs into breadwinners. This transition accorded greater legal rights to women and more economic responsibilities to men. While some theorists (Donzelot 1979; Lasch 1979) have seen this as the beginning of the end of patriarchy, it is better understood as a restructuring. The increased legal rights of wives and mothers were contingent upon observance of the ubiquitous adultery clause that ensured women's sexuality continued to be subject to male authority. Coupled with the labour laws that maintained women's dependence upon male support, this virtually guaranteed female subordination. The increased responsibilities of the patriarch-turned-breadwinner were necessary, in light of the sexual division of labour, to ensure the continued responsibility of private families for the costs of their reproduction. Finally, the expansion of welfare legislation completed the restructuring process by filling the authority and resource gaps created by the transformation of patriarchy.

While welfare expenditures did increase during this period, the primary thrust of welfare legislation was regulatory. The extension of state authority over children contained within welfare law eroded the patriarch's traditional near absolute authority over their offspring and centralized greater portions of that authority within the state.

The transformation of patriarch to breadwinner, the legal/social reinforcement of woman's role as reproducer and the intervention of the state in family life was designed to save the patriarchal family from the onslaught of industrialism. This accommodation took the form of the support-service family structure, a sexual division of labour that visited the burden of financial support upon the man and the burden of reproductive work upon the woman. This structure ensured, at one and the same time, women's continued dependency upon men and private familial responsibility for the costs of reproduction. While this accommodation did ensure that women's labour was reserved primarily for reproduction, it did little to address the issue of income resources for the expanding unit of dependants, characteristic of the support-service family structure. Prophetically, the last federal inquiry to be called in 1913 was the Commission to investigate the Increase in the Cost of Living in Canada.

PERIOD II:
1914–1939

The support-service family structure — the new face of familial patriarchy in the twentieth century — was built upon a much more precarious economic base than past reproductive systems. While this structure did ensure that women's labour would be reserved primarily for reproduction, it had no capacity to ensure that the necessary income resources for reproduction would be secured. Given the combined effect of social reforms that reduced the number of breadwinners per family and demographic changes that increased the number of dependants per family, the support-service family structure was characterized by increasing costs of reproduction without commensurate increases in income. This was expressed at the societal level as a conflict over the allocation of income between production and reproduction.

While the contradiction between production and reproduction was manifest and dealt with as a labour-allocation problem in the first period, it resurfaced as an income-allocation problem in the second period. The focus on income was shaped, not only by the strategy and impact of state intervention in the previous period, but by other structural changes that increased the salience of the income-allocation issue and influenced the pattern of state intervention in the second period.

One of the most important structural developments of this period was the increasing costs of reproduction resulting from the increasing ratio of dependent to productive members within the family unit. Increased longevity combined with child labour laws, compulsory education and a rising age of legal adulthood to swell the ranks of dependants at both ends of the age continuum, while the number of breadwinners within a family was limited by age/sex restrictions within the labour statutes. To compound these pressures, the encroachment of the labour market into domestic production, along with the process of urbanization, further eroded extra-market options for supplementing a family's livelihood.[1]

A second factor that highlighted the income-allocation issue was the change in the organization and focus of class struggle during the second period. The increased organization of labour together with the granting of universal suffrage enabled labour to press its demands more effectively on the shop floor and in the legislatures. Labour's more direct access to government via suffrage, reform parties[2] and labour MPs coupled with their limited success in wresting a family wage from employers expanded the focus of their struggle and altered the nature of their demands. Organized labour played an important role in broadening the issue of income allocation beyond an exclusive focus on work and wage issues, by including demands for social-welfare schemes on their political agenda.

Finally, the shift in the labour supply-demand ratio from the first to the second period influenced the manner in which the contradiction between production and reproduction became manifest. Attention to allocating labour to the reproductive sphere is highest in periods of labour shortage, as was the case in the first period. However, the second period was characterized by a declining demand for labour as evidenced by the dramatic shift from an aggressive open-door immigration policy in the first period to a selective and restrictive policy characteristic of the second period (Dirks 1977, 260). In the absence of a labour shortage, the importance of allocating labour to reproduction declined and, with the combined effects of the above structural pressures, income allocation emerged as the central problem for the state in its ongoing struggle to regulate production and reproduction.

Although labour legislation and family law, in the first period, had successfully entrenched age/sex divisions of labour and restructured spousal and generational rights and obligations, these statutes proved extremely limited as mechanisms for redistributing income. Family law could only affect the distribution of income resources within the family. Labour law was circumscribed by powerful resistance to any attempt to alter the wage-determination process.

Caught between the inviolability of the wage-determination process and the cost of living crises it provoked, the state "solution" was to develop a system of redistributing income outside of the wage-labour system. Thus, welfare law emerged as the critical legislative mechanism of intervention in this period. Welfare legislation had the scope that family law lacked, as well as a critical location that permitted it to compensate for the inflexibility of the wage-determination process without fundamentally challenging it. Because the welfare-state strategy evolved at the provincial level (which had the jurisdictional authority to develop the system, but lacked the resource base to fully exercise that authority) this period is best understood as transitional.

Capital, Labour and the Economy

In the twenty-six years that make up the second period, the Canadian economy experienced a number of expansions and contractions that influenced the relations between capital and labour. Two constants, however, stand out during this period: capital's relentless drive toward concentration and monopolization and labour's relentless struggle to earn a living wage. These characteristics of an emerging modern economy shaped the parameters within which labour and capital developed their strategies and pursued their interests.

The second period begins with a recession only temporarily alleviated by a war economy. Pentland (1968) points out that government reliance on market forces to manage the war economy resulted in serious misallocations of resources as well as uncontrolled price increases that eroded the real wage levels. Thus, returning soldiers and Canadian labour in general faced the same problems of unemployment and declining wages that had prevailed prior to the war. As a result, labour militancy was high, there was a growth in organized labour and shop-floor politics was a major focus of labour's struggle for a living wage.

Pentland's study of labour relations in Canada reveals an enormous wave of unionization after 1915. *Labour Gazette* records indicate that this same period had a high incidence of strikes and lockouts, the most frequent cause of which was wage disputes. Throughout this period of intense union activity and labour militancy, however, real wages did not rise (Pentland 1968). "In 1929, before the Crash, the Department of labour judged that a Canadian family of four needed between $1,200 and $1,500 for the minimum comforts of life. Its own figures showed that 60% of men and 82% of working women earned less than $1,000 a year" (Morton and Copp 1980, 125).

A number of factors came together during this period to broaden the issue of income allocation from one exclusively between worker and employer to an issue involving populace and state. The International Labour Organization (ILO), founded after the First World War, played an important role in articulating and promoting labour's interest in social-welfare policies. The ILO's welfare policies were increasingly included on the political agendas of organized labour in Canada. In addition, the granting of universal suffrage in

1920 enabled the working class to have more direct access to government. The opportunity to elect a labour MP or MLA was not insignificant given that the majority of Canadian workers were still unorganized,[3] and the vote was for many their only means of political expression.

Although the extension of suffrage did not result in the immediate formation of a consolidated workers' party, it did make a substantial difference in workers' representation in parliament. More important perhaps than the absolute increase in labour, progressive and populist representatives was the change in the strategy of these members. After 1921, labour MPs led by Woodsworth became committed to the concept of an independent left and labour group that would persistently keep the viewpoint of labour before the House and country. "The efficacy of a minor party exercising a crucial vote in a balance of power situation between disciplined parties was well illustrated in 1926 when the labour group extracted an old age pension concession in return for legislative support for King" (Robin 1971, 273).

The enactment of the Old Age Pension Act in 1927 initiated a reallocation of millions of dollars of income annually, highlighting the benefits to the working class of a labour presence in the House. By the end of the second period, approximately 40% of all Canadians 70 years of age and over (186,154 individuals) were recipients of transfer payments amounting to $28,886,000 annually (Urquhart and Buckley 1965, Series C300–12)—a powerful victory in the income-allocation struggle that few, if any, union struggles could match. While labour was always sympathetic to welfare issues, the difference that emerged during the 1920s was the systematic inclusion of social-wage strategies on the agenda of organized labour, as well as the emergence of an independent labour group in the House, which could press these issues in the interests of all labour organized and unorganized.

In the 1930s there was a consolidation in the electoral strategies of labour with the founding of the Co-operative Commonwealth Federation (CCF). In addition, this decade witnessed a revival of shop-floor politics with the onset of a major organizing drive by American industrial unions in Canada. Thus, labour responded to the crises of the Depression with a dual strategy: pushing for a more equitable distribution of income through wage increases from employers and social-wage initiatives from the state.

Capital, having the strategic upper hand during this period, continued to favour minimal, sporadic government intervention until 1930. However, the upheaval of the Depression shook the faith of many in the benign operation of market forces creating some powerful and vociferous supporters of state intervention within the business community. Two factors seem to have contributed to this change in attitude toward government intervention. First, the severity of economic disorganization had the effect of visiting the costs of market forces upon the business community itself. Second, the severity of social disorganization had the effect of reminding business, in a manner reminiscent of the turn of the century, of their dependence upon the stability, harmony and consumption patterns of the population. In other words, the dislocation within and between the productive and reproductive spheres reached such proportions during the Depression that the business community had to search beyond itself and the invisible hand of the market place to find a way out of its problems. Its solution was to turn to the state.

The old faith in market forces waned as the costs of those forces began to be borne by the business community itself. One of the earliest manifestations of this was the breakdown of informal price fixing mechanisms due to expansion, overproduction and consequent fierce competition. Once the costs of competition could no longer be passed on to the worker or consumer, competition — the hallmark of free enterprise — was increasingly seen as problematic. Stability, growth and rationalization, conditions essential to the monopolization process, became the new leitmotif of capital. Under the euphemism of "state-encouraged industrial co-operation," business called upon the government to severely restrict competition through the regulation of pricing, production and marketing practices. "What the business community ultimately wanted was self-government — to control the state agencies established to enforce a set of rules business men evolved for themselves" (Finkel 1979, 29). Evidence of state responsiveness is seen in the Royal Commission on Price Spreads (1934), the Natural Products Marketing Act (1934) and the Dominion Trades and Industry Commission Act of 1935 (Finkel 1979, 30).

As the Depression deepened, the deteriorating condition of the population touched even the most stable of industries. Falling demand, falling prices, bankruptcies and, perhaps most important of all, political unrest led a number of influential and forward-looking business men to see a link between regulated industry (production) and regulated welfare (reproduction). While there was much debate within the business community over which policies would be best, the frequency and urgency of the debates and the assumption of greater state intervention contained within them indicates a distinct change in attitude from the earlier period. Business men began to argue that the business community itself had a vested interest in the development of welfare programs. The words of Raoul Dandurand, Liberal leader in the Senate and influential business man, are indicative of this new awareness: "When I think of them and of the inevitably slow process of reabsorbing into industry those who are now unemployed, I feel more and more concerned that if our capitalist system is to survive we shall have to establish a contributory unemployment system to tide our people over periods of economic depression (Finkel 1979, 91).

In summary, the economic conditions of the second period saw labour and capital moving, at different rates and with different blueprints, towards the demand for ever greater government intervention. Furthermore, these demands increasingly focussed upon and articulated the need for comprehensive welfare schemes to ameliorate the irreconcilable wage conflicts between labour and capital and to cushion both interest groups from the severe problems associated with unregulated business cycles.

Labour Commissions and Inquiries

In 1913 the Prime Minister responded to increasing unrest over rising prices by calling the Royal Commission to Investigate the Increase in the Cost of Living in Canada. It was largely a fact-finding mission and did not result in any specific recommendations. The inquiry does, however, provide us with detailed information on the cost of living situation in Canada up to 1913. The commission found that while the average wages in manufacturing had increased forty percent from 1900 to 1910 the average cost of living had risen fifty percent. Furthermore, the commission reported that the wage increases of unskilled workers and immigrants were far below the norm for workers in manufacturing. The most dramatic cost of living increase was that of housing, which increased sixty to seventy percent in the ten-year period. One of the consequences reported by the commission was that the number of families living in one room had increased by seventy-four percent, from 4.3% of all Canadian families in 1900 to 5.7% in 1910 (*Cost of Living Inquiry* 1915, 48). The increase in prices had long been justified by producers as being a result of rising wages. However, the commission reported that the wage bill to employers dropped from 23.5% to 20.6% during this period. The commission also conducted a small sample study of family budgets in the City of Winnipeg and, not surprisingly, found that the likelihood of a family falling into debt was directly related to the number of dependents it had to support (*Cost of Living Inquiry 1915*, 5.2: 1019).

The recession of 1913–14 added job insecurity to the existing problem of income insecurity, and the Ontario government responded by calling for an inquiry into unemployment. The recommendations of this commission advocated increased state involvement generally and the extension of welfare programs in particular to resolve labour problems. The commissioners called for greater state involvement in providing for the population in times of need and in regulating labour demand cycles. In the former case, the commission recommended that the province develop a separate department of welfare and introduce systematic provincial funding of relief programs generated through taxation, which would permit greater government regulation of welfare programs. It further recommended that the province set up and fund training programs for social workers to staff the new bureaucracy.

The post-war labour unrest, which culminated in the Winnipeg General Strike, provoked a number of inquiries that focussed explicitly on wage-price disparities as the central problem. In 1919 the Premier of Manitoba called for a royal commission to inquire into the cause of the general strike. The testimony of James Winnig, President of the Trades and Labour Council, emphasized that the cost of living crisis was a major cause of the high level of labour unrest in the province at the time.

Having received a wide range of testimony, the Manitoba commission identified nine causes of industrial unrest ranging from profiteering to employers' refusal to recognize the right to collective bargaining. The commissioners concluded that the most critical factor, however, was the wage-price disparity. In contrast to the ruthless anti-labour role the state played in terminating the strike, the commissioners advised a more balanced, sympathetic role for the state. Having concluded that labour's grievances were well founded, the commission expressed their vision of state responsibility as follows:

It must be apparent to all that a system of capital and labour should continue to exist. There must be something to provide the necessary incentive to effort or progress will cease. It would be as bad for Labour as for Capital if the incentive to capital to press forward were withdrawn, but it is the office of Government to see that these two important factors maintain proper regard for each other. If Capital does not provide enough to assure Labour a contented existence with a full enjoyment of the opportunities of the times for human improvement, then the Government might find it necessary to step in and let the state do these things at the expense of Capital (*Report of the Royal Commission to Inquire into the Cause of the Winnipeg General Strike* 1919: 27).

While the commission was not instructed to make recommendations, they nevertheless advised the development of a progressive system of taxation to facilitate the redistribution of wealth. "It is submitted that there should be a scheme of taxation of those who can afford it and application of wealth to the reasonable needs of the others in the community whose lot in life has not been favoured" (29). The idea that labour problems cannot be resolved solely within the confines of labour legislation is clearly expressed in the report.

Concurrent with the Manitoba inquiry, the federal government called for a national inquiry into industrial relations in Canada. This inquiry, also referred to as the *Mather's Commission*, identified the wage-price disparity as the central problem in labour relations. "...the high cost of living was assigned as one, if not the chief, cause of labour unrest. The opinion was frequently expressed that if that problem could be solved, and the equilibrium established between the wages and the cost living, labour unrest would largely disappear" (*Mather's Commission* 1919, 8). Taking this evidence to heart, the commission focussed equally upon labour conditions/legislation and welfare conditions/legislation. With regard to labour, the commissioners called for immediate legislation to establish minimum wages and maximum hours of employment in all provinces. They also recommended that suitable action be taken by the government to insure the right to organize, the right to collective bargaining and the payment of a "living wage" (19).

The commissioners' other recommendations anticipate and endorse what amounts to the basic framework for a modern welfare state — compulsory contributory state insurance. "We recommend to your Government, the question of making some provision by a system of State Social Insurance for those v/ho through no fault of their own are unable to work, whether the inability arises from lack of opportunity, sickness, invalidity or old age" (8). They further endorse state regulation of public works for the relief of unemployment, government assistance for public housing and the extension of equal opportunities in education. These recommendations were endorsed by the Liberal party at their 1919 convention. A similar scheme was again proposed by the Select Standing Committee on Industrial and International Relations in 1928 and received the support of the House of Commons in May 1929. Despite all this discussion and apparent approval, no universal social-insurance programs were introduced in the 1920s, leaving these concerns to be discussed once again during the 1930s.

In summary, the inquiries during this period revealed a consistent pattern of concern over the income-allocation problem, all responded to this problem by advocating greater government intervention, and many included as a corollary to labour-law reform a strong recommendation for state social-insurance programs.

Labour Legislation

The second period like the first was characterized by a high degree of legislative activity measured both by the introduction of new statutes and by the number of amendments to existing labour laws (see table A2.8 New Labour Laws in Ontario and Manitoba, Period II). The primary challenge of this period, to which all legislation that is reviewed here had to respond, was the issue of income-allocation. However, this does not mean that the legislation set in place in the first period to protect or restrict female/child labour could be abandoned or revoked. The income-allocation issue did not replace but was added to the ongoing concern with labour allocation. The state continued its commitment to differential protection of female/child labour (see table A2.9. Ontario Labour Legislation: Changes in the Regulation of Female and Child Labour, Period II). Most of the activity with regard to maintaining the sexual differentiation occurred through amendments to existing acts. The major thrust of the amendments to the protective legislation during this period was to eliminate loopholes and exemptions from the existing acts. There was no reversal or abandonment of the policy of differential treatment for female/child labour. In fact, there are moderate attempts to extend the principle.

Of more interest, during this period, are the limited attempts by the state to use labour law to address the problem of income allocation. Two types of labour legislation were introduced to deal directly with the income problem. The first was the Workmen's Compensation Act, which was rewritten in the second period and provides much more comprehensive coverage and represents a substantial reallocation of income. The second included the Minimum Wage Acts, the Manitoba Fair Wages Act and the Ontario Government Contract, Hours and Wages Act. These acts represented an attempt to provide a floor under which wages could not legally drop, and during this period they were highly selective in their application and in their determination of minimums.

The original Workmen's Compensation Act established the principle of employer's liability for workers' injuries on the job. The act was based on the concept of individual (employer or corporate) liability and reliance on the courts to determine the validity of a claim and the compensation deserved. The adversarial court system was difficult, expensive and time consuming for all parties involved. Initially, the legislation had the effect of discouraging claims because of legal costs. Furthermore, the fact that the burden of proof of negligence fell to the claimant resulted in few cases settled in favour of workers. However, as workers became more organized, the amount of litigation and the size of the settlements and the success of the claimants all increased.[4] In 1910, the Ontario government called a Royal Commission to inquire into the Workmen's Compensation Act with the support and co-operation of the Canadian Manufacturers' Association. Four reports and three years later the commission recommended a complete redrafting of the law.

The commissioners recommended a new program based

upon the concept of collective rather than individual liability and the replacement of the courts by a workmen's compensation board that would handle claims and administer the program. The board was to be empowered to classify industries according to number of employees, accident rates and other factors and assess appropriate annual payments the industries must make to a collective accident fund. A new act was passed in Ontario in 1915 adopting the recommended program. Manitoba followed suit in 1916. The new Workmen's Compensation Act gave the state an active role in determining rates of assessment and compensation through the board and prompted the development of a complex bureaucracy to administer the act. For employers the program operated as an insurance fund, and as such they supported it; for workers, it meant a more stable, accessible system for making and receiving claims. The Workmen's Compensation Board was the first state program to administer and guarantee massive transfers of income resources from employers to those employees who qualified. In the first thirteen years of operation the board collected millions of dollars in assessments on industries and between 1915 and 1927 had paid out over $63 million in benefits to qualified employees (*Report of the Workmen's Compensation Board, Ontario, 1928* Sessional Papers 28.3: 19).

The second type of labour legislation that attempted to address the income-allocation problem did so through setting minimum-wage regulations. In addition to the better-known Minimum Wage Act, there were also the Fair Wages Act in Manitoba and the Government Contract, Hours and Wages Act in Ontario, which provided minimum-wage protection to employees on government public-work projects. Manitoba introduced the Fair Wages Act in 1916, establishing a Fair Wages Board to determine minimum wage and maximum hours for all classes of workers employed in the construction of public works for the province; but it was twenty years later before Ontario passed a similar statute, using as its model the federal Fair Wages Act (SC 1930, c.20).

The more comprehensive law was the Minimum Wage Act, which called for a board to be established to determine and enforce wage minimums for women and youths. During this period, there was no concept of a provincial minimum wage. The legislation stipulated that minimums should vary by trade, region, skill and age of worker. When this act was amended to include men, toward the end of this period, sex became another category upon which wage minimums varied — with male wages consistently set higher than females wages. The act required that a greater share of the surplus be returned to the worker as wages and in theory could effect a considerable reallocation of income. The legislation empowered the boards to check employers wage sheets and prosecute in cases of violation.

The first Ontario board set out its guidelines as follows:

The Board is fortunate in the nature of its task, which rests upon an economic and moral principle so simple and convincing that all admit its cogency. This principle is the right of the worker to live from her work. ...It does not fix wages, but sets levels below which wages may not fall. (*Report of the Minimum Wage Board Ontario, 1922* Sessional Papers 73: 5)

While the principle may have been simple and convincing, the enforcement proved to be quite another matter as the Commission on Price Spreads revealed. There was a multitude of loopholes whereby employers could circumvent the law, and many employers simply violated the law without ever being discovered. However, the act did establish the principle of government intervention in the wage-determination process, a principle that became increasingly acceptable to employers as the monopolization process required, not only standardized pricing and marketing, but more standardized labour costs as well (Price Spreads Inquiry, 1937 c.9).

All of these legislative activities had one common effect and that was to dramatically increase government involvement and regulation of the labour process necessitating a much expanded labour bureaucracy to meet the task. The legislation enacted in the second period greatly expanded the administrative and regulatory functions of the government, resulting in the emergence of a complex and full-blown bureaucracy by the end of the period. By 1939 Ontario had introduced eight new administrative boards as well as a separate department of labour, and Manitoba introduced six new administrative boards and a labour bureau.

The Ontario Workmen's Compensation Board provides a good example of the growth in administrative work throughout this period. Once the board was established the number of claims brought forth grew astronomically. Prior to the change in the law, 1912 was a particularly active year with 36 claims brought to court. In contrast, the first year the board was established it received 17,033 claims. This rate escalated by approximately 10,000 additional claims annually, and in 1923 the board received 61,109 claims and dispensed well over five million dollars in compensation (*Report of the Workmen's Compensation Board Ontario, 1924* Sessional Papers 51: 16). The employment bureaus grew at an equally rapid rate in Ontario as regional offices opened up throughout the province requiring, by the end of the period, a full-time staff of 111 (*Ontario Public Accounts* 1940). The increase in Manitoba was similar although less dramatic, given the smaller population and the less industrialized economy.

However, with the passage of the Labour Bureau Act and the Fair Wages Act, the staff increased tenfold from 1913 to 1917 (*Manitoba Public Accounts* 1917).

In both Manitoba and Ontario the staff responsible for workplace inspections and the boards responsible for Fair Wages and Minimum Wage Acts increased as their tasks and responsibilities expanded. Further, new boards designed to handle industrial disputes at the provincial level were added to the labour bureaucracy, requiring ever more complex labour departments. Thus, by the end of the second period we find that the Ontario Labour Department had 230 full-time staff and an annual budget of over $500,000. Manitoba's Labour Bureau had 50 full-time staff and an annual budget of $90,000, a fifth of the expenditure of Ontario for a province with a fifth of the population.[5]

The operation of the labour bureaus also reveals the growing tendency to regard welfare programs as part of a comprehensive approach to labour problems. One of the first tasks assigned to the new Ontario Department of Labour was to investigate the need for a mothers' allowance program in the province. The Labour Department conducted the investigation, recommended adoption of the program and played an important role in selecting and advising the new board when the legislation was passed (*Report of the Department of Labour Ontario, 1921* Sessional Papers 16). In Manitoba and Ontario the labour departments played a critical role during the Depression in issuing relief certificates, maintaining statistics and administering the vast relief programs of the time. In Manitoba the labour bureau was given over almost entirely to administering relief programs, and for five years (from 1935 to 1939) the only reports submitted by the bureau were relief reports. In addition to these specific "welfare" services, the administrative experience the province gained in the operation of the early boards, like Workmen's Compensation, served as a model for the development and administration of welfare departments.

Constructing Social Patriarchy

By the last quarter of the nineteenth century, the increasing contradiction between reproduction and production called for a reformation of the wage-labour system and a transformation of patriarchy. This transformation involved three component processes: first, the erosion of the patriarch's legal authority over women and children, a corollary of which was a shift in the legislation from father/husband's rights to father/husband's responsibilities; second, the increasing assumption of that authority by the state; third, the provision of resources to subsidize the familial unit of reproduction. In the first period, changes in family and welfare law were designed to respond to the labour-allocation problem. The focus was on keeping women in the home. As a result, the bulk of legislative activity was concentrated in the first and second processes — the more regulative aspects of state intervention — with minor legislative attention to the third, more supportive aspect of intervention.

In the second period, the shift in the manifest problem from labour to income allocation demanded a new legislative strategy and a shift in emphasis to the second and third processes — increasing state authority over and subsidization of the reproductive unit. One of the obvious consequences of this new strategy is a dramatic change in welfare philosophy, legislation and expenditures compared to relatively minor developments in family legislation. This is indicative of a larger process: as the state welfare apparatus expands it tends to absorb more and more issues and regulations previously located within family law, and the distinctions between welfare and family law that were quite clear in the first period become less clear. The increasing integration of family and welfare law reveals a complementarity of tasks rather than a confusion of responsibilities. While welfare law was the critical mechanism of state intervention in this period, family law played an important role in defining the limits of that intervention.

Family Law

The income allocation problem was addressed to a limited extent in family law by the increasing clarification of rights of dependants and obligations of providers to ensure the most equitable division of resources within the family unit. However, because access to income resources lay largely outside the family, its redistributive effects were in most cases minimal. This then raises a question of why we see ever greater delineation of familial rights and obligations given its limited impact on income allocation for family members. A possible explanation lies in the fact that, while such careful specification of familial obligations might have limited internal (family) impact, it had significant external impact in terms of clarifying the parameters within which state subsidization would occur.

The increasing pressure for a social wage and the extension of welfare programs raised a disturbing possibility of overburdened breadwinners abandoning their dependants to the state. The introduction of each new welfare measure was invariably coupled with more detailed laws of familial obligation to ensure that state support would only be received when all available family resources had been exhausted. For example, we find a coincidence of the enactment of the Old Age Pension Act with the introduction of Parents Maintenance Acts and a tightening up of maintenance laws with the introduction of Mothers' Allowance. In short, we may best understand the legislation in family law during the second period as an attempt to entrench the concept of privatizing reproductive costs as a check upon the growing pressure to socialize those costs. While the state did indeed proceed to socialize some of the most pressing and unavoidable costs, it did so with the clear understanding stated in the law that the obligation to support the nation's dependent population lay first and foremost with their relatives. Thus, the developments in family law make most sense as a necessary corollary to the reigning welfare philosophy of means tested, crisis intervention aid and a studied avoidance of anything suggesting universal plans.

The most striking feature of all the new family legislation in this period is the apparent imbalance between Ontario, which added seven new pieces of legislation to the statutes introduced in the first period, and Manitoba which only brought in three new statutes while repealing the two earlier Infants Act and Illegitimate Children's Act (see table A2.10. New Family Legislation in Ontario and Manitoba, Period II). However, most of the regulations present in Ontario family law appear in Manitoba largely under the Child Welfare Act. The integration of family-law issues into welfare law appears first in Manitoba — a reflection of Manitoba's earlier development of welfare policies and legislation.

The principal of equity in property rights between husband and wife had been established in the first period; however, the issue of custody remained mired in patriarchal tradition. Although the first period saw the extension of a mother's right to claim custody under certain circumstances, the concept of father as rightful guardian until proven unfit predominated. However, in 1922 in Manitoba, the Child Welfare Act asserted the concept of joint guardian rights between mother and father, and in 1923 Ontario followed suit with an amendment to the Infants Act. The entrenchment of the principal of equity had two important consequences. First, it acknowledges women's rightful claim to guardianship of their children. Second, in asserting the mother's right as being equal to the father's, they eliminated the infamous adultery clause, which had only applied to women and had automatically disqualified her as guardian had she committed adultery. This removed one of the most critical legal sanctions of the sexual double standard. The adultery clause, however, remained intact in the Maintenance and Protection Acts in both Ontario and Manitoba throughout the second period.

The pattern of rights and obligations introduced in the legislation of this period (see table A2.11. Family Law: Clarification of Familial Rights and Obligations in Ontario and Manitoba, Period II) had the predominant purpose of entrenching the tradition of familial responsibility for reproductive costs. A brief examination reveals a consistent pattern of extending rights to dependants and obligations to presumed providers. This effects a complete reversal of familial patriarchal law, which extended rights to provider and obligations to dependants. However, this reversal was essential to preserve familial economic responsibility as a necessary concomitant to social patriarchy. Thus, whether we are talking about spousal, parental or filial relations, the law always operates to extend dependants' rights to family income and to enforce obligation to provide on the part of productive members.

In summary, this period marks a transition towards a growing acceptance of state subsidization of the reproductive unit within clearly defined boundaries, and family law serves to define those boundaries. Therefore, the pattern and direction of family law in the second period can best be understood in conjunction with the expansion of welfare legislation and programs.

Welfare Commissions and Inquiries

Canada's experience in World War I brought about a new set of expectations concerning the state's obligation to the population. Given the high price of the war effort to the Canadian working class (sixty thousand soldiers died), few politicians were willing to disagree with the growing sentiment that the quality of life, and particularly the security of the population, must be improved. The formation of the International Labour Organization (ILO) gave substance to these sentiments by promoting specific social-insurance programs that were added to the agenda of organized labour, referred to by commissioners in a variety of inquiries and endorsed by various political parties including the Liberals at their 1919 convention. Losses on the battle field gave new authority to those voices that pressed for better child care and family-support services on the grounds that our population was our greatest natural resource. Such concerns were given specific focus after the ministrations of the Canadian Patriotic Fund[6] had accustomed citizens to the support and supervision of large numbers of fatherless families. Thus, the postwar years witnessed a growing demand articulated in both Labour and Welfare Commissions for modernizing the whole process of relief assistance throughout the country.

During the second period we see, for the first time, commissions and inquiries specifically addressed to welfare issues. The Ontario government called four provincial inquiries: into the Ontario School for the Blind in 1917; into the Care and Control of the Mentally Defective in 1919; the Royal Commission on Public Welfare in 1929; and an inquiry into the Mental Hospitals Act in 1938. In the same period Manitoba called three commissions: the Public Welfare Commission in 1919; the Royal Commission on Child Welfare in 1928; and the 1931 Commission on the Welfare of Blind

Persons. Among these commissions three inquiries addressed the overall problem of welfare services and played a critical role in redesigning welfare services, laws and bureaucracies (1919 Public Welfare Commission, the 1928 inquiry on Child Welfare in Manitoba and the 1930 Ontario Royal Commission on Public Welfare).

Manitoba, which had been the centre of the most bitter post-war labour struggles, was one of the first provinces to act on this new initiative with the formation of the Public Welfare Commission in 1919. During a year of research and investigation, the commissioners studied existing welfare services concentrating on finance, supervision and control and filed three reports. They outlined five principles for a modern welfare system beginning with: "Responsibility of Government in seeing that the primary needs of all children are provided for from one source, and that the reasonable needs of the handicapped and less fortunate of its citizens shall be adequately supplied" (*Report of the Public Welfare Commission Manitoba, 1919* Sessional Papers 29). The other four principles outlined steps to achieve the goal of the first principle including: government direction on all welfare funds whether public monies or private contributions; government inspection and regulation of all welfare institutions and agencies, whether public or private; and the creation of a separate welfare department or portfolio to administer a public welfare program. The commissioners' recommendation of a government-appointed public body for the purposes of inspection, research and development of welfare programs was implemented through the Act Respecting Welfare Supervision that was passed the same year. Their final report contained a draft of the Manitoba Child Welfare Act (based on the Missouri Children's Code Commission) that was passed in 1922. The commissioners' work gave Manitoba the distinction of being the first province in Canada with a comprehensive child-welfare act.

The second Manitoba commission, the Inquiry on Child Welfare in 1928, was in response to the public campaign to reform the administration of the Child Welfare Act and the Mothers' Allowance program led by the Winnipeg MLA, W. Ivens. Ivens argued that there were insufficient funds allotted to child welfare in general and Mothers' Allowance in particular. The government, embarrassed by the negative publicity in the same year that it had set up the Department of Health and Public Welfare, appointed Charlotte Whitton, the epitome of the new breed of professional social reformers and executive director of the Canadian Council on Child Welfare, to conduct a commission of inquiry.

Most of Whitton's report is a history of the policies behind the Manitoba Child Welfare Act and the funds dispersed for child welfare through the act. Her report undoubtedly pleased the government under attack as it presented the welfare programs in Manitoba at the time in a very favourable light compared to programs in other provinces. She pointed out that Manitoba had the highest per capita expenditure on Mothers' Allowances of any province and that the Mothers' Allowances were higher than the monthly allowances provided either by Workmen's Compensation or city welfare (*Whitton Report* 1928, Pt. III: 65). Whitton concluded that Manitoba had the most comprehensive child-welfare act in the country.

In spite of the glowing nature of her report, she did have some recommendations for improvements in the letter and administration of the law. The biggest problem she found was that, while Manitoba had passed a commendably comprehensive child-welfare act, it did so without having any administrative facilities to enforce it. According to Whitton the Child Welfare Division in the Department of Public Works created in 1924 lacked the administrative capacity to implement the act. She strongly recommended that trained and qualified social workers be recruited by the division to administer the programs. In addition to these major recommendations she also advised some rewriting and clarification of the child-welfare statutes and came down particularly hard on the necessity of enforcing maintenance laws. Consistent with the dominant welfare philosophy of the time — the idea that families are first and foremost responsible for their members — she rejected the idea of extending Mothers' Allowance to divorced or deserted women. Instead she advocated the adoption of a statute similar to the Ontario Child Maintenance Act that would provide for the imprisonment of parents defaulting upon their economic responsibilities. While the Whitton Commission did result in some administrative reshuffling and amendments to the Child Welfare Act, it is most significant as an historical document of the philosophy and practice of social welfare in the 1920s.

Ten years after the Manitoba Public Welfare Commission conducted its inquiry, Ontario initiated a similar inquiry to determine the necessity of reorganizing its welfare programs. The report of the Ontario Public Welfare Commission released in 1930 gave ample evidence of the need to reorganize and upgrade the system. The commissioners had inquired into the conditions and services in general, mental hospitals, houses of refuge, jails and correctional institutions, services for handicapped children and the operation of general child-welfare programs. As a result of their exhaustive review, they put forth an equally exhaustive list of recommendations. At the general organizational level they called for the creation of a Public Welfare department and the expansion of programs to provide trained social workers to administer the welfare programs. They also recommended new legislation to deal with hospitals and charitable institutions and the repeal of the old Charitable Institutions Act. The commissioners recommended an increase in or extension of the hospital facilities and charitable institutions, substantial increases in funding and the enactment of laws requiring cities to provide houses of refuge.

Their recommendations on child-welfare programs had particular significance for the family. They recommended substantial increases in government funding of child-welfare programs including a doubling of the allotment to orphanages, increased funding for CAS and a reorganization of the Children's Aid Branch. Supporting the move to de-institutionalization, the commissioners recommended that private homes caring for children under CAS supervision should qualify for the same provincial subsidy as orphanages. They also emphasized the need to reorganize and systematize the operation of Industrial Schools. Characteristic of the attitudes of the time, the recommendations for extended funding and support for children was coupled with several recommendations for tightening up on both the letter and the enforcement of maintenance laws for paternity suits, desertion and divorce. Government response to this report was nothing short of dramatic. One year later the Ontario legislature passed four new and comprehensive welfare laws including the establishment of a separate Public Welfare Department, thus, completing the first steps in revamping its welfare system.

In spite of the common concerns for welfare issues shared by both labour and welfare commissions, their approaches were distinctly different and worth noting. The labour commissions tended to adopt the ILO strategy of advocating broad social-insurance schemes that presumed a connection to the labour force, such as unemployment insurance or pensions plans. The welfare commissions addressed the needs of those who were largely marginal to the productive system, typically, women and children. In short, labour commissions addressed the reproductive needs of productive workers, while welfare commissions addressed the needs of those largely confined to reproductive work. Furthermore, the labour commissions' recommendations were of broad scope and could not easily be funded at the provincial level. The welfare commissions confined themselves to programs operating at the provincial level and subsequently had a more dramatic impact upon legislation and administration of the welfare systems in both Manitoba and Ontario. We should not, however, conclude that the labour commissions were ineffective. In spite of the financial and constitutional problems their proposals posed, they saw the realization of a national pension plan in the second period and the realization of much of their recommendations in the post-war years.

The welfare commissions played an important role, not only in instituting and supporting significant income-allocation programs like the Mothers' Allowance program, but they also served to construct a legal and administrative structure that facilitated the vast expansion of welfare programs in the subsequent period.

Welfare Legislation

The defining feature of social patriarchy is the particular combination of state support and state control, which shifts the locus of power in patriarchy from the head of household to the state. Welfare legislation in the first period consisted largely of dismantling the old patriarchal system and substituting state authority for the waning authority of the patriarch. Legislation in the second period, however, is more characteristic of the operation of social patriarchy combining support and control in increasingly balanced measures.

As documented by the welfare and labour commissions

the state was under mounting pressure to expand its welfare role. However, expanding welfare budgets under the old model of welfare delivery, in which the destitute were typically institutionalized, would be extraordinarily expensive and administratively cumbersome. The extension of state authority over the family generally and children in particular, in the first period, had the effect of greatly increasing the number of state wards. In addition, there was a growing number of elderly people dependent upon state support because of the combined effect of increased longevity and decreasing familial resources.[7]

At a time when welfare legislation and practice was based on the principle of institutional relief, expanding welfare budgets would create the possibility of an endlessly growing population of institutionalized state dependants. The fiscal, organizational and social consequences of coupling extended state authority with institutional relief were overwhelming. The CAS in Ontario had long complained that the institutionalization of dependent and neglected children was not only bad care but bad economics.

Unwilling to retreat from the extension of state authority but unhappy with the escalating costs of the way in which it was carried out, Manitoba and Ontario pursued identical legislative strategies — selective de-institutionalization, expansion of non-institutional relief programs and comprehensive enforcement of familial economic obligations through both welfare and family law. Such a program, however, necessitated a complete reorganization of the existing welfare systems including the establishment of separate departments of welfare. Overall, the reorganization had the effect of centralizing the control of the welfare system at the provincial level within provincial bureaucracies.

Manitoba not only had a greater volume of legislation but preceded Ontario in the initiation of welfare statutes (see table A2.12. Welfare Legislation Enacted in Ontario and Manitoba, Period II). The consolidation of family and welfare acts in the new Manitoba Child Welfare Act (1922) suggests that concern with reorganization and support did not detract from the continued commitment to increasing state authority over the family. Two particular clauses served to greatly expand the authority of the state in family matters: the adoption clause made the state the ultimate authority in all adoption cases, and the children-of-unwed-parents clause accorded paternal authority to the state. Ontario accomplished the same control in two separate acts — the Child of Unmarried Parents Act and the Adoption Act in 1921. Prior to these statutes the state's authority over adoption was limited to cases over which CAS supervision had been extended, usually cases of unwed mothers. However, with the new adoption act the state determined all of the conditions for adoption, including eligibility, overruling parental wish and/or community tradition.

The commitment to extending state authority was perhaps most pronounced in the supervision and control of children born out of wedlock. The new act provided that a representative of the state automatically be appointed guardian of the child, either jointly with the mother or solely — there was no longer any requirement of proving neglect. However, while the mother increasingly lost control over her child, the act reaffirmed her liability for the support of the child, even if she was deemed unworthy of custody, and the child became a state ward. The state's concern with enforcing the concept of privatizing the costs of reproduction led to the clause that permitted the state to remove the child from the mother if she refused to press a paternity suit (1926 SM, c.4 s.12). The concern with enforcing paternity suits led to an unusual clause that permitted the mother to lay information against more than one man (1925 SM c.3 s.83). This amendment put an end to the classic defense men had used, which was to get another man to testify that he also had intercourse, and therefore, paternity could not be ascertained. With the new amendment, the willingness of another man to so testify was greatly reduced because he stood the risk of being held jointly liable.

In addition to the above major developments, both Manitoba and Ontario continued to amend their acts to add new criteria for declaring a child neglected. By 1924 the Child Welfare Act in Manitoba listed sixteen different conditions under which a child would be made a ward of the state, including children who used profane language, had possession of obscene literature or frequented pool halls (SM c.30 s.29). An amendment to the Ontario Child Protection Act permitted the state to apprehend children whose parents did not provide adequate medical, surgical or remedial care (1919 SO c.65). This clause was also incorporated in the Manitoba new Child Welfare Act. In addition to specific welfare laws, there were other statutes, such as the School Attendance Act, that further defined parents' obligations and the state's authority. During the second period, the School Attendance Act in both Ontario and Manitoba increased the age for mandatory attendance to sixteen years, creating a further condition for the apprehension of children by defining parents as negligent who were unwilling or unable to enforce attendance (1922 SM c.2).

Reorganization of the Welfare System

While the number of dependent and destitute citizens increased and the demands on state coffers to support them increased, state control over their care and disposition was, for the most part, limited to regulatory clauses in the Charitable Institutions Act. Care of the destitute of all ages was provided by a vast and uncoordinated web of private agencies, municipal refuges and provincial institutions. Furthermore, the old institutional patterns of relief were increasingly coming under criticism, not only in terms of the quality of care they could provide, but because of the increasingly high costs of institutional care as documented by the Welfare Commissions in Manitoba in 1919 and Ontario in 1929. The two categories of the population most frequently institutionalized because of destitution were children and the elderly.

The Children's Aid Society, following the inspiration of their founder Kelso, had long favoured the normalizing influence of family life and been critical of the institutionalization of children. Given that the CAS was the agency primarily responsible for the apprehension and disposition of children, their opinion held great weight. In addition to this philosophical orientation, the care of the young could be more easily de-institutionalized. While neglected or dependent children could be redistributed throughout the population via adoption or foster homes, maintaining the privatization of most of their costs, the dependent elderly could not be so easily placed. As a result the de-institutionalization program was selectively applied. Children's institutions increasingly became temporary shelters or specialized as reformatories. Under pressure from the CAS, the Ontario and Manitoba governments began to subsidize foster homes at a rate equivalent to the funding of children in orphanages. Although orphanages did not close, the proportion of neglected children they cared for declined.

Ontario came under increasing criticism for using industrial schools and female refuges to care for destitute children and children sent by juvenile court. The old Industrial Schools Act was amended over the second period to ensure that industrial schools specialized as reformatories (1931 SO c.60 and 1939 SO c.51), and dependent and neglected children would be assured other placements (1927 SO c. 92). Female refuges were designated as women's reformatories (1913 SO c.79).

Refuges that had been established to house destitute adults were reclassified as old-folk's homes. This was a typical pattern in Ontario, which had a large number of refuges in operation. In Manitoba, where there was not a well-developed system of refuges, the Old Folks' Homes Act of 1916 provided funds and regulations for the establishment of such homes. In 1927 the passage of the federal Old Age Pension Act provided some alternative to institutionalization. The provisions of the act were soon adopted by both Manitoba and Ontario. With the federal government first assuming fifty percent of the costs and later seventy-five percent (1931), this greatly relieved provincial expenditures.[8] The provision of a small monthly subsidy to the needy elderly took some of the pressure off institutions and permitted the elderly poor to live on their own or contribute to the cost of staying with their families.

While the welfare commissions approved of these developments, they strongly recommended that they be accompanied by a systematic reorganization and centralization of the welfare system under greater control of the provincial government. Why Manitoba took the lead in this area and preceded Ontario by ten years in the process can be explained by the different histories of the two provinces. Ontario had a much more highly developed system of municipal and private charitable institutions dating back to the mid-nineteenth century. While the system was clearly inadequate to meet the demands of the twentieth century, its existence ameliorated some of the immediate crises of relief delivery and forestalled the development of a more modern system. Manitoba, unlike Ontario, had a much less well-developed private and municipal relief system and a much more dramatic influx of immigrants in the early twentieth century. The lack of charitable institutions made the development of noninstitutional relief programs more pressing and necessary. Thus, Manitoba was the first province in the country to introduce Mothers' Allowances and criteria for eligibility were consistently more liberal than those in Ontario.

The form of welfare delivery was clearly changing. De-institutionalization and greater government involvement and control distinguished this period from the first. However, three fundamental principles of welfare philosophy from the nineteenth century remained intact: first, the conviction that support conferred (if not morally required) the right to control; second, the belief that support of dependants was properly the responsibility of family and should only be assumed by others in cases of crises when all existing familial support was depleted; and finally, like the philanthropists of the nineteenth century, the legislators and social workers of the early twentieth century had an entrenched patriarchal vision of the world and women's role within it. Because women and children had always been major recipients of welfare, a function of their marginality to the wage-labour system, the patriarchal vision of women's proper role became an important determinant of the application of supportive legislation. An examination of the Mothers' Allowance Act and its application reveals all three principles in operation and indicates the underlying patriarchal assumptions built into the developing welfare state.

One of the consequences of the sexual division of labour supported by labour and family law was the frequent inability of mothers to support their children in the absence of a male breadwinner. Death, desertion or disability of a husband would often result in the break-up of the family and the institutionalization of the children. The Mothers' Allowance Act was a recognition of these conditions and an attempt to resolve the problem by paying this particular group of mothers a monthly income to stay in the home and care for their children. As such, the act indicates the state's continued commitment to the allocation of labour resources to reproduction.

From the beginning then, Mothers' Allowance was conceived of not as charity but rather as a salary. While the concept of salary was designed to remove the stigma of charity from the recipients, it also removed destitution as the major criterion for qualification. Thus, two categories of most frequently destitute women, unwed mothers and deserted women, were automatically excluded from coverage. In the former case, unwed mothers had in the eyes of society and the law already proved by virtue of their condition that they were unworthy of state support. In the case of deserted women, they were seen to be the responsibility of their husbands. Ontario relented somewhat in an amendment in 1921 providing eligibility to deserted mothers if they could prove their husbands' whereabouts had been unknown for at least five years and, hence, all attempt at enforcing maintenance had failed. Neither province relented on the issue of supporting unwed mothers, in spite of the fact that both provinces had accorded the state automatic parental authority over their children.

The concept of salary was used by administrators of the program to justify their selectivity in accepting applicants and the close supervision of recipients:

The members of the Commission do not wish applicants to be considered as applying for charity; rather, the mother when in receipt of an allowance is to be regarded as an employee of the Ontario Government receiving remuneration for services rendered in the proper care of her children. It is the duty, therefore, of the Commission and of the local board to investigate carefully the fitness of the applicant for her position. (*Report of the Mothers' Allowance Commission, Ontario, 1922 Sessional Papers 89: 59*)

They [commissioners] believe that the Province should satisfy itself that it is employing the right kind of women to bring up its future men and women, and that when the contract of employment between the mother and Province is signed, and the mother is in receipt of her salary, that the Province should satisfy itself that the services rendered for that salary are accomplishing what was intended.... (*Report of the Mothers' Allowance Commission, Manitoba, 1918* Sessional Papers 5)

The operation of the Mothers' Allowance program gives a good indication that the state's move toward noninstitutional relief did not require any abdication of its claims to authority or control. On the contrary, the terms of acceptance onto the rolls of Mothers' Allowance allowed far greater scrutiny of households than before. In the first year of operation of the Mothers' Allowance board in Ontario, seventeen percent of the recipients were removed from the rolls on the grounds that they were inadequate mothers or had failed to provide a good home environment (*Report of the Mothers' Allowance Commission, Ontario, 1922* Sessional Papers 89: 27). The exercise of moral entrepreneurship went hand in hand with the support of needy families requiring a growing bureaucracy to scrutinize recipients and administer programs.

Welfare Bureaucracy

Because welfare law is regulatory rather than adversarial, its enforcement is dependent upon the development of an administrative bureaucracy. The growth of a welfare bureaucracy can be considered as a measure of the state's commitment to enforcing the legislation. Because the law usually provides some measure of discretion to the administering body, a look at how the welfare bureaucracy operated gives some indication of the assumptions and ideas about family life built into the application of welfare legislation. Finally, the assignment of responsibility to enforce certain pieces of family law to the welfare bureaucracy indicates a growing awareness of the unsuitability of an adversarial system in managing reproductive relations.

By the end of the second period welfare administration far outstripped the more established labour departments in budget and staff. In Manitoba the Department of Health and Welfare had an overall budget of two and a half million dollars and a full-time administrative staff of sixty-nine for the welfare division (*Manitoba Public Accounts* 1940). In Ontario the budget of the welfare department was over thirteen million dollars, and they employed a full-time administrative staff of one hundred and ninety persons (*Ontario Public Accounts* 1940–41). Manitoba's commitment to welfare and its administration is underestimated by the above figures because during this period two of the largest welfare programs, old-age pension and unemployment relief were administered by the Department of Labour.

If we exclude the emergency relief programs necessitated by the Depression, we see that three pieces of legislation — Child Welfare, Mothers' Allowance and the Old Age Pension Acts — accounted for the greatest increase in administrative costs and staff. The reason why these acts accounted for most of the welfare bureaucracy at the time was because of the extensive investigative work they involved.

During the first period Manitoba and Ontario had largely entrusted the administration of the child-welfare acts to the CAS. It operated as a series of local volunteer philanthropic agencies that permitted the intensive investigative work required by the acts to be conducted at minimal cost to the state. However, during the second period, the attempt to centralize the operation of the welfare system resulted in the CAS becoming increasingly integrated into the welfare bureaucracy.

A report of the Ontario Department of Welfare shows how funding was used to increase the accountability of the agencies while preserving their distinctive status as a private agency. In 1934 a survey of all the societies in the province conducted by the welfare department led to the development of regulations upon which provincial funding was determined.

> placing the Department in an entirely new relation to the local Societies. The local Societies retain their autonomous character but they are graded on the quality of the work done, the type of organization established, the system of records installed and the qualifications of the staff. Grants ... are paid on the basis of the grading. (*Report of the Minister of Public Welfare for the Province of Ontario [R.M.P.W. ... Ontario], 1935* 19: 4)

While these regulations clearly gave the state greater co-ordination and control over the agency, it also meant greater administrative staff and expense to enforce them.

In the case of the Mothers' Allowance and the Old Age Pension Acts, investigative staff were required to ensure that the applicants and beneficiaries conformed to the criteria of the means-tested programs. For example, throughout the 1920s and 1930s, Manitoba and Ontario had a rejection rate of 25–30% for applicants of Mothers' Allowance and a cancellation rate of 15–18% for recipients. An indication of the amount of work that went into such investigations is contained in the 1935 report of the Family Allowance Commission of Ontario. The report states that during that year there were 7,418 families in receipt of the allowance, and the commission conducted 38,137 family visits. This meant that the average family on allowance was subject to five inspections a year. "In the same period, 1,333 allowances were for various reasons cancelled. Of these, 47% was due to the activities of the staff investigators" (R.M.P.W. ... Ontario, 1932 Sessional Papers Pt. 4, 20). These inspections were costly in terms of staff and travelling costs (administrative expenses that year came to $83,085), however, they were deemed necessary to ensure that only the "deserving poor" benefited. By 1939 Ontario pooled their inspectorate for Mothers' Allowance and Old Age Pension giving them a full-time staff of fifty seven and an annual budget over $100,000 (R.M.P.W. ... Ontario, 1940 Sessional Papers Pt. 4, 19: 9).

While means-tested programs were the only form of non-institutional relief at the time, and both provinces had to develop a bureaucracy to administer them, the interpretations of eligibility varied between Manitoba and Ontario. Kenneth Bryden's (1974) analysis of old-age pensions in Canada indicates that Ontario had some of the strictest criteria for eligibility. "...the proportion of the seventy and over age group in that province (Ontario) receiving pensions (full or partial) averaged about one-third, a substantially lower figure than in any other province" (Bryden 1974, 101).

In addition to these more usual forms of reallocating income, the welfare department was also assigned the responsibility of negotiating paternity suits. Throughout the

1930s, Ontario averaged 2,000–2,500 illegitimate births annually, which accounted for 4 to 4.5% of all births. In the same time period Manitoba averaged 500–600 illegitimate births annually or 3.6% of all births (Kubat and Thornton 1974). Provincial officers working out of the welfare department were charged with investigating the putative fathers and negotiating filiation settlements. This involved a considerable amount of investigative work, and both provinces were able to collect settlements in about one-fifth of the cases (*R.M.P.W. … Manitoba and Ontario, 1932–39* Sessional Papers). In these cases the supportive and regulative roles of the welfare state were particularly intertwined.

The growing integration of family and welfare law reveals the state's commitment to privatizing the costs of reproduction at the same time that it was engaged in a process of socializing some of these costs. The adversarial system provided by family law resulted in an incomplete enforcement because family members often were simply unwilling to take their providers to court. In the case of filiation payments to unwed mothers, maintenance payments to deserted wives and support for the elderly destitute (from their adult children), the benefits accruing to the plaintiff were often not sufficient to motivate them to go to court and endure the economic and psychological costs associated with a court hearing. Therefore, the letter and the application of welfare law was designed to motivate the reluctant dependants through a variety of measures to have their day in court. The most common means of pressuring people to take their designated providers to court was to deny them eligibility for relief. This was a pressure built right into the operation of means-tested welfare programs, which fell particularly hard upon deserted wives, unwed mothers and the destitute elderly. The unwed mother had the double incentive of ineligibility and potential loss of custody of her child if she did not file a suit; and finally, the provincial officer took over the task of pursuit and negotiation with the putative father regardless of the wishes of the mother. What existed in family law as a right to dependants became translated through the operation of welfare law into an obligation.

The investigators of the new welfare programs operated as investigators of family resources, locating husbands who could afford maintenance and adult children who could afford to support their elderly parents. In short, the welfare workers became the invisible plaintiffs pursuing potential providers to save the state the expense. As such, the new welfare workers facilitated the enforcement of family law by locating potential providers and putting the onus of support upon them. This process would operate quite independently of the wishes of the dependant.

The growth of welfare bureaucracies in the second period was the result of attempts to centralize operations to expand the supportive and regulatory work of the state. Built into the delivery system of these bureaucracies was a continued commitment to the sexual division of labour, which assigned women the primary role of child care and men the primary role of breadwinner. This is evident in the letter and application of Mothers' Allowance and child-welfare laws. The Child of Unmarried Parents Act and its enforcement is fraught with punitive patriarchal clauses that discriminate against unwed mothers. The automatic appointment of the state as guardian, in lieu of a husband/father, ensures that even in the absence of an internal authority, mothers will be accountable. This clause fulfils one of the most fundamental requirements of patriarchy, that women do not control the conditions of their own reproductive labour.

The reinforcement of the support-service family structure (female-homemaker, male-breadwinner) was a central organizing principle in the development of provincial welfare systems. The original purpose in the legislative support of this family structure was to ensure that women's labour was largely reserved for reproduction. However, the structure was inherently unstable because families were increasingly composed of dependants with a single breadwinner to provide. Family and welfare law developed and intersected to provide legislative reinforcement for the increasingly unstable family structure. Family law aggressively enforced the legal obligation of family members to support their kin, while welfare law evolved to provide support only to those who, through no fault of their own, were without a breadwinner. The welfare office became the "provider" for recipient families, claiming for itself the same level of scrutiny and control accorded to the traditional patriarch.

War, Depression and the Growth of Federal Welfare

Two national crises occurred in this period — World War I and the Great Depression — that changed the course of federal involvement in welfare. Federal welfare activity during the first period was minimal; there were no welfare commissions, only a few federal statutes dealing with veterans' benefits, no welfare bureaucracy and a minuscule budget allocated to welfare.

The First World War, however, brought an end to this era of non-involvement. First, federal responsibility for veterans and their dependants escalated dramatically, going from a budget of thousands of dollars prior to the war to annual expenditures between forty-five and seventy-five million dollars during the second period. The traditional responsibility of the federal government had gone from one easily resolved by giving away crown land, to a long-term fiscal responsibility for veterans and their dependants. Second, and most important, the presence of the Convention of Labour at the

Treaty of Versailles called for the signatory states to work towards the provision of social security programs within their nations. This call was taken up in Canada by the Trades and Labour Congress and a significant number of Members of Parliament who brought the issue of welfare into the federal House of Commons.

With welfare on the national agenda, it began to appear as a central theme in federal commissions and inquiries. A number of Royal Commissions on labour recommended the pursuit of national social-insurance schemes. In addition, there was the 1922 Royal Commission on Pensions and Re-establishment and, later, the 1937 Royal Commission on Dominion-Provincial Relations, which sought to redefine taxation and welfare policy between the two jurisdictions. Finally, during this period, there were two special committees of the House called in 1924 and 1925 to inquire into the development of a national old-age pension plan.

Accompanying this increasing debate in the federal House was an increase in welfare legislation. In contrast to the inactivity of the first period, the second period saw the introduction of eighteen new welfare statutes (see table A2.13. New Federal Welfare Legislation, Period II). This dramatic increase in legislation was accompanied by an even more dramatic increase in welfare expenditures: 2% of the national budget in 1914 to 20% of the overall budget in 1939 (Leacy 1983, Series H19–34). The increase in legislation and expenditure was the result of three major programs: Veterans' Benefits, Old Age Pension and Depression Relief Projects. In 1939 these three programs accounted for fourteen of the eighteen new statutes and $137.4 million of expenditure out of a $138 million welfare budget (Leacy 1983, Series H19–34).

Federal entry into the welfare field mirrored the provincial experience: crises intervention and increasing expenditure without a systematic welfare policy or bureaucracy. The one exception to the crisis-intervention pattern of federal involvement was the passage of the Old Age Pension Act in 1927. This act was unique, given the history of welfare program development at the time. Most welfare programs were first introduced at the provincial level during this period, yet the Old Age Pension was always conceived of as a national responsibility. It had no provincial precursors and was never seriously considered at the provincial level.[9] There was no challenge to the pension act, although it involved legislation deemed to be in the jurisdiction of the provinces. In spite of these unique characteristics, the pension act, as an isolated piece of legislation, did not substantially change the character of federal involvement during the second period, nor did it provoke the development of a national social-insurance policy or a national welfare bureaucracy. In the absence of a federal administrative body, the provinces were left to administer the program as they saw fit, and the federal government's role was largely limited to paying the bill.

Up to this point I have been discussing the evolution of the welfare state without specific mention of the Depression because the majority of legislative and administrative changes that characterized welfare policy during the second period were largely in place prior to its onset. Although the effects of the Depression cannot be seen as the significant determinants of welfare policy in this period, the impact of the Depression upon the evolution of the welfare state is indisputable.

Throughout the ten years of Depression, the characteristic response of all levels of government was to struggle with the existing system to meet the overwhelming demands for relief. The only substantial change was the dramatic increase in federal government expenditure. This was, however, accomplished on an *ad hoc*, year-by-year basis and did not result in any substantial reordering of federal-provincial welfare legislation.[10]

As relief demands outstripped the resources of the provinces, the federal government's control of national revenue became essential if it was to rescue the increasingly indebted municipalities and provinces. Therefore, federal involvement in relief provoked a change in taxation policy during the 1930s. Although personal income tax had been introduced during the First World War, its impact upon revenue was limited. Personal exemptions were set at $1,000 for single and $3,000 for married persons, at a time when sixty per cent of employed males and eighty-two percent of employed females earned less than $1,000 per year. As a result the revenue generated by personal income tax was quite small. For example, in 1926, personal income tax generated $18.1 million or 5% of the total national revenue (Perry 1955, 1: 250).

In response to the relief demands of the Depression, the federal government reduced exemptions and raised the tax rate. By 1932, exemptions were reduced to $2,000 for married and $1,000 for single persons adding an additional 200,000 tax payers to the roles (Perry 1955, 1: 261). As the federal tax rate rose, most provinces that did not already have personal income tax introduced it during this period. Thus, the tax burden on the employed increased dramatically during the 1930s. Between 1929 and 1940, these new taxation policies increased personal income tax as a source of revenue almost 200%, going from 7% to 13.3% of all federal revenue. In contrast, corporate tax increased 60%, going from 11% of all revenue in 1929 to 16.9% in 1940 (Perry 1955, 1: 258). In the attempt to reallocate income, it was the wage earners who were hit the hardest. As incomes fell and a smaller proportion of the population was employed, the amount of revenue from wage earners doubled and the proportion of national revenue generated from personal income tax doubled.

Welfare Expenditures

The central strategy of the state in dealing with the income-allocation problem was the development of a system of reallocating income outside of, and noncompetitive with, the wage-labour system. In spite of significant developments in labour law, the most significant legislation in channelling income resources into the reproductive unit occurred in the welfare field.

The welfare-state strategy for mediating production and reproduction has usually been understood as a post-World War II phenomenon in Canada. A careful analysis of fiscal and legislative developments in this period, however, suggests that such a strategy was well underway prior to the war, although limited by its provincial location. It is interesting to note that the greatest leap in this period (650%) in all government welfare expenditures (municipal, provincial and federal expenditures) occurred between 1913 and 1921 when federal involvement was still quite limited (Urquhart and Buckley 1965, 53). Overall welfare expenditures in Canada rose from $15 million in 1913 to $100 million in 1921, reaching the level of $235 million by 1939 (see table 6).

This massive increase in social-welfare expenditures was associated with a shifting pattern of fiscal responsibility, as ever larger resource bases were necessary to cope with the escalating demand (see table 7). In 1913 the municipalities bore the brunt of welfare costs. By 1930, however, this burden had shifted to the province, and in the heart of the Depression, federal welfare expenditures came to equal that of the provinces.

In discussing the process of state absorption of the costs of reproduction, categories not traditionally calculated as "welfare expenditures" are included because they are clearly understood as part and parcel of the development of the

Table 6
Government Expenditure on Social Welfare,
by Level of Government and per Capita,
Canada 1913–1939
(In Millions of Dollars)

Year	Federal	Provincial	Munici-pal	All Gov-ernment	(Dol-lars) per Capita
1913	2.7	4.3	8.2	15.2	–
1921	58.6	22.8	18.8	100.2	11.42
1926	49.7	28.6	20.7	99.0	10.49
1930	73.0	52.2	31.5	156.8	15.38
1933	96.7	57.4	41.9	196.0	18.46
1937	126.4	101.5	39.0	266.9	24.20
1939	113.7	86.2	35.2	235.2	20.91

SOURCE: Urquhart and Buckley 1965, 53, Series B266–270.

welfare state. The criteria for including nontraditional categories, such as health, education and veterans' benefits, is their effect in transferring income or providing services to the population outside the usual operation of the wage-labour system.

Table 7
Dimension of Public Welfare Expenditures
in Canada (Other Than Relief)

	1913	1930	1937
Municipalities	53%	40%	29%
Provinces	30%	42%	36%
Dominion	17%	18%	35%

SOURCE: *Royal Commission on Dominion-Provincial Relations Report Book II*, 208, table 82.

Table 8

Federal Welfare Expenditures for Selected Years,
by Components and as a Proportion of Total Expenditures
(In Millions of Dollars)

Year	Total Expenditure	Health, Welfare and Education		Veterans Benefits	Total Social Expenditures	
	Amount	Amount	Amount	Amount	Amount	%
1914	246	3	—	1	4	1.6
1918	696	4	—	30	34	4.8
1922	411	7	2	48	57	12.9
1926	359	5	2	46	53	14.7
1930	442	17	1	57	75	16.9
1934	478	81	1	55	137	28.6

SOURCE: Leacy 1983, Series 19–34.

Total reproductive/social expenditures of the federal government, throughout the second period, increased from $4 million in 1914 to $137 million in 1934. As a proportion of the overall national budget the commitment increased over twenty-fold from 1.6% in 1914 to 28.6% in 1934 (see table 8).

The provinces, like the federal government, experienced dramatic increases in their welfare expenditures in spite of the fact that they had already made substantial commitments to welfare in the first period. Submissions to the Royal Commission on Dominion-Provincial Relations (1937) indicated that the per-capita welfare expenditures in the first period averaged $0.41 in Ontario and $0.37 in Manitoba. This increased to an average of $3.75 and $3.45 respectively in the second period. If education is included as part of the reproductive costs broadly defined, an equally dramatic increase in provincial expenditure is apparent. Per-capita education expenditure for the provinces rose from a first period average of $0.41 in Ontario and $0.85 in Manitoba to a second period average of $2.98 and $3.33 respectively. At the same time, municipal welfare expenditures also increased.

If the extension of welfare legislation was indeed the prime strategy of the state to respond to the chronic income-allocation problem of this period, the amount of income reallocated to the reproduction and maintenance of the population would indicate that this strategy was highly effective. The magnitude of the transfers (even prior to the Depression) were massive in comparison to the first period. At the height of the Depression, 1937, the combined expenditures of the provincial and municipal governments in Ontario reallocated over $47 million of income and services through the welfare system in that one year. For that same year Manitoba reallocated over $10 million. Thus, as a system for reallocating income, innovations in welfare law and its concomitant, tax law, achieved far more than labour or family law reforms.

While the large outlays in 1937 resulted from an immediate crisis, evidence that the income-allocation problem is endemic to the wage-labour system and not merely a function of the Depression can be found in the dramatically rising welfare costs that characterize the next period.

Summary

The primary manifestation of the contradiction between production and reproduction during this period was an income crisis for the reproductive unit. In response to this crisis, the central task of the state was the reorganization of income flows between the two spheres to stabilize the patriarchal family. This process involved a modification of the wage-labour system and an elaboration of social patriarchal functions. Evidence of the modification of the wage-labour system comes from labour laws, which sought to provide income protection for workers, for example, workmen's compensation and minimum wage, as well as to sustain and to elaborate on sexual divisions within the work place. The outcome of state intervention in the labour process was to preserve and solidify existing sexual divisions of labour and to provide for increased flows of income to the reproductive unit.

While the state intervened in the production process to accommodate certain reproductive necessities, it was at the same time involved in adjusting the patriarchal family to fit the economic system. The family law reforms of the earlier period were extended to increase the entitlement of dependants and increase the obligations of productive family members. The model for accommodation between patriarchy and production, characteristic of both the first and second period, was the support-service marriage structure, that is, the male breadwinner and the female homemaker. However, despite reforms in labour law and elaborations in family law, the costs of this accommodation outgrew the willingness of employers and the resources of families.

Caught between the inflexibility of the wage-determination process and the cost of living crises it provoked, the state solution was to develop a system of redistributing income outside of the wage-labour system. Welfare law emerged as the critical mechanism of intervention in the second period. New welfare legislation and the growth of welfare bureaucracies represented a further development of social patriarchy as the state expanded its supportive and regulatory roles to fill the authority and resource gaps created by the disjuncture between production and reproduction. In doing so, the state managed to extend its control over the family, maintain the principle of privatization of reproductive costs and provide a back-up system when family support systems broke down completely.

While the support-service marriage structure appeared to be the most viable accommodation between production and reproduction throughout most of the first and second period, major national and international events were soon to call this solution into question. The Depression highlighted the limits of state intervention at the provincial level, and the economic boom of the third period (1940–68) called into question not only the location of state mediation but its strategy as well.

PERIOD III
1940–1968

State mediation in this period was different in location, strategy and outcome from the earlier two periods. In the third period the federal government became the key actor in the mediation of production and reproduction — during the war, because it took over the management of the Canadian economy, and in the post-war years, because no other level of government had the necessary resources to do so.

From 1940 to 1947 the War Measures Act empowered the federal government to manage the economy and all matters of labour. As provincial authority was usurped, federal Privy Council Orders (PC) issued directly from cabinet replaced the usual legislative process including debate in the House. Under conditions of war the provinces suspended most legislative activity, and the federal government intervened in the relations of production and reproduction through direct management. In the post-war years the state returns to its mediating role and the usual legislative procedures, including significant provincial activity, are once again observed. While state intervention in the war and post-war years underwent different processes, I group these years together as Period III because of the similarities in the content and intent of state intervention.

The primary strategy for accommodating production and reproduction in the first two periods was the support-service marriage structure. The legislatively sanctioned and subsidized division of labour allocated women's labour and some income (via welfare) to the reproductive sphere without disruption of the productive sphere. However, within the changing political and economic structures of the third period, this accommodation became less and less viable, necessitating a significant realignment of labour and income between the two spheres.

In response to compelling structural pressures to provide more income to reproduction and more labour to production, the state introduced dramatic changes in its mediating strategy in the third period. The most dramatic of these was the state's removal of restraints on the use of female labour in production. This provided employers with the expanding labour supply they required under the conditions of full production, which pertained throughout most of the third period. However, this policy reversal also dismantled the critical base of the support-service marriage structure. As restraints were removed and women's labour flowed from reproduction to production, the state's support of the patriarchal family was limited to reallocating income to the reproductive sphere. Hence, the second significant change in state intervention strategy was the creation of the modern welfare state — the socialization of the costs of reproduction on a national scale. These two major policy developments, realized in a variety of labour and welfare statutes, brought about the strategic realignment of labour and income flows that distinguish the third period.

The policy changes of this period altered the dynamic between familial and social patriarchy. In the previous two periods state support of the patriarchal family was evidenced in three distinct functions of social patriarchy: first, the provision of resources to subsidize the reproductive unit; second, the regulation of the family, including the disposition of property, wages and children; third, the regulation of labour between production and reproduction, specifically the allocation of women's labour to reproduction.

In the third period these functions of social patriarchy

changed in relation to the restructuring of production and the state. The first function, socializing the costs of reproduction, expanded massively with the introduction of the welfare state. The second function, regulating family life, was redirected from control of service consumers to control of service providers. The third function, regulating the flow of labour between production and reproduction, devolved from the state to the market place. In this process of expansion, redirection and devolution, the state's relation to the family changed significantly.

While social patriarchal functions of the state continued and expanded, they did so primarily in the direction of support. The regulatory social patriarchal functions of the state were less relevant to the mediating strategies of the third period, hence, the uniquely benevolent quality of state intervention during the third period. However, this benevolence was symptomatic of the increasing displacement of the costs of reproduction from capital (production) to the state, a process that would have serious implications for the state, the family and Canadian society in the long term.

Patriarchy and Patriotism:
The War and Reconstruction Years
1940–1947

Canada's entry into the Second World War marked a dramatic departure from the conditions that prevailed during the previous period. The most significant difference was the eight-year period 1940–47 when the federal government managed the Canadian economy. Under these conditions, the usual operation of state mediation was dramatically altered. First, the War Measures Act superceded provincial jurisdiction over labour, designating labour legislation and mediation as federal matters. Second, the special Dominion-Provincial War Time Tax Agreements altered jurisdiction over taxation powers transferring provincial authority over personal, corporate and succession tax exclusively to the federal government, substantially increasing the federal government's revenue-generating power. Third, legislative activity in the welfare field ceased in Manitoba and Ontario, while it expanded dramatically at the federal level. Thus, not only was most provincial legislation suspended, but the pattern of state mediation was altered by the requirements of management. During the war years legislation was as frequently pro-active as it was reactive, introducing the state as an active protagonist along with capital and labour, at the same time as it attempted to fulfil its mediating role.

The economic changes that occurred during these eight years were as dramatic as the political developments. A war economy meant a boom economy, moving Canadians from a crushing depression to full production and full employment in one and a half years. With the rapid growth of the economy, capital and labour intensified their struggles over the division of wealth between wages and profits. However, the economic boom altered the power differential between the two protagonists. Ironically, prosperity made capital potentially more vulnerable because their vested interest in full production made labour's ultimate weapon, work stoppages, far more effective. If conditions of high demand and full production coincide with high employment, labour is in a particularly good position to further its demands. Such were the conditions that prevailed during the war years, and the strength of labour grew dramatically.

As the power differential between capital and labour became more evenly balanced, the potential for stalemate increased. The federal state, with its newly acquired power and mandate, was required to intervene in a far more direct fashion than ever before. As capital and labour approached a deadlock in the midst of the war years, the state formally inserted itself between the two protagonists, with the introduction of the Labour Relations Act. This act transformed key shop-floor struggles into legal bureaucratic processes that were much more amenable to routines and control.

Economic recovery coincided with reproductive recovery and the birth rate rose steadily from 1940 on. The competing pressures of production and reproduction were expressed in the early war years in the classic conflict between capital and labour over the wage. However, the combined effect of stalemate on the wage issue and the experience of a state-managed economy gave new expression to reproductive pressures in the later war years. Reproductive demands for income and services increasingly focussed on the state and gave birth to a powerful social consensus on the necessity of a national social security system.

The location of state intervention and the concerns of war

overshadowed the usual patterns of state mediation in reproduction during the war years. However, evidence of continued pressure on the state from the reproductive sphere lay in the public demand for a national welfare system, a system that, while not realized within these eight years, was undeniably launched within this period.

The War Economy

At the outbreak of the war the federal government was faced with the problem of rapidly increasing the supply of everything required for the war effort. However, the experience of the First World War had impressed upon the government the risks of leaving high speed economic development solely to private initiative. In order to achieve the desired economic expansion and avoid the inflation and profiteering that characterized the war economy of 1914, the government invoked the War Measures Act to control all aspects of the economy and established the Wartime Prices and Trade Board and the War Labour Board. "In fact, the government instituted what we might call socialism, capitalist style; during the war, Canada had a centrally planned economy in which market mechanisms were largely superceded by administrative decisions, while ownership of most of the productive capacity was left in private hands" (Phillips and Watson 1984, 23).

The object of wartime economic policy was victory in war, not economic development. However, the resulting growth in the Canadian economy was dramatic. Canadians were able to raise the real output of their economy by about two-thirds between 1939 and 1944 despite the massive transfer of workers to the armed forces. Between 1939 and 1942 private investment increased by 80% and public investment increased 201%. Under these conditions of rapid growth, the unemployment problem disappeared as it plummeted from 20% during the depths of the Depression to 1.4% during the war. Further, the structure as well as the size of the economy was changing. In 1939 less than 16% of the labour force was employed in the manufacturing sector. By the end of the war, this had risen to over 26%. Manufacturing reached its zenith in 1944 in terms of the percentage of the labour force employed in this sector (Phillips and Watson 1984, 23).

The rapid increase in employment in manufacturing, which doubled between 1939 and the end of 1942, involved a massive transfer of workers from other sectors, especially agriculture, into manufacturing. There was, therefore, a shrinkage of employment in sectors little affected by industrial clashes and a massive growth of the manufacturing sector in which the conflicting attitudes of employers and workers over the issue of collective bargaining were at their sharpest. This growth and a significant amount of labour discontent led to a rapid rise in union membership. Between 1939 and 1944 organized labour doubled its membership. This momentum continued on into the reconstruction period, and by 1949 unions had tripled the 1939 membership figure (Lipton 1973, 275).

Government management did prevent the inflation associated with the First World War. The strict controls protected real wages, and the average wage in production rose from less that $1,000 in 1939 to $1,400 in 1942 (Russell 1984, 60). However, to state that conditions were better than during the Depression does not indicate that the workers faired well during this period of rapid economic development. Government management did not prevent the economic burden of the war being placed squarely on the shoulders of the country's wage earners. Their share of national income declined sharply while the shares going to profits, rents and interest were well maintained (Pentland 1968, 205).

While capital was benefiting from a period of uninterrupted full production, labour found itself straight-jacketed by rigid wage controls. Wage controls, however, were only half the problem. Workers were called upon to finance the war effort through personal income tax. What small increases in wages workers were able to wrest from the war labour board were gobbled up by taxes. Income-tax exemption levels were systematically lowered to $660 (individual) and $1,200 (family) by 1942. By 1944 less than one-quarter of Canadian households were exempt from the provisions of the Income War Tax Act, introduced ironically during the last war as a "conscription of wealth." Despite the buoyant economy, labour found itself squeezed between wage controls and rising taxation to a point that threatened household subsistence.

During the war years taxes on corporations rose as well. However, their impact did not appear to threaten the resources of corporations as it did the workers. Quite the opposite occurred, in fact, as we can see by the expansion of manufacturing and the growth of Canadian industry in general. The stimulating effect of high corporate taxes was the result of the particular manner in which profits were taxed, exempted and returned to corporations. A standard of normal profits was determined based on the pre-war profit levels of each corporation as measured by their 1936–39 profit averages. All profit above that level was considered excess profit and taxed theoretically at 100% with a 20% post-war refund. Tax on normal profits was 18% in 1940–41 and 12% thereafter. However, the impact of the Excess Profits Act was far less spartan than it appears. Nearly half of the revenue generated by the excess profits tax was returned to industry through depreciation allowances, direct investment and post-war refunds.[1]

The fact that government management of the economy seemed to serve the interests of business quite well is not surprising since the war managers were recruited largely from the business community. The locus of government's planning and control of the economy was the Department of Munitions and Supply established under C.D. Howe, a wealthy Canadian businessman who became even wealthier as a result of the war industries he owned. On 29 April 1942 CCF leader, M.J. Coldwell, charged in the House of Commons that Howe's department was a concentration point for the Canadian Manufacturers' Association and its friends (Lipton 1973, 267). Both taxation and labour legislation at the time suggest that government economic policy was closely allied with the interests of business — full production, industrial harmony and low wages.

Managing Labour

During the war the federal government was the major actor in the area of labour legislation and mediation. All provincial labour laws were superseded by the War Measures Act. Privy Council Orders issued directly from cabinet replaced the lengthy legislative process and the necessity of a house debate. These changes in the location and process of state intervention altered the typical sequence of state activity — inquiries, legislative enactment and bureaucratic enforcement. As these processes merged in form and function, decision making became highly centralized.

The combined effect of the concentration of decision making and the massive mobilization of the labour force provides a unique opportunity to see the state struggle with wage- and labour-allocation problems in a direct and immediate way. The critical events in labour during the war were:

first, the massive employment of women; second, the intense struggle by labour for union recognition; and third, the conflict between workers and employers over the wage. Women provided a vast reserve of labour that was at one and the same time extensively utilized in the war economy and effectively contained within the rhetoric and contracts of temporary placement. While the strategy for women's employment emerged early, and seemingly effortlessly from an entrenched patriarchal tradition, the wage and union recognition struggles took longer to resolve. Because all three factors remained the "live" labour issues in the post-war period, state strategies not only served to manage the war economy, but set the course for post-war industrial relations.

By the spring of 1940 the war was heating up and Mackenzie King's Liberals were returned to office with a landslide victory. In June the government's War Labour Policy (PC 2685) was issued declaring the right to form unions and bargain collectively and banning strikes and lockouts in war industries. Industrial harmony was deemed essential to the war economy. The union recognition clause was designed to win the co-operation of labour on the no strike policy, a strategy that worked until it became evident that the government was preoccupied with wage-control policies and had no sympathy for union recognition. Evidence of the government's priorities is seen in the rapid succession of orders in council, which, with the exception of PC 2685, dealt exclusively with matters of wage restraint, mechanisms for wage enforcement and dispute settlement (see table A2.14. Privy Council Orders Pertaining to Labour During World War II, Period III).

On the heels of the Depression, full employment, full production and increasing productivity created an unrelenting pressure for wage gains. This force confronted the equally strong commitment of the state to contain inflation through wage controls. For example, in 1940 PC 7440 imposed severe wage controls limiting wage settlements to rates established during the 1926–29 period. The consequences of the order became evident shortly after its issue when workers from the Peck Rolling Mills in Montreal petitioned the War Labour Board for a wage increase. The board operating under the Industrial Disputes Investigation Act refused any wage increase on the argument that thirty cents an hour was higher than the 1929 level. In November of 1941 PC 8253 provided for a National War Labour Board with powers of investigation and recommendation on wages and conditions. Increases in basic wages were prohibited, save by permission of the Board. Finally, PC 9384, enacted in 1943, stipulated that a wage adjustment could be granted only where it was necessary to correct "a gross inequality or gross injustice" — and this commensurate with the employers' ability to pay (Lipton 1973, 269). Large numbers of workers found themselves earning less than fifty cents an hour, an income that even the war labour board acknowledged as inadequate to support a family (*McTague Report* 1943, 16).

Maintaining wage controls and industrial harmony became increasingly difficult as the war progressed. The Industrial Disputes Investigation Commission, first brought into effect to manage disputes in war industries in 1941, was extended by 1943 to cover any dispute situation perceived to be a "threat to the war effort" (PC 496). Nine regional War Labour Boards and a twelve-man National War Labour Board were empowered to set wage ceilings and enforce them. In addition to these major mechanisms of restraint and enforcement, nine Royal Commissions were called between 1940 and 1943 for the purposes of addressing wage disputes.

While the government expended more and more effort issuing and enforcing wage restriction orders, its disregard for the union recognition clause in the War Labour Policy became increasingly evident. Emphatic exposure of this attitude and a crystallization of public feeling about it came in 1941 with a number of explicitly anti-union acts on the part of the state. In a dispute at the General Motors engine plant in St. Catherines, the Minister of Munitions and Supply, C.D. Howe, promised RCMP protection for workers who broke the strike. In the summer the government ordered in troops to resolve a dispute between the Aluminum Company of Canada and a Catholic syndicate in Arvida, Quebec. Finally, two major strikes for union recognition, at the National Steel Car Plant in Hamilton and the Kirkland Lake gold mines, involving thousands of workers received no government support in their bid for unionization. Government leaders defended their refusal to enforce laws supporting collective bargaining as a sincere effort to avoid compulsion in industrial relations (Roberts and Bullen 1984, 113).

The government was not moved to reconsider its labour policies until threatened by a massive outbreak of industrial disputes. The trade union's no-strike policy, its contribution to the war effort, kept a lid on tensions for a while. However, by 1942 the cumulative effect of backlogged complaints, the wage-tax squeeze and unresolved recognition battles led to a dramatic increase in disputes. Strikes and lockouts doubled in number between 1941 and 1942 and doubled again in 1943. The number of workers involved in disputes in 1943 (one unionist in three) was about twice the number of the previous year — already high — and much more than in any earlier year of Canadian history, including 1919. In 1942–43 there was a loss of one and a half million person-days of labour. Furthermore, the strikes were concentrated in critical war industries, in manufacturing (steel, autos, aircraft and textiles) and in mining (Clement 1984, 90). In the winter of 1943 the threat of a general strike in steel loomed large and the national War Labour Board had lost all credibility.

Labour Inquiry Board

Under threat of a paralyzed economy the government was forced to rediscover its mediation role and come up with a strategy to end the increasing polarization between capital and labour. Labour's bottom line was recognition and wage gains — capital's bottom line was industrial peace and wage control. In February 1943 King disbanded the controversial War Labour Board and appointed a three-man board of inquiry to report on labour unrest and recommend the means to improve labour relations. The activities of the inquiry and the government over the next year reveal the complex process of compromise and containment. The public process was relatively simple involving one inquiry, one order in council and one act of parliament all accomplished within one year. The speed and apparent simplicity of the resolution was, however, the product of intense behind-the-scenes manoeuvering by top government officials.

One compromise emerged early and encountered little resistance. The events of the last two years made it clear that union recognition was unavoidable. However, the battle line was drawn, both within the inquiry and behind the scenes, over the wage issue. The first public indication of division among the mediators (the labour inquiry board) came with the submission of two reports to the government in August. A majority report was submitted by Justice McTague, the chairman of the inquiry and a prominent Conservative. The minority report was submitted by J.L. Cohen, the third member of the inquiry board and a prominent labour lawyer.

The two reports were in basic agreement in their recommendations for a system of compulsory collective bargaining, labour management co-operation and genuine labour representation on government boards in response to the recognition problem. Interestingly enough the McTague report, the voice of Conservatism and officialdom, was as adamant as the Cohen report in denouncing previous patterns of industrial relations and in recommending a system of compulsory collective bargaining, labour-management co-operation and genuine labour representation on government boards. These recommendations were followed and enacted in PC 1003, the precursor to the Labour Relations Act, the following year.

However, although they were both sympathetic to labour's complaints about wages and were critical of the existing wage orders, they differed significantly in their recommendations. Throughout the inquiry, labour consistently argued for the removal of wage controls for workers earning less than $0.50 an hour. Workers with substandard wages could then bargain freely to increase their wage, while workers earning more than $0.50 an hour would continue to be subject to wage controls. For labour the principle was an equitable return for their work, a principle shared and articulated by Cohen. Cohen strongly recommended the labour proposal as the only acceptable solution.

In McTague's report the focus was shifted away from the concept of an equitable share to the problem of family income — a perspective that was not publicly articulated in any of the inquiry hearings and whose origins are to be found only in confidential government documents of the time. In discussing low wages McTague states, "Rigid control at such a level of earnings in the case of a family is hardly defensible, politically and morally." While he acknowledged that labour's proposal was one option, he cautioned against a problem contained within it: "Such a solution would be based, however on the assumption that all such workers are heads of families — a completely unwarranted one" (*McTague Report* 1943, 17). Lifting controls on low wages would be a costly solution that would benefit all low-wage workers, when heads of households were in fact the workers deemed to have the most legitimate complaint.

McTague proposed that "Another answer would appear to be a system of family allowances to be paid for by the Dominion Government." While Cohen argued strenuously against family allowances as the solution, stating it would merely perpetuate and legitimate substandard wages, the *McTague Report* was favoured by government.

The language and recommendations of the *McTague Report* presented in its clearest form the logic behind and the link between the welfare state and contemporary industrial relations, that is, the necessity of providing for the costs of reproduction without disrupting the wage-determination process. The two major outcomes of the Labour inquiry were the Family Allowance Act and PC 1003 that established the Labour Relations Act.

The Family Allowance Act: A Wage Subsidy Program

Although the Family Allowance Act is strictly speaking welfare legislation, it provides the most accurate reflection of a particularly explicit process of compromise undertaken by the state on the issues of wage control at a point in time in which it operated both as manager and mediator of the Canadian economy and the Canadian population.

The Family Allowance Act was unique in a number of ways. First, the major beneficiaries of the program never asked for it — in fact, most Canadians had never considered such a program until planning was well underway. Second, although it was destined to become a critical component of the modern welfare state, welfare commissions, inquiries and departments had nothing to do with its development.[2] Third, the act owed its existence to three somewhat unlikely advocates: Under-Secretary of the State for External Affairs Norman Robertson, Governor of the Bank of Canada Graham Towers, and Deputy Minister of Finance W.C. Clark, the real architect of the program. All three were members of the powerful Advisory Committee on Economic Policy, and while only Clark had revealed any previous interest or commitment to labour or welfare issues, all were highly committed to the effective management of the war economy. In sorting out the actors and their motivations, it is important to remember that the members of the Economic Advisory Committee (EAC) were drawn from the Canadian business elite and represented the strong voice of business in government.

The driving force behind the development of the Family Allowances program was the stalemate between business and labour over wages. In order to mediate this struggle, the battle had to be removed from the shop floor and contained within the state terrain of inquiries, bureaucracy and legislation. Labour used the inquiry hearings to promote its position, while business worked quietly through the EAC.

The activities of the labour board inquiry were being closely watched by members of the EAC who were fearful for the maintenance of the Wage and Price Stabilization program. It was known that Prime Minister King would likely be sympathetic to the removal of controls on substandard wages. By 1943 King was of the opinion that it had been a mistake to freeze the low wage levels in the first place. "The Finance Department were responsible and they should never have frozen an increasing injustice" (Pickersgill 1960, 159). Members of the EAC were convinced that to opt for the removal of controls, no matter now limited, would ultimately jeopardize the whole stabilization program.

Although the inquiry was generating a lot of sympathy for labour, business held the trump card. Before the hearings were completed a powerful bureaucracy swung into motion to reframe the issue, construct the compromise and manage potential labour allies (including the Prime Minister and inquiry board members). The account of the behind-the-scenes events that gave Canada its first universal welfare program were all duly recorded in the confidential documents of the Department of Finance and the Economic Advisory Council, as well in as the private papers of key actors in the process.

In private memos to Prime Minister King, dated 8 June 1943, both Clark and Robertson separately reported on a meeting they had with Justice McTague the previous evening. Robertson states, "I think his [McTague's] mind is turning toward recommending the restoration of free collective bargaining for the adjustment of wage rates up to fifty cents an hour." He then related McTague's response to concerns about the impact of such a policy on the Wage and Price Stabilization program: "McTague thinks it might be possible to hold adjustments at the fifty cents an hour level, but is naturally not confident that this could be done" (King Papers C187885). While it is not indicated in the memos, it is likely that Robertson and Clark did more than express their fears; they probably also expressed what they considered the better alternative, family allowances. Clearly they had given the issue a lot of thought, for their memos to King outline the major arguments in favour of family allowances as well as touching on costs and jurisdictional issues. It is most likely that Clark and Robertson first planted the idea of family allowances in McTague's mind, as there was no previous reference to it as an option in the briefs before the Labour Board Inquiry.

On 13 July 1943 Towers sent a memo to the Minister of Finance warning of the dangers of tampering with wage controls:

It seems to me quite probable that the National War Labour Board will endorse the proposal for removing any ceiling on rates up to 50 cents an hour. If this is done, I think that the whole price and wage stabilization program will have to be abandoned in a comparatively short time. If rates below 50 cents are raised, it will be impossible to prevent increases in the wage of those now receiving more. In other words, there will be a fight on the part of labour — I think a successful fight — to maintain, in part at least, the existing differentials in wage rates. (Dept. of Finance Papers, 101-53-114)

One day after Towers's memo to the Minister of Finance, Clark came forward with a Finance Department document entitled "The Case for Children's Allowances," followed one week later by a working paper on family allowances from the same department, which included a report on family allowance programs in other countries, a summary of the literature and preliminary cost estimates (Finance Central Files, 101-53-114). Arguments and evidence were being compiled in anticipation of McTague's recommendations.

With the submission of the *McTague Report*, activities around the issue of family allowances increased. In early September a memorandum was sent to Mackintosh, Vice-Chairman of the EAC, entitled "Proposed Family Allowances Scheme for Canada" (Finance Central Files, 101-53-114, Vol. 1). On 17 September 1943 the Economic Advisory Committee summarized its position on the wage issue raised by McTague. Speaking strongly against any removal of wage restraints, it offered two broad alternatives: "a) A stronger re-inforced wage control policy directed to reducing the over-all increase in wage-rates that are being made but more flexible with regard to rates which are low by absolute standards. b) Children's allowances payable for all children without means test" (Finance Central Files, 17 Sept. 1943).

Working with the consistent opposition of the Minister of Finance, Ilsley, but with the support of the Economic Advisory Committee, Clark took the committee's recommendations to a meeting with Cabinet and McTague on the first of October. McTague argued strenuously against the committee's first alternative and supported the second. While seeing family allowances as the best solution to the wage problem, McTague cautioned against any public association of the two. "Also McTague was most emphatic about not allowing any discussion of family allowances to become a part of the labour policy as such. Rather they were to be considered in connection with a social security program" (King's Diary, 1 Oct. 1943: 859). Thus, while the internal (bureaucratic) strategy was well underway, the public strategy was now in the making.

To have introduced family allowances immediately after the McTague and Cohen reports had been received would have revealed that family allowances were being used as a protective device for the maintenance of the government's wage and price stabilization policy. In his radio address to the nation on 4 December 1943, King announced that the government was prepared to accept as a basis for a revised labour policy the main proposals on which the Majority and Minority Reports had been able to agree. In doing so, King sidestepped the issue at the heart of the controversy between the two reports — family allowances in lieu of removing wage restraints. To ensure that no association between wage policy and family allowances be made, the reports were held up on a variety of contexts and not released for a year.

In the meantime a great deal of work remained in promoting family allowances within the government. While King appreciated the necessity of disassociating the two issues and acted accordingly, his initial response to Clark's proposal was far from enthusiastic: "I pointed out that to tell the country that everyone was to get a family allowance was sheer folly; it would occasion resentment everywhere" (King's Diary, 1 Oct. 1943: 859). From January to June 1944 Clark presented the Cabinet with a steady flow of memoranda, working papers and statistical analyses promoting the adoption of the family allowance scheme. A brief review of the major arguments presented by the Finance Department to Cabinet is most revealing of the significance of this particular welfare program to the government's role as mediator of production and reproduction.

While cabinet was exhorted to never discuss family allowances as a part of labour policy, the internal documents made the connection quite clearly. "Children's allowances are the most direct and economic method of meeting the current strong demand for relaxation of wage control in respect of the lower wage rates. If current dissatisfaction of lower-paid workers is met by allowing them unrestricted wage bargaining (and thus promoting union organization) a good deal of industrial strife and stoppage of essential work must be expected" (Finance Files, 101-53-144 14 June 1943: 3–4). Family allowances were argued for, not only as a means of rescuing the wage stabilization program and restoring industrial harmony, but also as a basis for developing a competitive post-war economy. "Children's allowances are likely to protect Canada's ability to compete with other countries in world markets. In the long run, minimum wages and average wages are likely to be pushed higher in the absence of family allowances than they would be if this supplementary equalizing measure were in effect" (Finance Files, 101-53-144 14 June 1943: 5).

As public pressure for social security measures mounted, the Finance Department invoked the arguments of British and Canadian welfare inquiries pointing out that wages could not be made responsive to family size. Their analysis of the 1941 census brought this point home with shocking clarity. The census revealed that, of all gainfully employed, 48% were single, 20% were married or widowed with no dependent children, 13% were married or widowed with one dependent child and 19% were married or widowed with more than one child. Further, the census indicated that 84% of all dependent children came from families with more than one child, the net result being that 19% of the gainfully employed supported 84% of Canada's dependent children (King Papers, C187877). In response to criticisms of the plan for a universal program, the Finance Department revealed, "An income ceiling would save little, a ceiling of $3,000 would exclude only 3% of all families" (Finance Files, 101-53-144 Sept. 1943: 5).

It was Clark's argument that the gap between wages and family costs fueled labour militancy. Since it was clearly demonstrated that the wage-labour system could not be made responsive to those costs, the options were either government subsidization of family costs or labour militancy and rising wages. It was a compelling argument made all the more so in the face of growing public pressure for social security programs. The cabinet supported the bill in June 1944, the first reading was in July, and the act passed unanimously in August of the same year.

While King had originally predicted widespread resistance to the scheme, the critics of family allowance were few and their arguments ineffectual. The English press remained critical of the program through the years 1943–45; however, they appeared to have little impact on public opinion. As media criticism escalated between 1943 and 1944, public opinion became more favourable. The first Gallup poll on family allowance, run in October 1943 when the idea was first talked about, revealed that 49% of Canadians thought it was a good idea, 42% a bad idea and 9% were undecided. When estimates of the cost of the program were included, support dropped to 43%. A second Gallup poll in 1944, one day after the act was passed, indicated that 62% of Canadians supported the program, 30% did not and 8% were undecided.

The Labour movement presented a half-hearted opposition in 1944 when the Trades and Labour Congress criticized the scheme "as a substitute for paying adequate wages to enable families to live in decency and health" (*Trades and Labour Congress Journal* 23 [1944]: 28). However, within a year they were reporting, "This congress has gone on record as approving, in principle, the payment of family allowances while emphatically declaring that such an allowance must not take the place of an adequate wage rate" (*Trades and Labour Journal* 24 [1945]: 13). It was clearly not politically popular to attack a program that offered to subsidize the income of families who could not adequately provide for their basic needs with wages alone. Cognizant of the politics involved, the Conservatives and CCF endorsed the program and limited all their criticism to smaller details of administration. Thus the only committed critic of Family Allowances, the Conservative Premier George Drew of Ontario carried on his vitriolic campaign in isolation and to little effect.

The family allowance issue had never provoked strong feelings on the part of Canadians. It was neither the object of popular demand nor strong opposition. The labour movement, which objectively had the most to lose, could not rally any significant opposition. It is curious that a program which was precedent-setting in a number of important regards could arrive so uneventfully.

The family allowance scheme was the most direct form of state mediation of production and reproduction. It was, in a way, a perfect compromise, neither pleasing nor offending capital or labour — as each faced worse alternatives in the absence of the program. While family allowances provoked some criticism from labour because of its blatant connection to low wage policy, it was merely a more obvious form of the "social wage" strategy that organized labour had backed since the inception of the International Labour Organization. Family allowances presented the compromise between capital and labour in its most naked form — subsidizing a wage system designed to ignore reproductive costs, only to perpetuate it. As such, few could find in the program much to get excited about, but fewer still could afford to do without it.

No other program draws attention to the lack of fit between wages and human welfare as explicitly as family allowances. The necessity for family allowances reveals the dynamic of the wage system that transforms reproduction (the most fundamental process of social survival) into a "universal risk." It leads one to question the rhetoric of "universal risk." What are child birth, sickness and old age if not natural processes of reproducing the population? And none of these can be adequately accommodated by the wage-labour system. The rhetoric of the welfare state identifies the necessity of state mediation while disguising the source of the necessity — the contradiction between production and reproduction. The history of the initiation of family allowances permits us to peek behind the disguise and see the essential purpose of the welfare state, the mediation of these two contradictory spheres.

The Labour Relations Act: Privy Council Order 1003

While the announcement of the Family Allowances Act was carefully orchestrated to belie its origin and intent, the second recommendation of the *McTague Report*, a labour relations act, was announced with much fanfare. This legislation was presented to labour as a great concession, a great victory to workers, and employers grudgingly accepted it. It was clearly an important moment in labour history: for the first time federal legislation guaranteed automatic recognition once a union gained majority support through a government-supervised vote. However, analysis indicates that the benefits to workers were not as unqualified as King suggested.

Prior to PC 1003 relations between capital and labour were by and large adversarial, with labour law providing only the broadest of parameters within which this struggle could occur. The greater the power differential between the two parties, the more likely the adversarial procedure would favour the stronger party. Thus, when capital was strong and labour weak or fragmented, such a system favoured capital, as evidenced by the slow growth of unionism between 1919 and 1935. The major avenue for labour to force recognition and/or settlements from capital was through strikes or threats of strikes. As labour became stronger during and shortly after World War II, strikes became a major source of disruption in an economy geared for full output. It was at this point that significant regulatory elements were introduced into labour legislation. PC 1003 provided for recognition and contract settlement through legal procedures that by-passed and explicitly penalized strikes for the attainment of either recognition or settlement.

While the Labour Relations Act was explicitly regulatory, once a unit had been certified, its regulations for certification maintained a strong adversarial element.[3] Unlike the protective labour legislation in which the regulatory element resulted in the state initiating and enforcing worker's rights (e.g., minimum wage, hours and conditions of work), the labour relations act required that workers petition the board under set conditions for certification and/or contract settlement. The law did not legislate certification on principle; organizers had to take the initiative and meet a set of criteria, that is, conform to the determination of the bargaining unit, which was outside of the organizers' control, and sign up a stipulated number of workers without full knowledge of what the real population of eligible workers would be.

The way in which application for certification worked, in fact, ensured that those workers concentrated in large industries and more easily organized (union membership doubled prior to 1944) would be readily acknowledged and certified. The criteria for certification, however, made it difficult for more fragmented workers, especially those in the tertiary sector, to achieve recognition. Those workers most in need of government intervention, to help even out the power differential between themselves and their employers, found the legislation unresponsive to the particular circumstances of their employment, which made it difficult in most cases to meet the criteria for certification. The old principle of equality before the law ensured that those who started out unequal remained so. This particular characteristic of the legislation — favouring the strong and ignoring the weak — became increasingly important in the post-war period as capital embarked upon a segmented-labour market strategy. It is interesting to note that when government itself was the employer it did not honour the principle of its own legislation. Federal and most provincial civil service workers were not legally permitted to unionize until the mid-1960s.

It is possible that PC 1003 granted no more than would have been achieved during the years (1942–1948) in which labour was in a strong bargaining position. The order achieved the effect of reducing strike incidents for sanctioning and enforcing agreements that labour was in a good position to win. However, while PC 1003 may have blunted the sharp edge of labour militancy during the war years, it similarly restrained and contained harsh employer policies when labour was weakened and divided. It acted, as mediation is intended, as a law of compromise — both sides agreeing to be regulated in order to avoid the high costs they would incur when the balance of power was not in their favour.

PC 1003 and all subsequent labour relations acts are an interesting marriage of regulatory and adversarial elements. The adversarial aspects left the initiative, risks and responsibilities with the workers, while the regulatory aspects protected against strikes and controlled access to certification. Workers' prerogative — withholding their labour — was effectively outlawed as a condition of coverage by the legislation. Capital's prerogative — to determine wages, to acknowledge or fight certification — continued to operate through a mass of rules and regulations which favoured the party with the larger legal budget.

Although PC 1003 did not alter the fundamental pattern of wage determination, it did introduce significant new protections for labour and a substantially increased role for the state in managing industrial relations. This would alter the process of class struggle for both protagonists in the post-war years. When government management of the economy was ended in 1947, most provinces quickly adopted Labour Relations Acts that were modeled, sometimes word for word, on the federal legislation. The pattern quite clearly was to involve the state much more directly in industrial relations as a critical third party. The result was a much more standardized means of arbitrating labour-management relations and a much heavier dependence upon formalized legal procedures. The effect was a post-war period of industrial harmony that remained virtually undisturbed until the mid-1960s.

Women in the War Economy

The third significant development in labour during the war was the massive employment of women. The declaration of war in 1939 pressed the state into an unprecedented role of recruiting women into production. This was in sharp contrast to the historic role of the state which restricted women's access to employment, in the interests of patriarchy. The years 1939 to 1944 saw a startling and rapid reversal of sixty-five years of limited labour force participation when 600,000 Canadian women entered the labour force (Pierson and Cohen 1984, 222). Sustaining the war effort was dependent, not only on drawing women into the labour force, but also upon their employment in "nontraditional" industries, particularly, war manufacturing. There was a potential that the exigencies of war would jeopardize the traditional patterns established by the "protective" labour legislation to restrict access and to segregate women's employment. Yet perhaps even more remarkable than the rapid recruitment of a female labour force was their rapid demobilization and/or deployment to other sectors after the war. The goal of the state, given its historic support of patriarchy and its concurrent commitment to the war effort, was to maximize the use of female labour during the war — not to support their integration into the labour market on a permanent basis.

A study by Ruth Roach Pierson and Marjorie Cohen (1984) documents a wide range of implicit and explicit discrimination in the recruitment, training and placement of women in the labour force, which served to maintain the principle of "male economic primacy." Even when labour shortages required women to directly replace men, the War Labour Board made it possible for employers to reclassify those positions. Invoking the traditional view that women's labour is more properly categorized with that of children and youth, and hence not the equal of men's, the War Labour Board approved lower wage scales for women:

> Women workers were considered together with youths and less experienced or less capable men who had to be engaged to perform work done before the war by experienced men. The Board was prepared to deal with applications made by employers for the establishment of new and lower paid classifications within an occupation for which classifications had already been made. (*Labour Gazette* 1950: 186)

In the reconstruction period, government launched large-scale retraining programs to prepare Canadians for post-war industry. The processes of restricted access and sexually segmented opportunities permiated retraining programs despite the official policy of sexual equality.

Married women were not eligible for the living and dependant allowances offered to individuals enrolled in the retraining programs because it was assumed their husbands would support them. A more serious barrier to women's employment was the Re-instatement in Civil Employment Act of 1942, which guaranteed that ex-service personnel be given back their pre-enlistment jobs. As a result all women who had worked in non-traditional employment replacing men could not make any claim to employment or further training in those occupations. The National Employment Services assessment of the projected labour demands for women gave prominence to traditional women's trades. As a result fully 85% of women taking government-sponsored vocational training courses were found in the following five occupational categories — commercial, hairdressing, dressmaking, nursing and prematriculation (Pierson and Cohen 1984, 232). In 1945 the government renewed the enforcement of the civil service regulations barring married women from working for the federal government.

While the state's motives and methods were unique to the war experience, the lesson — that one could achieve maximum utilization of female labour without permitting their integration within the labour market — became a critical and instructive lesson in the development of post-war employment patterns. In short, the analysis of war employment policies not only explains the deft reconciliation of patriarchy and patriotism but more importantly served as a "pilot project" for a segmented labour-market strategy so quickly adopted and so religiously adhered to in the post-war period. A segmented labour market was capital's solution to the age old dilemma of "having your cake and eating it too." Women had long been a source of cheap labour because of their marginality to the labour market and, hence, their limited bargaining position. The segmented labour-market strategy provided the means — through the employment of women in union-resistant sectors characterized by part-time, temporary and seasonal work — for maximum utilization of their labour while retaining their marginal status and, hence, their specific utility to capital.

The New Welfare Ideology

The war and reconstruction period was a watershed in Canadian welfare history. This period was like the first period in being a moment in Canadian social history of amazing and powerful social consensus. In both periods the public mobilized to demand dramatic state intervention to address serious structural imbalances between production and reproduction. The crisis of the first period gave rise to the Victorian Social Reform Movement, which identified the employment of women and children as a direct threat to the

Canadian family. The crisis of the third period gave rise to a new welfare ideology born from the reality that most Canadian incomes could not meet basic health, housing and nutritional needs.

The new welfare ideology was an achievement of public consensus equal in significance but substantially different in effect to the Victorian Social Reform Movement. The discourse of reform during the war and post-war years would shift the emphasis of state support for reproduction from the "protection" of female labour to the provision of income and social services to the family. Despite dramatic differences in their expression, both of these moments of social consensus force the attention of the state to the needs of reproduction and are an important measure of the pressure of the reproductive dynamic. In the former case, public demand called for a pattern of protective, supportive and regulative legislation, which underwrote the support-service marriage structure for over a half a century. In the latter case, the new welfare ideology, constituted a forty-year commitment of Canadians to the development of social welfare legislation that would provide a social security net for themselves and their families.

While the Social Reform Movement of the first period was explicitly oriented to reproduction, the welfare philosophy of the third period was not *consciously* familistic. The turn of the century call to rescue girls and women from factories, to protect their reproductive potential and promote family living, was so evidently pro-familistic that making the case for the pressure of the reproductive dynamic was simple and straightforward. In contrast, the pervasive demand for state intervention to provide income security and social services during the third period was not expressed or experienced as a specifically reproductive or familial issue. The demands for social reform in this period were expressed in general humanitarian terms that obscure the reproductive specificity of those demands.

During the third period, the Family Allowance program is the only intervention that provides us with an explicit view of the social/political calculus undertaken by the state in attempting to respond to pressures from production and reproduction. Subsequent programs were developed and implemented without the revealing circumstances of a head-on confrontation between capital and labour that made the Family Allowance strategy so explicit. Furthermore, subsequent policies tended to address the family more obliquely, focussing support on particular target individuals or categories, such as the elderly or the unemployed, rather than the family unit as a whole. As both the costs and some of the functions of reproduction became socialized, our awareness of these costs or functions as reproductive tends to be obscured. In the face of this tendency to only recognize as reproductive those activities and responsibilities that have remained privatized, it is important to understand that the welfare state is simply a more extensive response to the same competing pressures from production and reproduction that gave us the Family Allowance program.

By 1945 the concept of federal responsibility for social security was an accepted principle in Canadian politics. In addition, the negative pre-war image of means-tested welfare was replaced by a positive concept of social security — a right of all citizens to be insured against universal risks of sickness, old age and unemployment. This transition (initiated in the Depression and expressed in overwhelming popular demand during the war years) was the result of a build-up of structural pressures to socialize reproductive costs on a national scale. The government's dual mandate, managing the economy and the population — at a time when the two historic protagonists, capital and labour, were most evenly matched — brought home very directly the problems as well as the necessity of co-ordinating the contradictory sphere's of production and reproduction.

During the war years the government kept its fingers on the pulse of the nation through the monthly reports of the War Information Board. The board had an international branch that dealt with war intelligence and a domestic branch that gathered information on the public's response to wartime regulations and policies. The domestic branch extensively commissioned monthly public opinion polls, and it received regular reports from commissioned individuals all across Canada who daily monitored all forms of media. These reports are the best source of popular opinion during the war. From 1942 on, the documents of the War Information Board indicate that the major preoccupation of Canadians was a concern over post-war conditions in Canada. Throughout the war years Canadians' support for a more active, internationalist state and national social-welfare programs steadily increased. This concern was also expressed in growing electoral support for the CCF.

The increasing strength of labour and the CCF was impressing the government with the saliency of the welfare issue more effectively than had ten years of depression, misery and want. While need could be overlooked, the government found that it was troublesome to ignore strength. As labour was finding a stronger voice in its expanding organizations, the population at large was beginning to express itself in new voting patterns. The popular vote for the CCF rose from 8% in 1940 to 23% in 1942. In the years 1943–44, the CCF became the official opposition in Ontario, won victories in several federal by-elections, became the Saskatchewan provincial government and surpassed the Conservative and the Liberals in public opinion polls. The remarkable growth of the CCF had a significant impact upon

Prime Minister King and his cabinet. In 1943, the Minister of Health wrote to King expressing his concern: "There is no doubt that our government is unpopular. What of the rise of the socialism across Canada? It was for years a British Columbia and Saskatchewan freak but it is now definitely a national political menace" (Taylor 1978, 35).

Government had its own interests in expanding welfare programs. It was clear that a government without responsive post-war social and economic programs would not be a government for long. It was also evident that the end of the war would mean an end to government management of the economy and an end to the broad jurisdictional powers accorded the federal government as a war emergency. This left welfare as the major legislative mechanism for federal response to the growing demands of the population.[4]

Labour unrest in 1946–47 revealed that the Labour Relations Act on its own could not guarantee industrial harmony as workers militantly fought for an improved standard of living. The increased income that workers sought could ultimately come only from production. However, these gains could be achieved directly in the form of a rising personal wage or indirectly through the expansion of the social wage. The former option would mean a short-term vertical redistribution of wealth that would immediately cut into profits, while the latter option would mean a long-term horizontal redistribution of wealth that would raise the standard of living while minimizing the immediate costs to capital. The fact that the state chose the latter option should not suggest that the interests of capital were being violated, nor that they were the only interests being catered to. At a time when the two protagonists were most evenly matched, state mediation had to effect a real compromise. The welfare option appeared to be the only one that could simultaneously address the demands of workers for a higher standard of living while protecting the interests of capital in holding down wage gains and preserving industrial harmony.

The shifting balance of power between capital and labour during the war had quite simply pushed the struggle along to a new terrain — the interests, the antagonists and the contradiction had not changed, but the issues most certainly had. From 1943 on, the question was no longer whether the federal government should get involved in social security legislation but, rather, which programs, when and how? The government's role as mediator between production and reproduction, between capital and labour, was pushing it inexorably toward the construction of the modern welfare state. The war years marked the first critical steps in that direction.

Commissions and Inquiries

Between 1940 and 1945 ten studies or inquiries on welfare were released to the Canadian public. While they varied dramatically in terms of public impact and/or influence on policy makers, their greatest significance lies in the fact that they spoke, with one voice, the new ideology of the welfare state. Clearly, they articulated an idea whose time had come.

The stark contrast between the stagnation of the Depression and the rapid economic growth during the years of government management made a strong impression on the political thinking of Canadians. Traditional assumptions about the limited political role of the state were shattered. A national poll in 1943 indicated that 43% of Canadians were in favour of continued government management of the economy in peacetime, with 17% undecided. The better educated (48%) and the middle-income group (50%) were most in favour of the extension. In addition the sample poll revealed that two out of three Canadians would "like to see some 'great change' in our way of life after the war" (*War Information Board Report*, 3 Dec. 1943: 3). The changes Canadians were most anxious to see were: the elimination of unemployment, the expansion of social security, improved living conditions and a more equitable division of wealth. Furthermore, comparison studies conducted by the War Information Board revealed that Canadians (71%) were more highly committed to change and reforms than either the Americans (32%) or the British (57%) (*War Information Board Report*, 3 Dec. 1943: 3).

Chronologically, the generation and submission of reports reflected the rising tide of concern about post-war conditions. The report of the Royal Commission on Dominion-Provincial relations (*Rowell-Sirois Report*) was released in 1940, receiving little public or political attention as it was overshadowed by the urgency of the war effort. However, two years later the release of the British welfare inquiry report, the *Beveridge Report*, created quite a sensation in Canada. In the following year the Canadian populace and the government were deluged with welfare reports. The Report on Social Security for Canada (*Marsh Report*) was released in 1943 coinciding with the report of the Heagerty Commission on Health and the majority and minority reports of the War Labour Board Inquiry. In addition this same year saw the publication of two independent studies, one by Charlotte Whitton and the other by Michael Cassidy, which outlined their vision of the welfare state.[5]

In response to this intense public discourse and the increasing threat from the CCF the government established a House of Commons Committee on Social Security composed of forty-one members of Parliament. The terms of reference of the Committee were:

To examine and study the existing social insurance legislation of the Parliament of Canada and of the several provincial legislatures; social insurance policies of other countries; the most practicable measures of social insurance for Canada, including health insurance, and the steps which will be required to effect their inclusion in a national plan; the constitutional and financial adjustments which will be required for the achievement of a nation-wide plan for social security; and other related matters (Taylor 1978, 20).

In July 1943, after four months of hearings and deliberations, the House of Commons Committee endorsed the recommendations of the *Heagerty Report*, calling for a national health-insurance plan and advised that a conference of Dominion-Provincial representatives be held to discuss the proposed bill. In February 1944 a Cabinet Committee was established to draw up specific legislative proposals to present to the next Dominion-Provincial conference. In addition 1944 saw the completion and submission of the *Curtis Report* on a national housing policy. All of this intense study and debate culminated in the submission of the *Green Book Proposals*, the government's social-security package, to the Dominion-Provincial conference in 1945.

The report that had the greatest single impact upon crystallizing public opinion in favour of national welfare programs was the *Beveridge Report*. While a number of Canadian reports provided an equally well-articulated rationale and plan for the welfare state, Beveridge's report was the first to fall on the fertile ground of rising Canadian expectations. The *Beveridge Report* attracted the most extensive media coverage, headlining in all the major newspapers in Canada. The report became a reference point in public opinion polls, and Beveridge himself delivered a radio address over the national network of the CBC in May 1943 (*War Information Board Report*, June 1943).

The *Beveridge Report* was perhaps the most explicit in identifying the lack of fit between the wage-labour system and human welfare. Based on careful surveys of living standards in England between the two World Wars, he documented that from three-quarters to five-sixths of poverty resulted from the loss of earning power, and the remaining twenty to twenty-five percent was attributable to society's failure to relate wage to family size. "But a national minimum for families of every size cannot in practice be secured by a wage system, which must be based on the product of a man's labour and not on the size of his family" (*Beveridge Report* 1942, 154). In view of the systemic nature of the problem, he argued that short-term crises intervention or means-tested schemes were inadequate. He recommended that the state undertake substantial redistributions of income through social-security programs to compensate for the shortcomings of the system.

The Canadian reports reiterated Beveridge's arguments and gathered evidence that indicated that, even in wartime with all able-bodied men and women employed, basic needs were not being met for a substantial proportion of the population. The Curtis Commission documented the problem of inadequate housing for low-income groups, which in 1941 was identified as urban families of five with incomes of less than $1,200. This category accounted for approximately one-third of the urban population. Health reports indicated that in the 1940s only 43.7% of families of wage earners outside of agriculture had sufficient income to guarantee them a satisfactory nutritional diet (Guest 1980, 129). In addition Canada had developed the highest infant-mortality rate of all the developed countries in the British Empire (Taylor 1978, 5). Finally, the Heagerty Commission found that the majority of Canadians did not have sufficient income resources to provide for medical care for sustained or serious illnesses. Thus, the most basic requirements of adequate food, housing and health care were beyond the financial resources of a large number of Canadian families.

On the heels of all these inquiries the *Green Book Proposals* were developed in late 1944. The two reports, Rowell-Sirois and Heagerty, which were the backbone of the proposals, reflected the full range of government response to the demand for a more activist state. The *Rowell-Sirois Report* reflected the cautious, conservative, fiscally minded mood of the early war years, while the *Heagerty Report* shared the vision of social change characteristic of the mid 1940s. Despite their substantial differences these two reports were combined to form the body of the government's post-war social-security package.

The Royal Commission on Dominion-Provincial Relations was commissioned in 1937. Provoked by the fiscal and social dislocation of the Depression, it focussed on the constitutional and fiscal underpinnings of social-security planning. While accepting that some federal powers would have to be widened, the report remained strongly supportive of provincial autonomy. The commissioners' focus and philosophy resulted in a residualist approach to federal involvement in welfare — advocating federal responsibility for *only* those programs that could not be provided equitably and efficiently on a provincial scale. This limited category included the unemployed (employables) and the elderly. For the unemployed the commissioners recommended a two-tier system: a national unemployment-insurance program and a federal assistance program for the uninsured. The matters of health and welfare were seen to lie exclusively within provincial jurisdiction (Moore, Milton, Perry and Beach 1966, 20). Addressing fiscal issues, they recommended that the financing of welfare at the provincial level would best be accomplished through the provision of National Adjustment Grants payable by the federal government to each province on the basis of fiscal need. In return for these grants the provinces would vacate the fields of personal, corporate and inheritance tax. The commissioners expected that the implementation of these recommendations would put an end to the fiscal anarchy characteristic of the Depression, correct regional disparities and would respect provincial autonomy through the distribution of unconditional grants that would assist provinces in developing their own welfare programs.

The emphasis placed by the commissioners upon the rearrangement of taxation powers as the fundamental fiscal requirement for a comprehensive social-security system was the one recommendation strictly adhered to in the drafting of the *Green Book Proposals*. However, the incorporation of the Heagerty Health Commission recommendations in the *Green Book* was a clear departure from the *Rowell-Sirois Report*, which viewed health care as an exclusively provincial matter.

The *Heagerty Report* called for a joint federal-provincial program of health insurance, with the medical care and public health provisions administered at the provincial level with federal government assistance through grants-in-aid. The report envisaged the whole population being covered for medical, dental, pharmaceutical, hospital and nursing services. Recommendations did permit, but not encourage, provincial discretion in limiting benefits to those in low-income categories.

The *Green Book Proposals* were clearly a product of the Keynesian momentum of the late war years. Shaped by the considerable social and political pressure for an activist state, the *Green Book* revealed the federal government's willingness to take a quantum leap in the field of social and economic welfare. Some indication of the magnitude of the step lies in the fact that it took the federal government over twenty years to negotiate and implement the programming brought to the table in 1945. The federal *Green Book* outlined three broad goals. The first goal was to divide public revenues among government units efficiently. The second goal was to in-augurate social insurance against the hazards of illness and old age. The third was to co-ordinate the economic influence of all governments for the purposes of full employment. To this end the federal government proposed to assume full responsibility for old-age pensions for Canadians aged seven-ty years and over, to share in the cost of a public assistance scheme for the needy aged sixty-five to sixty-nine and to share in the cost of a national health-insurance scheme (Moore, Milton, Perry and Beach 1966, 22).

To ensure full employment the federal government would undertake to extend unemployment insurance by quick stages to all employees in Canada, to extend assistance benefits to unemployed employables not yet or no longer eligible for insurance benefits and to extend assistance to encourage anti-cyclical timing of public investment.

In return the federal government proposed the continua-tion of the Wartime Tax Agreement of 1941, which granted the federal government exclusive occupancy of the direct taxation field (personal, corporate and inheritance tax). The Dominion offered to pay a new unconditional subsidy of not less than $12 per head of their 1941 provincial population. These new subsidies were to supplant all existing statutory and special subsidies and unconditional grants previously in effect (Moore, Milton, Perry and Beach 1966, 22).

The position of the provinces in 1945 was not at all similar to their position during the war when they temporarily va-cated the direct taxation field. In 1941 the provinces, strug-gling with Depression debts and confronting the gloomiest year of the war, had adopted a co-operative posture. However, the particular combination of penury and patriotism that led to the War Time Tax Agreement was no longer to be had. The boom in the war economy had the more industrialized provinces anxious to resume their pre-war taxation jurisdictions. As expected, the "have-not provinces" — the Maritimes and the Prairies — were generally in favour of the federal offer since they stood to gain financially from the proposed arrangements. Quebec and Ontario, however, could not be persuaded to relinquish their taxation jurisdictions. After nine months of negotiations, the federal and provincial governments were stalemated and the *Green Book Proposals* were shelved.

Although the package was never to be implemented, the ideas embedded in the *Green Book Proposals* marked federal government social policy for the next three decades. Instead of the bold leap outlined in the *Green Book*, the history of Canada's welfare state was one of pain-staking negotiation around the jurisdictional pitfalls of ten diversely endowed and motivated provinces. Nevertheless, the die was cast. The pitfalls did not outweigh the structural pressures pushing towards a new activist role for the state. Labour and capital remained tenuously balanced in the post-war period of high employment — high production and the necessity to mediate even in periods of quiescence was not diminished. The war years were formative in giving momentum and direction to the new welfare ideology and in seeing the implementation of a number of key welfare statutes.

Welfare Legislation

Between 1940 and 1948 thirteen new federal welfare statutes were passed (see table A2.15. Federal Welfare Legislation, Period III, 1940–1947). Nine of the statutes dealt with veterans' benefits while the remaining four — the Unemployment Insurance Act 1940, the Family Allowances Act 1944, the National Health and Welfare Act 1944 and the National Housing Act 1944 — laid the ground work for the welfare state. By the end of the war two major social security programs, Unemployment Insurance and Family Allowance, were in place; a federal health and welfare department and bureaucracy had been created; and the federal government was actively involved in the funding and construction of housing. An understanding of why these statutes were enacted while others failed lies in an appreciation of the government's role as economic manager. Most particularly one might wonder why Family Allowances were instituted in preference to the National Health Insurance Bill. Contrasting the characteristics of these two proposals reveals the logic behind federal welfare legislation during the war years.

If one uses a political pressure or legitimacy model for explaining the introduction of social-security schemes, then health insurance should have been preferred on all accounts over Family Allowance. The national health-insurance proposal, the product of a two-year national inquiry, was aggressively promoted by the Minister of Health and Pensions and received broad media and public support. In fact, never has a proposed welfare scheme received so much support. Upon release of the *Heagerty Report*, the Canadian Medical Association, the Canadian Hospital Council and the Canadian Life Insurance Officers Association all commended the report and supported the principle of a national health insurance scheme (Taylor 1978). The forty-one members of the House of Commons Committee on Social Security endorsed the proposal for a national health-insurance plan and advised that legislation be prepared for the next Dominion-Provincial Conference. Finally, a Gallup poll on the proposed health bill showed eighty percent of Canadians approved of the scheme in 1944 and again in 1949. Despite overwhelming support and meticulous preparation, the health bill was not destined to be passed during the war. It was deferred in 1944 in order to implement the Family Allowances scheme.

The reason for this counter-indicated choice lies in the particular conditions of government mediation of production and reproduction during the war years. During this period the government was called upon to simultaneously manage the economy and the population. However, both as the experience of the Depression and the *Beveridge Report* had shown, "taking care of business" was not synonymous with taking care of the population. Nevertheless, in the position of direct management, the government was called upon to do both.

In this position the government opted for those programs that could simultaneously solve war production problems, as well as respond to the mounting pressure for social-security legislation. Using these criteria the National Health Insurance scheme had little to recommend it, as it would have virtually no impact upon production, in the short run. On the other hand Family Allowances made it politically possible for a government managing the economy to depress wages below their market value for the duration of the war. Unemployment Insurance and the National Housing Act had similar virtues of solving major war-management problems in the form of innovative social-security programs.

Of the four welfare statutes enacted during the war years, the Unemployment Insurance scheme had the longest history of consideration and debate. In spite of this fact, the process of passing the act had a hasty quality that was associated with war-time emergency, characteristic of most of the welfare legislation at this time.

An Unemployment Insurance Bill had been proposed by the Conservative government and passed the House in 1935. However, it was ruled *ultra vires* the same year, when the

Ontario government challenged it on jurisdictional grounds. When the Liberals took over the following year, Unemployment Insurance was in a state of suspended animation due to jurisdictional problems. At this time the new government was committed to a balanced budget and a reduction in federal responsibility for relief expenditures. Thus, the new Prime Minister King's only initiative was to appoint a National Employment Commission to study the issue, undoubtedly on the assumption that research was an acceptable excuse for inactivity. For when the commission submitted its report in 1937 strongly urging the immediate adoption of unemployment insurance, it occasioned a serious split between the civil service and the Cabinet (Struthers 1983, 180). The government delayed the release of the report and fought its recommendations announcing that without unanimous provincial support of constitutional reform there would be no consideration of an unemployment-insurance scheme until the tabling of the *Rowell-Sirois Report*. Thus, the Liberal government spent the first three years of their administration resisting all attempts to introduce the bill.

The outbreak of the war in 1939 changed the situation. According to the Labour Minister, the war itself had created a compelling new reason for unemployment insurance, "namely, the need for affording a cushion when we are faced with the problem of demobilization and the cessation of war industry" (Struthers 1983, 197). Convinced that unemployment insurance was a critical component of war management, King now actively sought out and received the co-operation of the provincial premiers. The last hold out, Alberta, agreed in the early months of 1940. On 10 July the British Parliament amended the BNA Act to give the federal government exclusive jurisdiction over legislation in the field of unemployment insurance. On 7 August 1940 the Unemployment Insurance Bill had passed the House and received royal assent.

The plan, like its predecessor the Employment and Social Insurance Act of 1935, was modelled on British legislation. In spite of the limitations of the act — excluding certain occupational categories and introducing the precedent of having benefits and contributions wage-related — it was the largest social-security program introduced in Canada up to that time. The program aimed at covering 75% of wage earners and included 4.6 million people in its first year of operation.

The Liberal government's dramatic about face on this issue appeared to have more to do with war management than with the plight of the unemployed. The insurance scheme offered the Liberal government an opportunity to kill two war-management problems with one stone. First, it offered a concrete and comprehensive response to the demobilization problem the government envisaged at the end of the war. As the governor of the Bank of Canada pointed out, post-war workers would "likely face unemployment with much greater resentment — to put it mildly — than displayed during the Depression years. In the interests of peace, order and good government Ottawa would have to assume full responsibility for the problem" (Struthers 1983, 206). Second, the generated funds (which would not begin to pay out for two years) would constitute a significant source of revenue for the war effort. "While contributions under the scheme (i.e., unemployment insurance) will not be a tax, they will, nevertheless, achieve this same purpose of diverting a proportion of the national income from present private expenditures to place it at the disposal of the government" (King Papers C187885, 15 July 1940). The Finance Department's predictions were correct. By 1945 the par value of the reserves of the fund stood at about $300 million and the accrued interest amounted to approximately $2 million.

With workers receiving only 6%, the "…Unemployment Insurance Act worked admirably well in transferring about $280 million throughout the war from the hands of labour to the coffers of the state" (Cuneo 1979, 15).

After five years of foot-dragging delay, the war provided the means (provincial co-operation) and the motives for a rapid introduction of unemployment insurance in Canada. But, regardless of the motives that lay behind it, it was a landmark piece of social legislation. In sheer administrative and financial terms, the Unemployment Insurance Act was a crucial milestone in the development of the Canadian welfare state. "In one stroke 3,000 new civil-service jobs were created and 1,600 federal offices were opened in cities and towns across the country" (Struthers 1983, 202).

In 1944, the year after the CCF overtook the Liberals and Conservatives in the public opinion polls, the federal government introduced three new welfare bills: The National Health and Welfare Act (1944 SC c.22), The National Housing Act (1944 SC c.46) and the Family Allowances Act (1944 SC c.40). The first act was at the behest of Ian Mackenzie, the Minister of Pensions and Health who thought a separate ministry would increase the momentum for the health-insurance bill he strongly supported. While Mackenzie never saw the implementation of the Health Insurance Bill during his term in office, the National Health and Welfare Act laid the departmental groundwork for the development of a federal welfare bureaucracy.

The National Housing Act was recommended in the *Curtis Report*, which advised large-scale federal intervention in the housing market with a special emphasis upon the provision of low-rental housing. This report researched and edited by Leonard Marsh viewed housing policy as part and parcel of a comprehensive social-security system. As conceived in the *Curtis Report*, the act would have a substantial impact upon the living conditions of low-income Canadians. This impact was relatively short lived, however, as federal involvement in the provision of housing lasted only as long as federal management of the economy.

In fact, the implementation of the full intention of the act was found only at those points in which housing policy intersected with war production or demobilization plans. During the war years, the agency administering this act produced a total of 45,930 war-time houses in centres where war industries were located. During the reconstruction period (1947–49) a home-building program entitled Veterans' Rental Housing aimed at building 10,000 homes per year as part of a national demobilization strategy (Guest 1980, 128). Once the government vacated the field of economic management, however, the low-income housing projects were given lower priority. Bowing to the primacy of the private market in the post-war period, program emphasis shifted to the maximization of private home ownership through the provision of low-interest mortgage monies. As a result, the program's major beneficiaries became the housing industry and middle-income families.

Although the implementation of the act did not reflect the intent of the commission in the immediate post-war period, the legislation itself set an important precedent for substantial federal subsidization of housing for Canadians.

Three of the four welfare statutes passed during the war had a direct link with the management of the labour force and the economy. The only exception was the act creating the Department of Health and Welfare. Unemployment Insurance generated millions of dollars for the war effort and provided a cushion during demobilization; Family Allowances made it politically possible to depress wages below their market value; and the Housing Act provided an essential infrastructure for rapid relocation of labour. The regulatory nature of state intervention during the war is not surprising given its dual mandate of managing the economy as well as the country. However, it is important to remember that state mediation is supportive as well as regulatory. The short-term utility of Family Allowances or Unemployment Insurance in the management of the war-time economy does not negate the long-term significance of these programs for the redistribution of income to reproduction. A look at the growth of welfare expenditures and the transfer of resources from production to reproduction that it entails will reveal the more benevolent face of the welfare state in this period.

Welfare Expenditures

To deal with the lack of fit between production and reproduction, the state was required to develop a system of reallocating income outside of, and noncompetitive with, the wage-labour system. In the earlier periods this took the form of allowances to people who were considered unable to work: mothers, the elderly or the disabled. The most significant change in the system for reallocating income during the war was the move, beyond welfare as a substitute for wages, to welfare as a subsidy for wages. The three major welfare statutes of the war years — Family Allowances, Unemployment Insurance and Housing — were specifically focussed on the able-bodied worker, who by virtue of circumstance (that is, had children, could not afford housing or was temporarily unemployed) was eligible for assistance from the state.

The legitimation of welfare for the employed dramatically increased the proportion of the population entitled to assistance from the state. By 1947 one and a half million Canadian families were recipients of family allowances and 4.6 million Canadians were registered with UIC (Unemployment Insurance Commission) (Urquhart and Buckley 1965, Series

C14–26). In addition, as the number of social-welfare recipients and expenditures grew so also did the federal bureaucracy, almost tripling from 46,000 to 125,000 in the eight years under review (Bird 1970, 299). By the end of the war it was clear that the federal government would, of necessity, be the key actor in the field of welfare in the third period.

More comprehensive programs required a national resource base to meet the increasing expenditure commitments. Rising national welfare costs surfaced early in the war years and escalated rapidly throughout the war despite massive military expenditures. Demands on the federal treasury increased as welfare expenditures increased from $140 million in 1939 to well over $700 million in 1947 (see table 9).

The war years were characterized by a pattern of consistent growth in state welfare expenditures, as well as a shifting pattern of fiscal responsibility. During a period of full employment and increased federal social expenditures,

Table 9

Federal Social Welfare Expenditures Classified
by Function for Selected Years 1939–1947
(In Millions of Dollars)

Year	Veterans	Health	Family Allowance	Welfare	Education	Total
1939	60	1	—	78	1	140
1941	58	1	—	51	7	117
1943	70	1	—	75	6	152
1945	402	1	173	111	14	702
1947	341	8	263	148	10	770

SOURCE: Leacy. 1983, Series H19–34.

provincial and municipal social expenditures increased as well. While the absolute expenditures of local governments increased, their relative importance declined in the face of rising federal involvement (see table 10).

Welfare expenditures in all jurisdictions increased from $345 million in 1941 to over $1 billion by 1947. Furthermore, while costs were escalating in all three jurisdictions, the most dramatic increase absolutely and proportionately occurred at the federal level. In 1941 social-welfare expenditures were more or less equally divided between the three jurisdictions; however, by 1947 federal expenditures accounted for 62% of all governments' social-service expenditures.

A final measure of the growing welfare mandate of the state is the increasing importance of social welfare in the overall pattern of government expenditures. Although

Table 10
Government Expenditures on Social Services*
by Level of Government, Canada 1941–1947
(In Millions of Dollars)

Year	All Government	Federal		Provincial		Municipal	
		Amt. $	%	Amt. $	%	Amt. $	%
1941	345	113	33	107	31	125	36
1943	393	141	36	118	30	134	34
1945	967	669	69	253	16	145	15
1946	1,327	960	72	189	14	178	13
1947	1,187	732	62	256	22	208	18

* Social Services — includes Welfare, Education, Health and Veterans' Benefits.
SOURCE: Urquhart and Buckley 1965, Series H148–160, H188–196, H176–187, H161–175.

government expenditures, in general, began to decrease after the war, social welfare expenditures continued to accelerate. As a consequence, welfare expenditures accounted for an increasing amount of total government expenditures (municipal, provincial and federal). By 1947 this had increased to 38% (Urquhart and Buckley 1965, H148–160).

As capital resisted workers, efforts to achieve a "family wage," pressure for income shifted to government. Welfare was reconceptualized as a subsidy for wages, and the provision of this "social wage" carried a very heavy price tag. A new pattern of increasing fiscal commitment to the family, at all three levels of government, had emerged. This pattern, evident by the end of the war, was essential to achieve the massive reallocations of income required to mediate production and reproduction in the third period.

Summary

The war and reconstruction period saw a dramatic growth in the Canadian economy under conditions that altered the balance of power between capital and labour. During this period the government was called upon to simultaneously manage the economy and the population. This mandate changed the structure and pattern of state mediation in two ways. First, as managers, government intervention in the spheres of production and reproduction became much more direct. Second, the locus of government mediation switched to the federal level. Under the pressures of war management, precedents were established for greater federal government intervention in labour relations and social welfare.

The new balance of power between capital and labour pushed the state to pursue policies that would at one and the same time cushion capital from the growing strength of labour and increase resources to the reproductive unit. This strategy resulted in the introduction of the highly regulative Labour Relations Act (PC 1003) and the expansion of the social wage. Despite massive war expenditures, the federal government's social-welfare expenditures increased steadily throughout the war years. Because the new balance of power between capital and labour persisted beyond the war years, the labour and welfare policies of the 1940s became prototypes for post-war social policy. Although the government retreated from active management to mediation after 1947, the dual strategy of regulating labour relations and expanding the social wage became the foundation for Canada's modern welfare state.

Post-War Canada
1948–1968

The predominant feature of post-war Canada was growth. The years 1948 to 1968 were characterized by a more or less concurrent growth in production, reproduction, capital, organized labour and the state. Post-war Canada appeared to have achieved that elusive goal of balancing production and reproduction. However, against this one-dimensional backdrop of growth and stability a major realignment of labour and income flows between production and reproduction was taking place.

During the war years it became evident that previous state strategies for mediating production and reproduction had resulted in a family structure that was heavy on dependants, light on providers and, consequently, chronically low on income. On the other hand production was in the position of experiencing an expanding market and high demand in the face of a very tight labour market. In the post-war years this imbalance resulted in divergent pressures for the two spheres. Reproductive pressures were expressed in a sustained demand for more income, largely directed to the welfare state, while productive pressures focussed on labour supplies and labour markets. Unlike the war years the immediate concerns of production and reproduction — labour and capital — did not appear to be on a collision course.

Two major centralizing processes realized in the post-war years determined the parameters, focus and direction of state response to the pressures of production and reproduction. First, the centralization of the state itself can be seen in federal control over taxation and growing federal responsibility for social-welfare programs. This expanded the resources and terrain of state mediation permitting the socialization of reproductive costs on a national scale. The second major process was the global organization of production facilitated by post-war trade and monetary agreements (Marchak 1991).

The global organization of production created the necessary conditions for a global labour supply. The consequences of production exceeding the boundaries of the nation state are many and varied. For the purposes of this study two factors are particularly relevant: first, the liberation of capital from any concern about reproducing a domestic labour supply; and second, the consequent shift in the value of women's labour from reproduction to production within industrialized nations. Under these conditions state mediation strategy in the post-war years was substantially different from earlier periods.

At the national level production increased as capital in Canada, including foreign capital, rushed to take advantage of the overwhelming demand for goods and services after the war. Thus, while the global restructuring of production resolved the long-term concerns of capital about cheap labour supplies, the immediate demands presented employers with circumstances similar to the war years — full production, full employment and a strong organized-labour movement. Once again, corporate interests looked to the state to maintain industrial peace and secure cheap labour supplies.

However, corporate interests were not the only interests that had to be dealt with by the Canadian state. The continued commitment of Canadians to secure a better standard of living maintained its momentum in the post-war period. This powerful social consensus was articulated in the demand for national welfare programs. This demand was directed to the federal government through electoral pressure, lobbying from organized labour and aggressive if unpredictable pressure from the provinces. With corporate interests pulling in one direction and the population, its labour organizations and the provinces pulling in the other, the potential for polarization and conflict was high. However, compromises negotiated in the post-war years produced a period of political and industrial peace of remarkable length.

The ability of the state to come up with the necessary compromises was rooted in the generation and circulation of enormous amounts of capital in the twenty years following the war and the apparent parallel, rather than conflicting, demands of the two spheres. The imbalance between production and reproduction was experienced by the family as an income shortage, whereas it was experienced and expressed by capital largely as a labour shortage. This permitted both spheres to exert strong pressure upon the state without coming into direct confrontation with one another, as had happened during the war years.

The state's response to demands from the reproductive sphere for income was the welfare state — the combination of services (medicare) and cash transfers (Family Allowances) that increased all state expenditure on social services, 1000% in the post-war period. Social-welfare expenditures rose from approximately $700 million in 1947 to nearly $7 billion in 1968 (Leacy 1983, Series H19–34). The rapid growth of the Canadian economy permitted the state to meet these demands and to extend an equally generous hand to capital.

The state's responsiveness to corporate interests was evident in both financial concessions and labour policies. Among these concessions were: the sale (at low prices) of government-created industrial capacity to private corporations after the war (Phillips and Watson 1984, 34), substantial post-war corporate tax rebates (Perry 1955, 346), a liberal open-door immigration policy, legislation facilitating the employment of women and a sympathetic reading of the

Labour Relations Acts, which maintained industrial peace but contained unionization.

Out of the pressures of the war years, both capital and labour made compromises. The position of capital with regard to organized labour was one of accommodation where necessary and automation where possible. In turn, labour's position was to accept the fact that the earned wage would never be sufficient and to direct considerable energy towards the extension of the social wage. Further distinction was added by the fact that this was a period in which the political-economic significance of women's reproductive labour plummeted, while their actual reproductive rates soared. All of these factors combined with the escalating level of state intervention to obscure the on-going dynamic of and contradiction between production and reproduction.

The state's assumption of responsibility for the social wage and the legislative management of industrial relations reduced the polarization between capital and labour by a partial fulfilment of demands and by a significant displacement of conflict between the two spheres to the electoral process and/or regulatory agencies. This displacement of conflict dramatically altered the form in which productive-reproductive pressures were felt within the system. In this period much of the action around resolving the competing pressures for income between the two spheres occurred at the federal-provincial negotiating table. While the pressures continued to occur because of the ongoing lack of fit between the productive-reproductive units, these pressures became rapidly translated into a bureaucratic form. For example, because demands for more income or services from Canadian families were felt first at the provincial level, provincial governments became the carriers of these expectations to the federal government where they became the focus of federal-provincial negotiations over taxation agreements and transfer payments. Similarly, labour-capital disputes over contracts, wages and unionization were quickly transferred to the Labour-Relations Boards activating regulatory agencies to resolve disputes that reflected the underlying conflict between the structures of production and reproduction. This was, of course, the intended effect of state mediation — to switch the terrain of dispute to more neutral grounds, to locate or create mechanisms for compromise.

During this period the competition between production and reproduction for income and labour resources was not only experienced and expressed differently, in one important regard it was substantially different. The active possibility of a global labour supply removed the imperative from the state to secure the long-term interests of production by "protecting" labour resources — securing the allocation of women's labour to reproduction. This was the first period since industrialization in which there was no political, economic or social pressure upon the state to restrict the use of female labour in production. In the absence of countervailing pressures, the state readily removed barriers to the employment of women, accommodating production's demand for more cheap labour for use in a rapidly expanding economy.

The substantial realignment of labour and income resources between production and reproduction undertaken in the post-war years was not, of course, without consequences. But it was not until the end of this period that evidence of a growing imbalance between production and reproduction appeared in the declining birth rate, the skewed demography, the growing ratio of dependent to productive members of society and in the flight of capital to avoid the high costs of Canadian labour.

Restructuring Reproduction

The post-war years in Canada witnessed a dramatic reversal in state policy towards the family. The state's support and subsidization of the family had been a two-fold process since the onset of industrialization: the allocation of female labour to reproduction and the direction of income resources to the family. In the post-war years the first function of state support was entirely abandoned. The state's support for reproduction switches from a process of allocating women's labour to reproduction to a process of allocating income and services to reproduction. This resulted in a restructuring of the labour force and a restructuring of reproduction, specifically, the erosion of the support-service marriage structure. It is interesting that the consequent shift of women's labour from the home to the work place occurred with so little notice and no controversy.

At the turn of the century the idea of women's employment encountered a wall of social resistance, gave rise to an international Social Reform Movement and over half a century of restrictive, pro-natalist legislation. One might wonder why the issue that mobilized a nation at one moment in history would pass without remark in another. The answer lies in locating the point at which the contradiction between production and reproduction becomes manifest in each period. One of the most important variables in determining this point is the birth rate. The long-term trend in wage-labour systems is for women's employment to be inversely related to birth rates, a visible indicator of the competing demands of production and reproduction.

At the turn of the century Canadians experienced the first impact of the wage-labour system upon reproduction. The impact was powerful because of the absence of any comprehensive social programs to cushion the blow. As a result, the inverse relation between women's employment and the birth rate was distressingly evident. In addition, the process of industrialization resulted in a serious disruption of the reproductive unit and a concentration of its casualties in urban centres across the country. Canadians came to see a relation between industrialization, urbanization, family dissolution, abortion, abandonment and the declining birth rate. While the underlying cause was the lack of fit between the wage-labour system and the structure of reproduction, the obvious manifest symptom was the employment of women and children. Thus, the process of saving the family and reducing all the social problems associated with its dissolution became synonymous with protecting women and children from employment. The result was the legislative engineering of the support-service marriage structure — the male-breadwinner, female-homemaker family ideal.

In the third period Canadians experienced the impact of the wage-labour system on reproduction through a cushion of social-welfare programs and a filter of unprecedented economic prosperity. The impact was neither harsh nor unfamiliar, and the tension that did exist focussed on the issue of income and social services. There was no need to "save" the family. Post-war family ideology was a celebration of the triumph of the nuclear family. The evidence was impressive; increased marriage rates, increased birth rates, a vibrant and growing population combined with a vibrant and growing economy. The reversal of the typical inverse relation between women's employment and birth rates was dramatic but somewhat misleading. The increased birth rate was a relatively short-lived anomaly; it lasted for fifteen years.[1] However, its impact on public attitudes to women's employment was much more profound.

The convergence of the baby boom with the first fifteen years of women's slow-but-steady absorption into the labour force obscured any awareness of competition between the two spheres for labour. While conditions in Canada converged to increase the domestic supply of labour, international conditions and liberal immigration policies were augmenting the adult labour supply. The rate of natural increase combined with the increased immigration rate[2] to suggest an unlimited supply of labour. Indeed the Canadian labour force doubled from four million in 1948 to eight million in 1968 (Leacy 1983, Series D8–55). Earlier resistance to women's employment based on concerns about labour supplies was nonexistent in the post-war period.

As the conditions of reproduction were changing to favour the employment of women, so also were the conditions of production. General improvements in the hours and conditions of work eroded the legal distinctions between male and female work. In addition, the rapid post-war development of the tertiary sector increased the number of temporary, part-time and full-time employment opportunities well within the regulations applied to female labour. The amenability (by structure and design) of this sector to part-time and temporary employment permitted the presentation of such employment as a complement to rather than a competition with women's reproductive responsibilities. The baby boom gave further credence to the new concept of the compatibility of employment with women's familial roles. Women's movement into the labour force was facilitated by the fact that women were recruited and hired into the expanding tertiary sector creating socially acceptable (pink collar) ghettos of women's employment, reassuring men in the "traditional" industrial sector that women's employment posed no threat to them.

The improved conditions of work and the part-time and flexible nature of employment obscured the underlying reality that the increasing absorption of women in the labour market amounted to an intensification of female labour. The intensification occurred across spheres as women's labour was increasingly in demand in both production and reproduction. At the beginning of this period, the 1941 census indicated only 4.5% of married women were employed; however, by the end of the third period, the 1971 census indicated that 33% of married women were in the labour force. Cross-sphere intensification involves an increase in the productive/reproductive labour ratio, that is, more hours of labour being expended in production in order to sustain a reproductive unit. The changing ratio was reflected in the fact that the majority (57%) of Canadian families had one wage earner in 1951 in contrast to the majority (64.9%) of Canadian families with multiple wage earners in 1971 (Armstrong and Armstrong 1978, 157).

This process constituted a radical restructuring of the reproductive unit, as well as the labour force. The support-service marriage structure based on the allocation of women's labour to reproduction would be seriously undermined. Ironically, the intensification of women's labour and the increase in the productive/reproductive labour ratio, processes that further subordinate reproductive interests to productive interests, are first experienced as beneficial to the family. The increased opportunities for women's employment, coupled with the extension of the welfare state addressed the immediate income shortage experienced by families. Because the needs of capital (for cheap labour) coincided with the short-term needs of the family (for income), this major transition in state mediating strategies and reproductive structure proceeded with little controversy or debate.

The reallocation of women's labour to production represented a structural subordination of reproduction to production; however, it also represented the potential for greater economic independence for women. Thus, while the reproductive unit was subordinated, the individual member who had anchored that unit, the wife/mother, was provided with greater freedom. As women's labour was increasingly utilized in production, the state's support for reproduction switched from allocating labour to allocating income to reproduction. As such the state was directly associated with increasing flows of income and services to the family and was *not* directly associated with limiting women's options in the labour force (although labour legislation did have this effect through omission). As a result the state and social patriarchy presented a uniquely benevolent face during this period.

In the halcyon days of the post-war welfare state, the restructuring of reproduction was, itself, not apparent, and hence its consequences were not anticipated. The proud, patriarchal pronouncements of Talcott Parsons and the whole school of nuclear family celebrants were premature in their assertion that the modern family was particularly well suited to the requirements of industrialized societies. In the absence of a "crisis of the family," state support for a critical under-pinning of the nuclear family was removed. As the state abandoned its role in allocating female labour to reproduction, the nuclear family would undergo a gradual but fundamental change.

By the mid 1960s the consequences of women's employment began to be felt. The traditional nuclear family was on the verge of becoming a minority, birth rates were down, divorce rates were up, abortion had once again become a central social issue, and women were beginning to articulate their anger with a double work load and fifty percent pay. These issues were articulated on a national scale in 1967 in the Royal Commission on the Status of Women.

Restructuring the Canadian Labour Market

In the post-war period, capital embarked on a course of protecting its income interests through management and control of the labour process, rather than direct confrontation with organized labour over the wage. The goal was to contain unionism and control the costs of labour. The method was a segmentation of the labour market, which could concede higher wages to organized workers while preserving a large category of unorganized low-wage workers. The segmentation strategy combined with the expansion of the tertiary sector dramatically increased the demand for low-wage, semi-skilled workers. Women constituted the largest pool of such labour in Canada and were, therefore, a key component in the segmentation strategy of capital. This strategy, in the absence of any countervailing pressure, resulted in the massive absorption of women into the labour force.

Studies in the US and Canada document the process and consequences of labour market segmentation in this period.[3] These studies indicate that the old division between large capital and small competitive capital became further refined with the rationalization of production and the differentiation of core and periphery industries. Core industries, characterized by stable product demand, had a vested interest in stable labour supplies. To keep their employees and keep them off the picket line these industries offered unionized jobs, with training opportunities, internal job ladders and job security. These jobs structured and drew upon a primary labour market, — skilled, unionized, white male labour, Canada's traditionally advantaged labour pool.

In contrast periphery industry — characterized by unstable product demand — and the growing tertiary sector offered non-unionized jobs, with little job training or promotional opportunity and minimal job security. This "secondary" labour market attracted unskilled, marginal labour such as women and immigrants, Canada's traditionally disadvantaged labour pool. Canadian studies, indicate that three of the four occupational categories absorbing large numbers of female workers during this period were organized in terms of secondary labour market characteristics — clerical, peripheral manufacturing and unskilled personal service workers.[4]

Studies of Canadian manufacturing from 1950 to 1970 conducted by Chan F. Aw (1980) and Pradeep Kumar (1974) provide evidence of growing discrepancies between core and peripheral industries, consistent wage differentials between the two sectors and little labour mobility between them. Kumar's study also provides additional information on the impact of the sexual composition of the labour force. He found that the sexual composition was the most significant factor in inter-industry wage differentials for workers of equal skill. His data revealed that a one percent difference in the proportion of females caused a five percent wage differential for unskilled labour and a three percent difference in wage rates of skilled labour (Kumar 1974, 68). The benefit of segmentation to employers is clear in a comparison of the average annual wage of women, $1,681 in periphery industries in 1967, to the average annual wage of men, $4,670 in core industries the same year (Ursel 1991, 446).

While capital had forged a new strategy out of the conflict and confrontation of the war years, organized labour remained focussed on its traditional male membership and industrial base. Labour was strong and united on a number of traditional labour issues, hours and conditions of work, vacations with pay, workmen's compensation coverage and minimum wage. Labour was perhaps most effective in its pursuit of the social wage, acting as a powerful national lobby that pushed reluctant governments to extend social services.

However, labour's ability to recognize and respond to the restructuring of the Canadian labour market was extremely limited, particularly in relation to the conditions of women's employment.

In the absence of any experience or analysis that would focus organized labour on women or the tertiary sector, labour lagged behind government and other organizations in its recognition of the growing role and importance of women in the workplace. Although the ILO ratified the equal pay for equal work convention in 1951, the first formal adoption of the equal-pay principle was introduced in Canada, not by a union, but by the Ontario legislature. In 1951 the Ontario government passed the Fair Remuneration for Female Employees Act. The first Canadian organization to recommend equal pay for work of equal value was not a union but a business organization. In 1956 the Canadian Federation of Business and Professional Women approved the ILO convention of equal pay, recommending that the federal government pass such legislation and that the provincial legislation substitute the term *equivalent work* for the original wording of "identical work" (*Labour Gazette* 1956: 1000).

Labour also failed to mount an effective resistance to a blatantly discriminatory revision to the Unemployment Insurance regulations in 1950. The revision disqualified women upon marriage from receiving UIC for two years unless they met special employment criteria. This revision was justified by the commission as a necessary measure to prevent "a drain on the unemployment insurance fund through claims from women who, on marriage, are really withdrawing from the employment field" (M.F. Greeg, Minister of Labour, *Labour Gazette* 1950: 1988). In the three months following the implementation of the amendment, 10,808 women were disqualified from UIC (*Labour Gazette* 1951: 446). During the seven years this amendment was in force, the number of married women in the labour force increased from 303,000 to 543,000. It was estimated by the Minister of Labour that the amendment served to disqualify 12,000 married women annually (*Labour Gazette* 1957: 1504). Despite the evident discrimination in the new regulations and despite the significant loss of income this meant for thousands of women and their families, the labour unions were once again underwhelming in their response.

In the 1950s and early 1960s organized labour did not have a strategy that could effectively counteract the segmenting trends in the labour force. While the wage gap between unionized and nonunionized sectors increased, unionized occupations decreased and nonunionized occupations proliferated. Between 1951 and 1971 mining, manufacturing and construction declined 7% in the percentage of the labour force they absorbed, while trade, finance and service increased their market share by 15% (White 1980, 39). Although labour presented a strong challenge to capital in the closing years of this period, by that time the labour market had fundamentally and irrevocably changed. The entrenched segmentation and gender stratification of the labour market had not only changed the way in which labour was structured and organized, but also changed the flow of labour between production and reproduction. Segmentation would continue to frustrate attempts at organizing labour, while the increased employment of women served to extract double the labour time in production in order to sustain a reproductive unit.

Labour Commissions and Inquiries

Labour commissions and inquiries, the first point of state involvement, are usually a good barometer of labour relations, and the post-war period is no exception. The quiescent 1950s gave rise to only two Royal Commissions dealing with the updating of the Workmen's Compensation Acts in Ontario (1949) and Manitoba (1957).[5] The tone of these commissions was conciliatory, and the goal of the inquiry was to extend benefits to workers.

In the 1960s the number of inquiries increased as all jurisdictions had to come to terms with two major problems; first, how to deal with the large number of increasingly restless government employees excluded from the Labour Relations Acts and, second, how to deal with rising labour militancy, wild-cat strikes and picket-line violence. The solution to the former problem was fairly straightforward and resulted over time in the systematic coverage of previously excluded employees under the Labour Relations Act. The second problem did not lend itself so readily to a solution. Evidence of mounting tension can be traced in the sequence of inquiries into labour disputes in the 1960s.

In 1960 Manitoba commissioned an inquiry into the Brandon Packers strike, and a year later Ontario commissioned an inquiry into labour-management relations in the construction industry. While both commissions had been called because of circumstances the labour boards had been unable to manage, there was a sense in the early 1960s that these cases were anomalies that could be prevented with some fine tuning of labour regulations. However, the sense that all that was needed was judicious revisions to the labour-board regulations came to an abrupt end with the widespread and alarming numbers of strikes and lockouts that occurred in the mid 1960s.

In 1965 the federal government called an inquiry into labour-management relations in the post office, and the following year the Ontario government called an inquiry into labour disputes. Finally, reminiscent of the circumstances leading up to the War Labour Board Inquiry in 1942 (when 33% of the nation's working time was lost through strikes and lockouts), the Privy Council of Canada commissioned the Woods Task Force on Labour Relations in 1966.

The Ontario commission conducted by Justice Ivan Rand held out a plan for restoring industrial peace that pleased employers and outraged the labour movement. The *Rand Report* recommended that unions become legal entities, able to sue or be sued, that mass picketing and boycotts be banned and above all that a labour court be created armed with sweeping powers to report on disputes and to end strikes and lockouts in industries deemed essential, all without appeal. "The Ontario government studied the report, thanked the author, listened to the uproar from labour ranks, and prudently buried the document" (Morton and Copp 1980, 262).

The Woods Task Force, on the other hand, received guarded welcome from unions, disapproval from employers and offered little comfort to governments looking for an end to industrial strife. The Woods Task Force reiterated the uncomfortable lessons of history; there are limits to which governments can manage or contain inherently adversarial relations, and even the most effective labour-relations boards cannot guarantee industrial harmony.

Labour Legislation

In the first and second periods and during the war years, state mediation of the labour process was explicitly interventionist and regulatory. In the post-war years, however, the restructuring of the labour market was a market-driven process, in which the state "co-operated." The strongest observation that can be made about state activity in this field is captured in the terms of omission and/or bias, a language of passivity or compliance rather than intervention. Omission and bias leave little evidence of decision making, no discussions of anticipated "cost-benefit." However, this passive posture on the part of the state was certainly not without consequence. Labour legislation in general and the Labour Relations Acts in particular had an effect consistent with and supportive of the segmentation strategy of capital.

Up until the widespread rebellion of labour in the mid 1960s it appeared that the state could meet the needs of capital and labour simultaneously. The reforms labour most consistently lobbied for, for example, minimum wage, workmen's compensation and hours and conditions of work, did not conflict with segmentation strategies and were accommodated by the state without much dispute. At the same time the state could accommodate the demands of capital for a plentiful supply of cheap labour (women and immigrants) and contain the spread of unionization (through a cautious implementation of the Labour Relations Acts), without unduly provoking organized labour. The characteristic features of state intervention in this period are accommodation to organized labour, disregard for unorganized labour and the implementation of routine management through the operation of labour-relations boards across the country.

The state's more conciliatory attitude to unions opened new avenues to labour to communicate their concerns directly to government. Labour leaders responded to their new legitimacy with an incremental reform strategy. The state in turn gradually implemented these changes (see table A2.16. New Labour Laws in Ontario and Manitoba, Period III, 1940–1968).[6] Beginning with the Employment Standards Act in Manitoba in 1957, both Manitoba and Ontario introduced a series of successive reforms throughout the 1960s to meet labour's demands on hours, wages and conditions of work. The last piece of the labour reform package to be put in place was the standardization of the minimum wage through amendment in 1960 in Manitoba, 1963 in Ontario and 1964 in the Canada Labour Code.

By the end of the third period organized labour had realized one of their major goals, the implementation of labour codes that extended basic employment standards for workers whether or not they had the benefit of a union contract. In the pursuit of this goal labour also participated, quite unconsciously, in the dismantling of legislative barriers to the employment of women. The success of organized labour in extending to men much of the protective legislation that previously included only women had the serendipitous effect of removing special restrictions on the use of female labour.

In contrast to the intense debate on women, their "nature" and their employment, which gave rise to the "protective" statutes in the first period, the elimination of women's protected status was accomplished with little debate or controversy. Nevertheless, the increasing presence of women in the labour force did require some specific legislative attention. However, the state's response to women's employment was decidedly uneven. Legislation removing barriers to women's employment was simple and straightforward, while legislation addressing issues of equity was weak and contradictory. This pattern revealed a legislative bias towards access rather than equity (see table A2.17. Labour Legislation and Statutory Orders Facilitating the Employment of Women, Period III, 1940–1968).

A good example of the uneven legislative response to women's employment is seen in the federal statutes of the time. In 1955 the federal government removed regulations prohibiting the employment of married women in the federal civil service. However, from 1950 to 1957, Unemployment Insurance regulations disqualified women upon marriage from receiving benefits unless special requirements were met. While employers were to have equal access to women regardless of marital status, women were not to have equal access to benefits. In 1956 the federal government passed equal pay legislation; however, for the next nine years the federal labour code specified unequal minimum wages for men and women. Unfortunately, this mixture of progressive and regressive legislation was not unique to the federal government. The move towards the principle of equal pay in the provinces was very uneven.

The first provincial legislation to specifically address women's employment was the equal pay act. The very first act was introduced in Ontario in 1951 as the Fair Remuneration of Female Employees Act.[7] However, Ontario continued for another twelve years to set separate and unequal minimum wages for men and women.

Manitoba introduced a Fair Employment Practices Act in 1953 and an Equal Pay Act in 1956. However, there was a four-year gap between the enactment of equal-pay legislation and the equalization of the minimum-wage regulations in Manitoba. In addition, both provinces and the federal government excluded civil servants from coverage under the Equal Pay Act until the 1970s.

In spite of the relatively early passage of the equal-pay legislation, it was a well-known fact that the statutes did little to reduce the gap between male and female wages. Its negligible impact was a result of both the wording of the legislation and its enforcement. The Ontario act called for "equal pay for the same work done in the same establishment," while the federal and Manitoba legislation called for equal pay for "identical or substantially identical work." However, in a labour force that was highly sex-segregated, women were most unlikely to obtain employment in the same occupations as men. As the Women's Bureau of Ontario reported, "It was discovered that classifying jobs as 'male' or 'female' was a greater obstacle to equality than separate wage scales" (*Ontario Dept. of Labour Annual Reports* 1968, 16). Thus, in the absence of equal-opportunity legislation, which was not introduced until the 1970s the concept of "same" or "identical" work served to disqualify the majority of working women.

Ontario's Fair Employment Practices Branch provides us with an excellent history of the first eighteen years of enforcement of the equal-pay legislation. These records reveal that the problems of the "letter of the law" were compounded by a very lenient enforcement of the act. First of all, the annual data on complaints indicate that putting the burden of initiation on the claimant resulted in a small number of complaints being filed. In ten of the eighteen years less than three complaints were filed annually; in five of those years there were no complaints at all. In the eighteen-year period 339 claims came before the Branch, of which 55% were dismissed, 15% withdrawn, leaving only 30% of the cases resulting in settlements. None of the 339 cases were prosecuted in court, and the settlements typically consisted of a wage adjustment not a fine (*Ontario Dept. of Labour Annual Reports* 1951, 68).

The one statute that appeared as a countervailing force against the creation of a cheap pool of female labour, the Equal Pay Act, was worded and enforced in such a manner as to amount to little more than window dressing. By all accounts the equal-pay laws had no appreciable effect upon women's wages during this period. However, the act that may have had the greatest depressing effect on women's wages was the Labour Relations Act. This act set out terms and conditions for certification that made it virtually impossible to unionize the tertiary sector in this period.

The tertiary sector was the litmus paper of industrial relations during this period. As the fastest growing occupational sector, it became a critical component of capital's segmentation strategy, the new frontier for labour and the primary location of women's reallocated labour. The terms and conditions set out in the Labour Relations Act — the inclusion of restrictive clauses at the provincial level, the exclusion of collective-bargaining rights for civil servants and, finally, the operation of the labour boards[8] — all served to impede unionization of the tertiary sector. Barriers to organizing the tertiary sector were essential to labour-market segmentation; they preserved the "secondary labour market" characteristics within the sector, not the least important of which were the low-wage rates. While the unionized sectors managed to maintain their wages above the industrial average throughout this period, the non-unionized sectors experienced wages well below the average (*Labour Gazette*, 1968: 202).

The biggest stumbling block for tertiary sector organizing involved the processes outlined in the Labour Relations Acts for the determination of the appropriate bargaining unit. The process permitted employers to develop two very effective strategies to defeat applications for certification. First, employers could argue for a unit so large as to abort any possibility of collective bargaining. This has typically been the strategy of bank administrators in Canada (*Labour Relations Law Casebook 1981: 161*). Second, the acts also permitted employers to prolong the dispute over the appropriate bargaining unit in order to substantially delay proceedings. This was the case in the Eaton's drive in 1947–50, in which the company succeeded in delaying proceedings for seven months through bargaining unit debates (Suffrin 1982).

During this period there is, perhaps, no better indication of government's attitude to organizing the unorganized than in its relation to its own expanding labour force. Between 1941 and 1971 government employees increased six-fold, health and welfare workers increased five-fold and education workers also increased by a factor of five (Leacy 1983, Series D56, 85). These million and a half workers were the backbone of the developing welfare state. Government, like most other employers in labour-intensive industries, dug in its heels on the issue of certification. Civil-service regulations explicitly denied the right to collective bargaining in all provinces (except Saskatchewan), and in the federal government. In addition civil servants were often excluded from other labour legislation, for example, equal-pay laws. Furthermore, most Labour Relations Acts excluded a large number of workers whose wages came from government coffers, for example, teachers, hospital labour and municipal workers. For almost twenty years this massive labour force remained outside of the usual protection afforded by the Labour Relations Acts. Not until the mid 1960s did the barriers begin to come down.

Labour legislation in general and the Labour Relations Acts in particular shared many of the same characteristics of the segmentation strategy of capital — accommodation to organized labour, routine management rather than crisis intervention and disregard for unorganized labour. The argument that the Labour Relations Act itself constituted a significant barrier to tertiary sector organizing is borne out by the fact that it was not until the act was revised to eliminate major exclusion clauses that the first significant breakthrough in organizing this sector occurred.

By the 1960s the gap between wages and productivity had risen to 30%, and both organized and unorganized labour were getting restless. This restlessness was translated into a new militancy as the strike rate increased steadily from 1962 on. The climax was reached in 1966 when 33% of the nation's working time was lost through strikes and lockouts involving 411,459 workers and a loss of over 5 million person days (Jamieson 1968, 397). A new feature of the strike situation in the 1960s was the number of government employees involved. As work stoppages and labour unrest spread in the public sector, federal and provincial governments found themselves in a position similar to that of the 1940s. If they didn't quickly establish a machinery for legal bargaining, they would find themselves caught in an escalating cycle of crisis intervention. Preferring a more stable atmosphere for labour relations, federal and provincial governments introduced legislation and/or amendments to extend bargaining rights to the civil service.

In 1965 Ontario granted collective bargaining rights to hospital labour (SO c.48), and in 1966 Ontario removed the exclusion of librarians, non-teaching staff and municipal workers from the Labour Board Act (SO c.76). In the following year (1967) the federal government passed the Public Service Staff Relations Act (SC c.71), providing collective bargaining rights for federal civil servants. The significance of the exclusion clauses can be appreciated when we consider the consequence of their removal: "...in one blow, 260,000 of the government's 400,000 employees gained the right to choose between arbitration or the strike" (Morton and Copp 1980, 261). When the 120,000 member Public Service Alliance of Canada entered the ranks of organized labour, it became the third-largest union in the country. Moreover, the federal example spread rapidly to the provinces, with Manitoba and Ontario following suit in 1971 (SM c.75 and SO c.67). The effect was dramatic. Organized labour, stalled at less than a third of the non-agricultural work force as late as 1964, boosted its share to more than 40% by the mid 1970s. Furthermore, the organization of government employees accounted for the largest increase in unionization of women, a 106% increase for women compared with a 40% increase for men (White 1980).

On the labour front, the third period closed much as it began — punctuated by industrial disputes, expanding unionism and demands for greater government intervention that once again tested the limits of state mediation. While the achievement of industrial and social harmony was, indeed, time limited, the reallocation of women's labour to production would have a more lasting effect. By the end of this period the labour force had been substantially restructured, and women's role in Canadian society was rapidly changing. Although the state was no longer called upon to reserve women's labour for reproduction, the state was under sustained pressure throughout this period to increase income and services to the reproductive unit. Thus, while women were moving out into the work force, the state was moving in with greater support and services for the family. The welfare state expanded to fill the gap between the private wage and human need and also, now, to compensate for labour losses.

The Making of a National Welfare State

Welfare ideology in the war and post-war years is marked by strong similarities and continuities. Most important of these was the sustained public demand for adequate social security and the continued commitment to the concept of entitlement. This new ideology not only resulted in greater state activity, but also in a shift in emphasis from regulative to supportive government interventions. This shift is largely a result of the introduction of universal programs. Both the philosophy and the actual administration of universal programs reduced the state's capacity to use its financial assistance as a lever for regulation of individuals or the family. When entitlement is extended to everyone, access to programs cannot be made dependent upon fulfilment of particular social standards, as was the case with Mothers' Allowance in the previous period. Intrinsic to universality and the concept of entitlement is the emphasis upon the state's responsibility rather than the state's right to regulate. Just as the individual patriarch experienced the transition from rights to responsibility in the second period, so did the social patriarch (the state) in the third period. In addition to the more benevolent policy thrust of universal programs, the sheer wealth of the period permitted even means-tested programs to proceed in a more open-handed less punitive way.

While this was a more generous period in social history, it was also a more bureaucratic one. The war years were the idea years, characterized by a large number of commissions and inquiries and broad-based public debate. The competition over income between capital and labour — production and reproduction — was explicit and explosive as the events of 1943 revealed. The connection between state mediation of the productive-reproductive dynamic was equally explicit as the documents recording the development of family allowances indicate. In contrast, the post-war years were the bureaucratic moment in Canadian social policy characterized by a limited number of commissions and a reduced amount of public debate.[9]

The state's assumption of responsibility for the social wage absorbed and transformed the expression of the productive-reproductive competition over income. While the pressures continued to originate with the lack of fit between the two spheres, these pressures became more rapidly translated into a bureaucratic form. Social-policy activity of the post-war period now occurred at the federal-provincial negotiating table; the actors were bureaucrats and politicians whose exercise of power and responsibility seemed far removed from the productive-reproductive dynamic they mediate. While the actors changed, the process remained the same — displacing the costs of reproduction to an ever larger resource base.

The provinces emerge in the post-war years as new and aggressive actors alongside the electorate and organized labour in the pursuit of greater federal financing of social welfare. Although the post-war years were characterized by provincial rebellion against the centralism of the war years, their rebellion was tempered by escalating social-welfare expenditures. The gap between provincial jurisdictional responsibility for health and welfare and the revenue generating capacities of their treasuries frequently led the provinces into aggressive advocacy of national cost-shared programs. The pressure to socialize the costs of reproduction created an unlikely alliance of provincial premiers, organized labour and the general electorate on a number of social-welfare issues. The entry of the provinces as strong and frequently querulous partners in the construction of the welfare state shifted the struggle for income to a new terrain — the federal-provincial negotiation table.

Provincial Welfare Legislation

Throughout the third period provinces were subject to two major countervailing pressures that shaped their legislation and their relation to the federal government. On the one hand, there was the combined effect of jurisdictional responsibility and mounting public pressure for social services, which pushed the provinces in the direction of liberalized statutes and extended benefits. The opposing pressure was the resource limitations of most provinces. Broad jurisdictional responsibility in conjunction with a narrow resource base has typically impelled provincial governments to establish mechanisms to limit their commitments to social expenditure. This was accomplished in the second period through the interaction of family and welfare law that aggressively enforced familial obligations while extending "means-tested" assistance only when all family supports had been exhausted.

The new philosophy of entitlement and the resultant move from means-tested to universal services changed the structure of social-welfare systems in the provinces, as well as throughout the nation. The concept of entitlement made the privatization strategies of the second period politically untenable. In the face of continued resource-based limitations, provinces had to accommodate increasing demands for social services with their structural predisposition to limit social expenditures. These countervailing pressures pushed the provinces to liberalize its legislation and services while off-loading its costs onto the federal government. Thus, the distinguishing features of provincial welfare activity in the third period are the systematic liberalization of social-welfare legislation and the growth of federal-provincial cost-shared agreements.

For the most part, provinces maintained their traditional focus on services to people marginal to production — women, children, the elderly and the disabled. As a result provincial legislation retained the quality of "substitute" for wages, while federal universal welfare legislation moved more boldly in the direction of "subsidy" for wages. Despite these limitations provincial legislation was unquestionably affected by the new social-service expectations of the Canadian electorate. Evidence of provincial response to these expectations is found in broader definitions of eligibility, a move away from means tests, a refocussing of regulative functions away from surveillance of service consumers towards surveillance of service providers and, finally, a redefinition of the role of welfare workers from moral entrepreneur to social advocate.

A brief review of the new welfare legislation in Ontario and Manitoba throughout the third period indicates that there was no new legislation passed during the war years, and that in the post-war years Ontario was more active than Manitoba (see table A2.18. New Provincial Welfare Legislation in Ontario and Manitoba, Period III, 1940–1968). In previous periods, the state's impact on the family was measured by the effect of welfare legislation on the disposition of property within the family, the disposition of children in cases of family breakdown or neglect and the allocation of resources to the family. In the third period, state activity in all three of these areas underwent substantial change as a result of the strong shift away from regulation toward support. Considerable legislative activity was involved in producing this effect. There were twenty new statutes in Ontario and eleven in Manitoba. However, what the state did not do is almost as revealing as what it did.

State control of the disposition of family property draws boundaries around which costs are socialized. In the second period the interaction of family law and restrictive welfare legislation served to maximize privatization. Not surprisingly, under the new wave of entitlement this approach was largely abandoned. Family obligations were less rigorously enforced, and restrictive welfare legislation was either rewritten or ignored.

In the second period two welfare acts — The Child of Unmarried Parents Act and the Parents' Maintenance Act — became synonymous with very aggressive investigative teams seeking a legal reallocation of family resources to keep applicants off the welfare roles. The Parents' Maintenance Act remained on the books in both Ontario and Manitoba throughout the third period; however, it simply ceased to be enforced. Enforcement required the maintenance of a team of investigators who would regularly check the financial status of the families of elderly recipients of social assistance. The introduction of a universal Old Age Pension in 1951 (SC c.18) removed all fiscal incentive to carry out such enforcement. Manitoba went so far as to introduce the Old Age Pension Debt Cancellation Act to terminate court cases in which the state was suing to regain funds from the families of elderly welfare recipients (1954 SM c.23).

The Child of Unmarried Parents legislation also experienced a lapse in enforcement as well as amendments that altered the thrust of the act from regulation to support. Two of the most regulative and punitive clauses were written out of the legislation in the 1950s. Specifically, the Ontario clause (1921 SO c.54 s.10) that provided for the appointment of a provincial guardian just because a child was born out of wedlock and the Manitoba clause (1926 SM c.4 s.12) that empowered the state to assume sole guardianship if a mother refused to press a paternity suit were removed.[10]

In the second period these statutes mobilized an aggressive bureaucracy of provincial officers devoted to seeking out and obtaining child support from putative fathers. Manitoba and Ontario's welfare reports were filled with detailed accountings of the number of illegitimate births, fathers located, support agreements achieved and the number of court cases initiated by the provincial officer when agreements could not be reached. In contrast, in the third period mothers were no longer required to press paternity suits under threat of losing their children, and the overall activity of the departments shifted from hunting down putative fathers to assisting unwed mothers to secure necessary social supports (*Manitoba and Ontario Dept. of Public Welfare Annual Reports*, 1948–68). Both the amendments and the change in enforcement policy reflect a move away from regulation and privatization towards acceptance of public responsibility for family support.

In addition to reducing their regulative relation with the family, Ontario and Manitoba also introduced a large number of statutes that extended their supportive role. A review of this legislation reveals a much more benevolent posture on the part of the provinces both in regard to the allocation of resources to the family and the disposition of children. Because the extension of financial support to families was a precondition for greater benevolence in the disposition of children it will be considered first.

Perhaps the most direct example of the provinces increasing support for families was the systematic extension of eligibility and coverage in the provision of Mothers' Allowance. Prior to the war Mothers' Allowance was circumscribed by a long list of eligibility requirements: it excluded families with only one child, it excluded the divorced and the unwed, it required a long period of provincial residency, and heaped on top of all of these limits were a series of moral and behavioural requirements. However, shortly after the war the impact of the new welfare ideology began to be felt at the provincial level. By 1948 both Ontario and Manitoba began to remove the barriers to eligibility and extend the benefits within the Mothers' Allowance program.

The impact of these amendments was substantial. Despite a booming economy and near to full employment rates, case loads in Manitoba and Ontario grew as eligibility broadened. In 1951 Ontario had an average monthly enrolment of 7,500 families at an annual expenditure of $6.5 million, by 1961 the enrolment had increased to 9,800 families at a total expenditure of $12.8 million (*Ontario Dept. of Public Welfare Annual Reports* 1948–62). Manitoba experienced a similar but proportional increase, although their accounting is less detailed than Ontario.[11]

As the material conditions for support began to change, so also did the attitude of the bureaucracy administering Mothers' Allowance. In the second period these allowances were regarded as wages for childcare and as such it was the "duty" of the administrators to "investigate carefully the fitness of the applicant" (*Report of the Minister of Public Welfare, Ontario, 1922* Sessional Papers 89: 59) and "to satisfy itself that the services rendered ... are accomplishing what was intended" (*Report of the Minister of Welfare, Manitoba, 1918* Sessional Papers: 5). This approach placed the family under intense bureaucratic scrutiny. However, in the post-war period Mothers' Allowance were redefined as a government responsibility. In accepting as inevitable the lack of fit between family and economy and accepting government responsibility to fill the gap, post-war policies removed the moral requirement, as well as the economic necessity for aggressive surveillance of recipients. The role of the case workers was rapidly redefined from that of moral entrepreneur to family advocate.

This new mood of entitlement was found, not only in the allocation of resources to the family, but also in a new attitude toward the disposition of children. In the first two periods, the state extended its authority over children greatly increasing the number of children who became wards of the state. However, this pattern began to be reversed in the third period making way for a new philosophy — the best way to help children was to help their families. While this philosophy was generously infused with the "milk of human kindness," it also served to advance the de-institutionalization policies introduced in the second period.

Maintaining a child in its own home was the next logical step in the process of de-institutionalization. It presupposed the extension of support to disadvantaged families so they could care adequately for their children. As these material prerequisites were being put in place in the third period, the administering departments and their staff changed their attitudes and goals accordingly. While the measure of success in the second period was the number of children under care, the third period measured success by the declining rate of apprehension. Support began to replace suspicion as the predominant approach of case workers to families. An early reflection of the new mood is revealed in the 1946 Manitoba Welfare report, in which it was asserted that "the object of the Welfare Division is to try wherever possible to keep children in their own homes" (*Manitoba Dept. of Health and Welfare Annual Report* 1946: 199). This sentiment of apprehension as a final resort was voiced in the Ontario Welfare report of 1951–52. "Where adequate preventative services are developed, the child is removed from his home only when all other means of rehabilitation have failed" (*Ontario Dept. of Public Welfare Annual Report* 1951–52: 23).

While child-welfare workers gave every evidence of support for this new phase of de-institutionalization, the Ontario government sought to reinforce the process with financial incentives. In 1956 the government altered the grant structure to the Children's Aid Societies:

….a new provincial grant structure has been devised for all societies. These grants will be based upon the amount of time devoted to the prevention and repair of family breakdown which should result in reducing the proportion of the child population in the case [sic] of societies. These grants are intended not only to serve the social interests of the community but, through keeping to a minimum the number of children maintained at public expense, to effect a considerable saving to the tax payer (*Ontario Dept. of Public Welfare Annual Report* 1956–57: 56).

The rising birth rate made governments increasingly appreciative of the cost effectiveness of keeping children in their own homes. The restructuring of grants to Children's Aid Societies was seen to produce the desired effect, and in 1960 the Ontario government proudly announced that "… the proportion of the child population in the care of welfare agencies continued to decrease — 45% in ten years" (*Ontario Dept. of Public Welfare Annual Report* 1959–60: 16).

In the third period rising birth rates, increasing social expenditures and the process of de-institutionalization combined to create a new more benevolent approach in child welfare. The construction of the modern welfare state created a fiscal as well as a bureaucratic structure in which everyone had something to gain by keeping the family together. This material reality quickly became reflected in the pro-family ideology of the social-service experts of the day. However, at the very point in which everyone was becoming so keen on keeping children in the home, women were increasingly working outside of it. As the rising birth rate and increased longevity increased the burden of dependants upon the family, the family's major labour resource was exiting into the work force. Thus, in addition to a down-scaling of regulation and an up-scaling of support, during this period the provinces were also called upon to assume some of the functions of the reproductive unit.

Ontario, being the more industrialized province and the first to feel the impact of women's employment, led the way with legislation that provided for personal care services as well as financial support. The introduction of the Homes for the Aged Act (1947 SO c.46), the passage of the Day Nurseries Act (1946 SO c.17) and the Homemakers' and Nurses' Services Act (1958 SO c.37) reflected the growing recognition that financial support was only part of a state program for subsidizing the family. While childcare and care of the elderly were provided in the past for orphans or indigents, it became an expectation in this period that, even in the presence of able-bodied parents and relatives, the state had a responsibility to provide child and elder care.

This new responsibility was most manifest in this period in the provision of personal-care homes for the elderly. In fact, it was in this field that the provinces first departed from the means-tested principle. Prior to 1947 Ontario and Manitoba's only commitment to residential care for the elderly was contained in acts pertaining to charitable institutions. However, in the post-war period both provinces extended their responsibility beyond the limit of "the indigent" in an attempt to meet the demand for institutional care for the elderly. Demographic changes as well as social changes were increasing this demand. The Ontario Department of Public Welfare reported a 172% increase in the elderly population between the years 1911 and 1951 compared to an 82% increase in the total population of the province (*Ontario Dept. of Public Welfare Annual Report* 1952: 15).

Ontario, with the greater population and the greater problem, led the way in 1947 with the Homes for the Aged Act (1947 SO c.46 and c. 31). While the act in 1947 increased the breadth of provincial responsibility, the amendments and consolidation of the act in 1949 put some real teeth into the legislation (1949 SO c.41). The amended act required every municipality to provide for a home for the aged, and it specified provincial responsibility for regulations and funding for the construction and maintenance of these homes. "Under the new program, admission to a Home for the Aged is based on the need for care and no longer primarily on financial need ..." (*Ontario Dept. of Public Welfare Annual Report* 1952: 15).

The primary thrust of the Ontario legislation was institutional, and the removal of the means test resulted in a significant expansion of municipally run, provincially financed, old-folks' homes. The number of beds increased from 3,000 in 1948 to 14,000 in 1968, and provincial expenditures rose from approximately $1 million in 1948 to over $56 million in 1968 (*Ontario Dept. of Public Welfare Annual Report* 1968–69: 48–49). Manitoba's response was much slower because population pressures were much less urgent. Nevertheless, they followed suit with the Elderly Person's Housing Act (SM c.14) in 1956 and the Elderly and Infirm Persons' Housing Act in 1964 (SM c.17).

While the spirit of entitlement directed the provinces away from surveillance of service consumers, the new burden of responsibility increased the provinces' surveillance of service providers. The increasing flow of public monies to social services and the introduction of new specialized services resulted in a large number of statutes directed to their regulation. In fact, of the twenty new statutes introduced in Ontario, fourteen specified new or extended regulation of services and institutions, while none added any further capacity to regulate recipients. This was also the case in Manitoba where six of the eleven new statutes provided for regulation of agencies or institutions; none added to the regulation of recipients.

Through this legislation special-care homes and services became subject to very specific rules and licensing procedures. For example, in Ontario in 1948 only 45% of their 164 nurseries in operation were licensed; however, by 1967, 98% of the 441 nurseries were fully supervised and licensed (*Ontario, Dept. of Family Services Annual Report 1968: 19*). The provinces were still the primary regulative body among the three jurisdictions; however, the focus of their attention on agencies and services rather than recipients resulted in a much more humane atmosphere and much better treatment of recipients.

Because of provincial jurisdictional responsibility for health, education and welfare, the rising expectations of the Canadian electorate were visited first upon provincial treasuries. Provincial involvement in socializing the costs of reproduction escalated steadily throughout the third period. All provincial social expenditures (health, education and welfare) increased from $27.29 per capita in 1941 to $802.58 in 1971 (Moscovitch and Albert 1987, 21, 22). While these increases succeeded in providing more income and services for Canadian families, they played havoc with provincial treasuries. Although provincial budgets were expanding rapidly, keeping pace with the growth in GNP, social expenditures were clearly outstripping overall growth.

Social expenditures in Manitoba grew dramatically in the post-war period (see table 11). As a percentage of the total provincial budget, social expenditures increased from 26% in 1944 to 62% in 1968. Manitoba's social expenditures multiplied 46 times from $4.7 million in 1944 to $216.2 million in 1968.

The growth of social expenditures was equally dramatic in Ontario (see table 12). Ontario, as a wealthier province, was in a better position to handle these costs, but nevertheless, they saw social expenditures move from 34% of their overall

Table 11

Manitoba Social Expenditures* for Selected Years
by Category and as Percentage of Total Budget
(In Millions of Dollars)

Year	Education	Health	Welfare	Total Social Expenditures	Social Expenditures: As % of Total Provincial Budget
1944	2.3	2.4		4.7	26%
1948	4.9	3.8		8.7	31%
1952	7.0	8.4		15.4	37%
1956	11.7	12.1		23.8	40%
1960	29.6	20.6		50.2	58%
1964	38.7	20.8	18.8	78.3	60%
1968	109.8	72.7	33.7	216.2	62%

* Gross Expenditures Including Federal Reimbursements
SOURCE: *Manitoba Public Accounts 1944–68*

Table 12

Ontario Social Expenditures* for Selected Years
by Category and as Percentage of Total Budget
(In Millions of Dollars)

Year	Education	Health	Welfare	Total Social Expenditures	Social Expenditures: As % of Total Provincial Budget
1944	15.6	13.3	10.2	39.1	34%
1948	38.9	20.2	11.8	70.9	49%
1952	67.7	44.6	24.6	136.9	44%
1956	100.0	59.3	27.0	186.4	44%
1960	204.4	89.0	44.6	338.0	46%
1964	388.4	126.6	60.6	575.6	51%
1968	732.1	320.7	198.2	1,251.0	49%

* Gross Expenditures Including Federal Reimbursements
SOURCE: *Ontario Public Accounts 1944–68*

budget in 1944 to 49% in 1968. Ontario's social expenditures multiplied 32 times, increasing from $39.1 million in 1944 to $1.2 billion in 1968.

From 1948 to 1961 the burden of the welfare state fell most heavily on the provinces (Moscovitch and Albert 1987, 30). While education and health placed the largest burden upon provincial treasuries, social welfare costs were also weighty. In 1957 the Ontario Director of Public Welfare drew attention to the heavy share of welfare expenditures absorbed by the provinces. He reported that 61.9% of direct welfare expenditures were provided by the province, 19.3% by the federal government and 18.8% by the municipality. If we include the costs of the municipal grants, in aid of welfare and social services, Ontario's actual share of welfare costs for its residents was 71% (*Ontario Dept. of Public Welfare Annual Report* 1956–57: 2). The outcome of the liberalization of provincial social-welfare policies, the baby boom and increased longevity was a powerful fiscal squeeze for the provinces. Their only recourse, in a period in which the populace remained committed to a "better quality of life," was to transfer costs to the federal government. During the third period we witness a remarkable range of provincial behaviour in relation to the federal government — accommodating in their ready acceptance of constitutional amendments (for Old Age Pensions) at one moment, aggressive in their pursuit of a national hospital insurance program at another moment and equally aggressive in their resistance to a national health insurance program a decade later. The one factor that makes sense of the variety of provincial postures on national welfare programs is its impact on provincial treasuries.

Negotiating the Welfare State

The federal government's response to the new spirit of entitlement was outlined in the *Green Book Proposals* of 1946. In essence they offered to implement all the major national welfare programs (pensions, health, extended UIC and cost-shared social assistance) in return for sole occupancy of three major tax fields. Rejection of the *Green Book Proposals* left the provinces vulnerable to rising social expenditures, which gave the provinces a motive for and interest in national welfare programs. Rejection of the *Green Book Proposals* left the federal government in a vulnerable revenue position as they now had to regularly renew and renegotiate occupancy of the personal, corporate and excise tax fields with the provincial governments.

Throughout the post-war years provinces with escalating

expenditures and restrained revenues confronted a federal government with restrained expenditures and insecure revenues. Tipping the scale of this revenue-expenditure imbalance in favour of the development of a national welfare state was the continued commitment of the electorate to a comprehensive social-security system. Thus, the politics of socializing the costs of reproduction in this period followed a dual and for the most part mutually reinforcing cycle. Every four years the federal government confronted the populace at election time, and every five years the federal government confronted the provinces at national taxation-agreement conferences. Between 1948 and 1968 there were seven federal elections and five taxation agreements; thus, there were very few years in which pressure was not exerted on the federal government.

When electoral pressure waned, provincial fiscal pressure peaked. In the mid to late 1950s, during a period of relatively conservative attitudes on the part of the electorate and declining influence of the CCF and organized labour, fiscal pressure on provincial treasuries served to keep social-welfare reform on the federal agenda. This fluctuating pattern of pressure that created the modern welfare state is illustrated in the sequence of election and taxation agreement cycles and federal welfare legislative response (see table A2.19. Federal Social Welfare Legislation by Taxation Agreement and Election Cycles, Period III, 1940–1968).

In the first cycle of federal-provincial negotiations, the major social-welfare statute to be introduced was the Old Age Security Act (1951 SC c.18), which provided universal pensions to Canadians seventy years of age and over. The adoption of the important principle of universality in this legislation was the product of combined pressure from the public and the provinces. The election of 1949 had many of the elements of the more volatile mid 1940s. There was strong electoral pressure for reform of the Old Age Assistance program; the CCF was still a force to be reckoned with provincially; and organized labour mounted a strong lobbying effort to eliminate the means test from Old Age Assistance. As a result reform of Old Age Assistance became a major election promise of all three parties during the 1949 campaign.

In addition to the mounting political pressures, provincial fiscal pressure was critical to the realization of the act. In order to implement this legislation, a constitutional amendment was required. The provinces' co-operation on this matter reflected the fact that they really could not afford to do otherwise. Even the increasingly independent Quebec agreed to the amendment. Although the provinces were only responsible for 25% of the costs of the former scheme, Ontario reported in 1951 that their Old Age Assistance payments accounted for 42% of their total welfare budget (*Ontario Dept. of Public Welfare Annual Report* 1951: 53). Other provinces subject to the same demographic pressures were experiencing a similar increase in costs for supporting the elderly.[12]

In the same year the federal government also introduced two companion pieces of legislation, the Old Age Assistance Act (SC c.55) and the Blind Persons Act (SC c.38) to reaffirm its cost-sharing responsibilities for these two categories previously covered under the former Old Age Assistance Act. These acts provided federal aid to the provinces of 75% of the cost of allowances for the blind and 50% of the cost for assistance to persons aged 65–69, subject to means tests. The last piece of legislation introduced in this cycle was the War Veterans' Allowance Act, which extended benefits to veterans.

The provinces' goal of off-loading social-welfare expenditures onto the federal treasury was achieved in this cycle largely through the Old Age Security and Old Age Assistance Acts. As a result of their implementation federal expenditures on the elderly leaped from $76 million in 1951 to $323 million one year later and reached the level of $1.5 billion in 1968 (Leacy 1983, Series C79–91).

By the next cycle of federal-provincial negotiations (1953–57), the political climate had mellowed: the Liberals received a comfortable majority in the 1953 election, the CCF had suffered political setbacks, and organized labour was in the midst of internecine warfare. As a result, the primary pressure for federal welfare legislation came from provincial premiers struggling with mounting health, education and welfare expenditures. Incremental reforms were introduced in 1953, 1954 and 1956 as the federal government assumed responsibility for education costs of veterans' children (1953 SC c.27) and a heavier cost-sharing role for the disabled (1954 SC c.55), for housing (1954 SC c.23) and for the unemployed (1956 SC c.26). However, the big push from the provinces centred around the Hospital Insurance Act (1957 SC c.28).

While provincial expenditures on all social-welfare programs were increasing rapidly, expenditures on health were escalating at an even more alarming rate. All provincial expenditures on health went from $30 million in 1941 to 7 times that amount ($214 million) in 1951 and increased another 4.5 times to nearly $4 billion by 1961 (Moscovitch and Albert 1987, 22). In the 1950s, hospital funding was the primary source of the problem. Hospitals, over time, had come within the sphere of provincial public financing, while medical care remained a private service.

British Columbia, Alberta, Saskatchewan and Newfoundland dealt with the problem by developing provincial hospital-insurance programs. Manitoba and Ontario responded by commissioning studies and inquiries. In the early 1950s Ontario and Manitoba looked to Royal Commissions for audits of hospital financing and to advise on improved mechanisms for accountability. Despite the fact that both provinces were increasing their funding, hospitals continued to be plagued by deficits. In one year alone (1951), 72 hospitals in Ontario had deficits amounting to $3.5 million (Taylor 1978, 111). Provinces without a public insurance plan were increasingly involved in deficit financing of hospitals. This upset provincial budget processes and left the provinces with their traditional relationship to hospitals — limited control and regulatory powers — despite their growing fiscal responsibility.

In addition to the problem of deficit financing, there was also the problem of inadequate facilities. In 1951 the Ontario Health Survey Report had set as a minimum requirement 5.5 active treatment beds per 1,000 population. In 1954 both Ontario and Manitoba were still short of the goal at 4.4 beds per 1,000. In fact, Manitoba had one of the lowest per capita expenditures on health care in Canada (Taylor 1978, 178).

In 1954 Premier Frost of Ontario, requested a detailed study on hospital financing. This study, the *Taylor Report*, revealed that the only provinces that were meeting or exceeding the recommended ratio of 5.5 treatment beds per 1,000 were the provinces with hospital insurance plans. Furthermore, the report indicated, while these provinces succeeded in providing near universal coverage and adequate hospital funding, their costs were not rising any faster than the costs in Ontario. Being a political realist, Frost saw hospital insurance as inevitable; being a fiscal conservative, he was unwilling to absorb the costs without substantial federal assistance. Frost took the *Taylor Report* to the federal-provincial taxation conference in 1955 to lobby for a national hospital-insurance plan. Provinces with plans in operation joined Ontario in pressing the federal government to take some specific action on health insurance (Taylor 1978, 131).

The advocates of a National Hospital Insurance Plan included the electorate, the Canadian Congress of Labour and the premiers of British Columbia, Alberta, Saskatchewan, Ontario and Newfoundland. The opponents of this plan included the Canadian Medical Association, the Canadian Hospital Association, the Canadian Life-Insurance Officers Association and the Canadian Chamber of Commerce. This odd alliance of organized labour, social credit, CCF and Conservative provincial governments against important sectors of the business and professional establishment testifies to the compelling fiscal pressure being exerted upon provincial treasuries. In the end, the provinces prevailed, and the Hospital Insurance Act was proclaimed in 1957.

While the other legislation during this cycle increased federal cost-sharing, the Hospital Insurance Act was most important in extending the principle of universal entitlement and in achieving a substantial transfer of costs from the provincial to the federal treasury. Federal health expenditures rose from $62 million in the year prior to the legislation to $132 million the year after implementation. Costs continued to rise to over half a billion in 1967, the year prior to the implementation of Medicare (Leacy 1983, Series H19–34).

The third cycle of federal-provincial negotiations (1958-1963) was less eventful in terms of social-welfare activity. In 1957 a Conservative minority government was elected, a year later they received a majority, organized labour was still largely on the defensive, and the CCF seemed contained in Saskatchewan. At the federal-provincial taxation conferences attention was directed to revenue-sharing rather than expenditures, and the first federal offer of joint occupancy of the personal income-tax field was made. The federal government did live up to its election promise — amending the pension acts of 1951 by increasing the universal and the means-tested benefits from the original $40 a month to $65 by 1962. However, only one new welfare statute was enacted during these years. The Vocational Rehabilitation Act (1961 SC c.26) providing federal cost-sharing with the provinces for training of the disabled.

During these years there was discussion of extending federal involvement in health care through a national medical-insurance program (Walters 1982). However, Prime Minister Diefenbaker adeptly forestalled any difficult decisions by appointing a Royal Commission on Health in 1961. Thus, the Conservatives came to the end of their term in 1963, having played a very limited role in the construction of the welfare state. Perhaps their greatest legacy was the appointment of the Royal Commission on Health, which was destined to play a critical role in the realization of the last of the universal programs to be implemented by the federal state.

The fourth cycle (1963–66) was the decisive period for the implementation of a national welfare state. Within the four years, 1963–66, ten new welfare statutes were passed that extended federal cost-sharing in health, education and social welfare, created the first national contributory pension plan and brought in the last universal social program, Medicare. This extraordinary level of legislative activity was a response to the resurgence of social-reform pressures in the 1960s. The divided labour movement became united (1956) and formally allied with the CCF (1961) in the New Democratic Party. Labour militancy was on the upsurge, and pressures for social reform were mounting.

After seven years in opposition the Liberal party read the mood of the electorate and ran on a social-welfare platform in the election of 1963. The strategy succeeded in bringing them into power, but only as a minority. Nonetheless, the liberals began their agenda of reform immediately with a number of important but noncontroversial "housekeeping" acts. The Established Program Financing Act (1964 SC c.54) provided a formula for federal cost-sharing of educational and health expenses that eliminated the conditional grant mechanism.[13] The Canada Assistance Plan (CAP) (1966 SC c.45) provided for fifty percent cost-sharing for all provincial social-welfare costs, consolidating the separate commitments to categorical groups that had accumulated over time. This consolidation extended the coverage to include all social-assistance expenditures and replaced the provincial means test with the federal needs test, broadening eligibility to the working poor.

In the 1960s welfare rolls throughout the country expanded dramatically producing a 129% increase in the number of recipients between 1961 and 1971 (Leman 1980, 3). The implementation of CAP in 1966 substantially increased the federal share of these rising expenditures. In 1963 the Ontario Department of Public Welfare reported a recovery of $35 million from the federal government on a budget of $92 million — a 38% recovery. In 1967–68, the year after implementation of CAP, the same department reported a recovery of $115 million on a budget of $190 million — a 60% recovery (*Ontario Dept. of Public Welfare Annual Reports* 1963 and 1968).

In addition, in 1964 the federal government passed two acts that attempted to respond to the social and demographic consequences of the baby boom. The Youth Allowances Act (SC c.23) extended family allowances to children up to eighteen years of age who remained in school, and the Canada Student Loan Act (SC c.24) provided financial assistance for the first wave of the baby boom pursuing post-secondary education.

In the subsequent two years the federal government undertook to implement the Canada Pension Plan and Medicare without benefit of a majority in the house. However, much like the implementation of the universal pension plan, these major pieces of the welfare state were put into place through the combined influence of political pressure and cold hard cash. In 1965 the federal government succeeded in enacting the Canada Pension Plan Act (SC c.51) and its companion act, the Guaranteed Income Supplement (SC c.52) was passed a year later.

The process of developing a contributory pension plan was begun in 1963, taking three years of tough negotiation between the federal government and the provinces before agreement was reached. Although the provinces have always shown a great interest in the federal government assuming more responsibility for the costs of the elderly, the Canada Pension Plan became the focus of some major jurisdictional wrangling.

The federal government took a first stab in presenting a general formulation of a contributory scheme to the federal-provincial conference in July of 1963. It outlined a basic "pay-as-you-go" plan, without any federal contributions, that would come into full effect after a ten-year transitional period. In response, Quebec announced that it would develop and administer its own plan, while the other provincial "heavy weight" at the table, Ontario, was fractious (Bryden 1974, 166). A year later the federal government returned to the negotiating table with Bill C-75, which attempted to give more details and accommodate provincial interests. The primary difference in the second offer was an attempt to win provincial co-operation (accrued at the end of the ten year transition, with the offer the *half*, the $2.5 billion fund would be made available to the provinces for investment. At this point, Quebec presented their own detailed plan, which was more comprehensive than the federal scheme, with a broad range of survivor, death and disability benefits.

While the Ontario government and the insurance industry tried to provoke resistance, the overwhelming popularity of the plan among the electorate and the promise of greater federal funding eventually silenced detractors (Bryden 1974, 162). The final offer put forward by Ottawa resolved jurisdictional problems by advancing the more generous "Quebec" scheme with an opting-in or opting-out provision. Quebec, as announced in 1963, opted for their own provincial scheme, the Quebec Pension Plan. However, all of the other provinces opted-in, attracted by the increased offer of a $4.5 billion fund, *all* of which would be available for provincial investment.

This scheme did have the indirect effect of reducing future provincial expenditures on the elderly through better overall provisions for the retired. However, the direct effect upon provincial treasuries, the $4.5 billion solution, clearly won the favour of the provinces. The companion piece of legislation, the Guaranteed Income Supplement, was originally designed as a temporary measure to provide coverage for the elderly during the ten-year transition before full benefits from the contributory plan would become payable.[14]

The same year that the pension-plan negotiations were concluded, the Royal Commission on Health released its report providing the opening volley in the struggle to implement the last major statute in the Canadian welfare state. In a reversal of the process leading to the implementation of the Hospital Insurance Act, the Medicare struggle had the federal government taking the lead with the provinces doing their utmost to block the legislation. This time the federal government was aligned with the Canadian electorate, organized labour and the NDP against the opposition of the business and professional establishments as well as three provinces — Ontario, Quebec and Alberta. With the exception of Saskatchewan the other provinces took a wait-and-see attitude.

The provincial turnabout on Medicare, couched in the rhetoric of free enterprise, was largely an act of fiscal protectionism. All the provinces had assumed some of the costs of medical care for the poor in their province through their social-assistance programs. However, that was as far as most provinces wanted to go. They, along with their business and medical allies, favoured a national means-tested plan. The provinces' resistance to the federal insistence upon a universal plan was based upon straightforward cost considerations. With a universal program, provincial health-care costs would escalate even with federal cost-sharing, because universality would increase accessibility and hence utilization. Whereas provinces were willing in the 1950s to antagonize their traditional conservative constituents in order to transfer provincial hospital costs to the federal government, they stood firmly alongside that same constituency to oppose a federal program that would inevitably increase demands on their provincial treasuries.

The Medicare plan lacked the powerful monetary lever wielded in the pension plan, but it did have the influential backing of the Royal Commission on Health (the Hall Commission), which crystallized strong enough public support to sway the balance in its favour. The *Hall Commission Report*[15] provided critical legitimacy and support to a minority government faced with an economic down-turn, well-organized opposition and a waivering cabinet on the eve of implementing the largest and the last of the *Green Book Proposals*. As such it occupies a prominent position in Canadian social-welfare history.

The irony of Canadian health insurance is that, at the most politically auspicious moment for its implementation in 1944, the Liberal government shelved the plan only to revive it twenty years later in the face of one of the most well-organized opposition lobbies in Canadian social-welfare history. At the time that the Royal Commission on Health was conducting its inquiry, a major polarization was underway across Canada on the issue of health insurance. While it was generally understood and accepted that a federal-provincial health-insurance plan was on the political agenda, a clear division was developing on what such a plan would look like. In the early 1960s three provinces — Ontario, British Columbia and Alberta — had developed health insurance for the uninsurables, the low income, "poor risk" group rejected by private insurance companies. On the other hand Saskatchewan had proceeded with a universal provincial plan and, despite the hostile reaction of the medical profession, was proving it would work. The question was means-tested versus universal health insurance, and the Hall Commission was called upon to advise on the issue. The ruling of the commission in favour of universal health insurance was a serious blow to its opponents.

Buttressed with the *Hall Commission Report*, the federal government took their Medicare proposal to the federal-provincial conference in 1965. Initial provincial response was low key, with only Alberta and Quebec expressing clear opposition to a plan that would be universal, compulsory, publicly administered and portable. However, in the subsequent months during another federal election campaign, the provinces' opposition increased. The Liberals returned once again as a minority government and moved quickly to bring in their Medical Care Act (SC c.64), which passed third reading in December of 1966. Despite the apparent speed with which the program moved from proposal stage to legislation, every inch of the way was marked by opposition, and the opposition continued to mount in the two years between enactment and implementation.

The federal government did not require any constitutional amendments; thus, they proceeded to pass the legislation as an enabling act. Provinces could choose to opt in and receive fifty percent cost-sharing or opt out and receive no cost-sharing. This, of course, put the provinces in the position of providing or denying their citizens a universal health plan. The combined effect of political pressure and the fifty percent cost-sharing could not be resisted. Saskatchewan and British Columbia led the way in 1968; Nova Scotia and Manitoba followed in the spring of 1969 with the big three critics, Alberta, Ontario and Quebec, joining in the fall of the same year. By 1972 all the provinces and the two territories were in the federal Medicare plan. The provision of universal medical insurance was destined to be the federal government's single largest social-welfare expense. Prior to implementation of Medicare, federal expenditures on health in 1967 were half a billion dollars. However, by 1972 when all the provinces had entered the plan, costs rose to $1.6 billion and continued to rise steadily (Leacy 1983, Series H19–34).

Medicare, the object of the last big struggle over welfare in this period, marked an end to an era of rapidly expanding social programs. Between 1951 and 1968, twenty federal statutes were passed leading to an even greater number of provincial statutes, since the welfare state was built on joint federal-provincial programs. The pattern of legislative response can be seen in the response of Manitoba and Ontario to the federal statutes initiated in this period (see table A2.20. Joint Federal-Provincial Welfare Legislature in the Federal, Ontario and Manitoba Governments, Period III, 1940–1968). By 1968 the legislative structure for a national welfare state was in place, and a decade later the fiscal consequences of that structure became manifest. Between 1946 and 1978 GNP had increased four-fold, total government expenditures increased six-fold and social-welfare expenditures increased eighteen-fold (Moscovitch and Albert 1987, 31). The costs of mediating production and reproduction had become very high. The necessity of socializing the costs of reproduction on a national scale becomes evident when we compare the fiscal capacities of the provinces to the federal government.

Welfare Expenditures

Throughout the third period the federal government had the greatest share of the nation's revenue through their control of the two major tax fields — corporate and personal income tax. Federal resources were so much greater than provincial resources at the beginning of this period that in 1941 federal social expenditures of $150 per capita used only 8% of their budget while provincial social expenditures of $27 per capita used up 35% of their budget (Moscovitch and Albert 1987, 22–23). The necessity and inevitability of harnessing the federal treasury to the task of socializing the costs of reproduction are indicated by the sheer magnitude of the costs of state intervention in the third period.

At the beginning of this period, 1941, the social-welfare bill for health, education and welfare for Canada was $381 million. By 1977, a decade after implementation of the major welfare statutes, the social-welfare bill for the country had increased to over $63 billion (see table 13). This level of growth was only possible through socializing the costs of reproduction on a national scale. The federal universal programs and the federal-provincial cost-shared programs reviewed above were the mechanisms for nationalizing these costs.

Nationalization meant centralization; thus, the construction of the welfare state altered the relation between federal and provincial governments, as well as the relation between state and family. "The principal force behind increasing centralization in a number of countries has been the growing relative importance of social expenditures, most of which in most countries tend to be made centrally" (Bird 1970, 171). While Canada has not experienced a "classic" centralization process (particularly since the agreements in the 1960s provided greater provincial occupancy of the major tax

Table 13

Social Expenditures by Jurisdictions in
Amounts and Proportion of Overall Social Expenditures,
for Selected Years 1931–1977
(In Millions of Dollars)

Year	Federal		Provincial		Municipal		Total
	$	%	$	%	$	%	
1931	130	38	61	18	154	45	345
1941	145	38	110	29	126	33	381
1951	949	52	616	34	261	14	1,826
1961	2,238	41	2,338	43	850	10	5,425
1971	8,765	35	11,252	44	5,286	21	23,302
1977	24,357	38	28,330	45	10,704	17	63,391

SOURCES: Moscovitch and Albert 1987, 21–23, tables 5–7.

fields), we do see an unambiguous process of increasing federal responsibility for social-welfare expenditures.

Regardless of how the federal and provincial governments negotiated access to revenue, the outcomes on the expenditure side were consistent throughout the third period. All jurisdictions with taxing authority were called upon to allocate more and more of their overall expenditures to social welfare. Both the number of dollars expended and the percentage of each jurisdictional budget allocated to social expenditures increased steadily.

Social expenditures came to absorb ever greater proportions of the overall expenditures in each jurisdiction. The percentage of the federal budget committed to social expenditures rose from 29% in 1931 to 53% by 1977. The provinces and municipalities experienced a similar process of seeing an ever greater proportion of their overall budget being expended on social services, from 32% and 45% respectively in 1931 to 65% and 51% respectively in 1977 (see table 14).

At the beginning of the third period the federal and provincial government together were spending about $200 per person on social services; by the end of the period it had increased to close to $2,000 per person, and by 1977 it was nearly to $4,000 per person (see table 15).

In 1977 the average government input to an average Canadian family (two parents, two children) was $15,324.76 (4 x $3,849.90). This same year the average industrial wage was $13,089.44 (*Labour Gazette*, 1977: 578). This comparison highlights the increasing displacement of reproductive costs from employers to the state and the increasing reliance of the Canadian family upon the social wage. This massive public financing of the private family was the cost of the political and industrial stability that characterized most of the third period.

The process of mediating production and reproduction in the third period led to the development of the modern welfare state. An historic development in Canadian social history that was necessary in order to annually reallocate billions of dollars of income and services to Canadian families outside of the wage-determination process. Absorbing the costs of

Table 14
Per Cent of Jurisdictional Budget Expended
on Social Welfare, for Selected Years 1931–1977

Year	Federal*	Provincial*	Municipal
1931	29%	32%	45%
1941	8%	35%	43%
1951	26%	49%	34%
1961	34%	61%	42%
1971	41%	67%	56%
1977	53%	65%	51%

* Including transfer payments
SOURCES: Moscovitch and Albert 1987, 21–23, tables 5–7.

Table 15
Per Capita Social Expenditures by Jurisdiction
for Selected Years 1931–1977
(In Dollars)

Year	Federal	Provincial	Municipal
1931	43.24	18.38	61.62
1941	157.03	27.29	184.32
1951	260.49	89.79	350.28
1961	360.94	210.13	571.07
1971	99.14	802.13	1,793.72
1977	1,975.92	1,873.98	3,849.90

SOURCES: Moscovitch and Albert 1987, 21–22, tables 5–6.

reproduction on a national scale required the state to reorganize itself, change its taxation and expenditure patterns and alter its relation to the family. The impetus behind these dramatic social and political transitions was the necessity to accommodate reproductive requirements in wage-labour system inherently and purposefully unresponsive to those requirements. Our measure of the fundamental nature of reproductive relations and their on-going pressure on the system lies in the fact that governments throughout Canada and in other industrialized nations undertook this massive transition in social, jurisdictional and fiscal policy precisely because reproductive requirements had to be met.

Summary

State mediation of production and reproduction in this period involved a major realignment of labour and income between the two spheres. The consequences of this realignment were fundamental in terms of changes to the structure of society, the structure of the family and the structure of the labour force. The social and political unrest of the 1960s was both a symptom of and harbinger for the new society created by the substantial realignments undertaken in the post-war period. While the social reformers demanded the best of the realignment strategy, providing the impetus necessary to complete the social-welfare package promised in the 1940s, the critics and rebels in the 1960s identified the worst of the realignment strategy, the injustices and inequities upon which the social compromise of the 1950s was built. In doing so, the critics created the possibility and the context in which patriarchy would be "exposed" in the latter part of the twentieth century.

For twenty years the realignment process involved a massive flow of income into the family and an equally massive flow of female labour into the workplace. All the while this restructuring was underway, the dominant ideology extolled the nuclear family ideal — father-breadwinner, mother-homemaker. However, by the mid 1960s even the ideologues could not ignore the evidence of change — the nuclear family was on the verge of becoming a minority, birth rates were down, divorce rates were up, abortion had once again become a central social issue, and women were beginning to articulate their anger with a double work load and fifty percent pay. As women joined the ranks of the rebellious in the labour movement and the student movement, they discovered and challenged the legislation and institutions that restricted their rights and freedoms. They exposed the patriarchal practices embedded in our public institutions — discovering the dynamics of social patriarchy.

In response to this new angry constituency, the federal government appointed the Royal Commission on the Status of Women with a broad mandate "to inquire into legislation, regulations and policies that concern or affect the rights of women" (PC 1967-312, *Report of the Royal Commission on the*

Status of Women 1970, vii). Unexpectedly, the commission tapped into a public sentiment as pervasive and powerful as that which gave rise to the Social Reform Movement at the turn of the century. Much as the *Beveridge Report* became the signal document for the new welfare ideology, so the Royal Commission on the Status of Women became the bench-mark for the second wave of feminism.

The response to the Royal Commission was overwhelming. The commission received 468 briefs, 1,000 letters, 890 witnesses at public meetings and 40 specially commissioned studies (*Report of the Royal Commission on the Status of Women* 1970, ix). The commission had become the mechanism for publicly and formally placing the "women's issue" on the political agenda. As such it was an exhaustive process, fraught with differences and controversy. The seven-member commission produced five formally submitted documents: a majority report with 165 recommendations, a minority report and three separate statements by signators of the majority document identifying specific concerns, primarily around abortion.

The report contained a well-documented list of inequities and discrimination against women manifest in the workplace, in the home, in the public institutions of education, law and government and throughout government policies from taxation and childcare to immigration and citizenship. For the first time in Canadian history the patriarchal structures and assumptions of our society were examined and presented for public scrutiny. The indictment was powerful. The commission revealed the inequities upon which traditional institutions were built, acknowledged the irreversibility of women's extended role in production and gave clear warning that the consequences of women's new role would be far reaching and fundamental to the structures of our families, our work and our society.

While the Royal Commission on the Status of Women dealt with all the same symptoms of disjuncture between production and reproduction that provoked the Victorian Social Reform Movement, the response options available in the 1970s were quite different from those of the 1890s. The centralization of production and the availability of a global labour market had fundamentally changed the value of women's labour in Canada. There could be no return to the "protection" of female labour and the legislative underwriting of the support-service family structure. The recommendations and reforms resulting from the Royal Commission would further erode the legislation and policies that had allocated women's labour to reproduction. It was no longer structurally possible to "rescue" the family at the expense of women. In the struggle to liberate the individual women who had sustained and anchored the family, the contradiction of production and reproduction would reappear, in the subsequent period, as a labour crisis in the family and a demographic imbalance in the society as a whole.

The Royal Commission changed the language of Canadian social and legal policy by placing patriarchy on the political agenda. The historic problem of co-ordinating production and reproduction, work and family life, would no longer be limited to the partial expression obtained in the struggle between capital and labour over the wage. The conditions for a comprehensive and direct expression of this conflict were contained in the articulation of women's dual role in our society. Women became the literal as well as the political embodiment of the conflict between production and reproduction, their "issues" being the issues of co-ordinating the requirements and responsibilities of work and family life. By seriously considering the status of women, the Royal Commission exposed the patriarchal premises of state mediation strategies, brought closure to a period of complacency and ushered in a new wave of state intervention. As such it is fitting that this inquiry concludes this hundred year review of the relation between production, reproduction and the state.

State mediation in the third period did succeed in securing a temporary moment of balance between production and reproduction, albeit under uniquely auspicious conditions and even then at a very high cost to the treasury and the Canadian family. But it was only a moment. The third period ends, much as the previous two did, with the conditions of mediation within the period becoming the conditions of crisis in the next. What is unique about this period is the magnitude of the resources rallied to effect a "resolution" and the restructuring of reproduction permitted in the process. Events subsequent to this period suggest that the challenge of mediating the two spheres returns in crisis proportions. This time, however, fewer options are available to the state than in the third period.

PART 3

The State and the Future
of Patriarchy

The questions that remain upon completion of this historical review of family-state relations in Canada, centre around the changing patterns of state mediation and social patriarchal functions. The state does have a vested interest in supporting and sustaining patriarchal structures, because patriarchy is the means of organizing and controlling reproduction in class societies. The review of state-family relations through all three periods documents the transition from a familial patriarchal system to a social patriarchal system as a means of maintaining patriarchal family structures and, hence, of managing reproduction within a wage-labour system. As the dynamic of the wage-labour system eroded traditional patriarchal functioning, the state intervened to assume regulatory and supportive functions previously performed by the familial patriarch.

Key to the operation of patriarchy, as a set of social relations for controlling reproduction, has been its ability to structure women's access to a means of livelihood contingent upon conforming to particular reproductive policies. In wage-labour systems this amounted to keeping women economically dependent upon men so that marriage and presumably procreation would be the predominant career choice for women. The development of the support-service family structure, in which the growing division between production and reproduction was accommodated and reflected in the sexual division of labour between the male-breadwinner and the female-homemaker, marked the period of most complementary functioning of familial and social patriarchy. This was achieved through state control of the allocation of women's labour, state regulation of the disposition of children and property within families and state support of the increasingly vulnerable reproductive unit.

In the third period, however, the state's ability to control the allocation of women's labour was lost as a result of the global restructuring of production. The global organization of production created a global labour supply (Caporaso 1987; Kolko 1988). The existence of a vast, underpaid labour supply in the Third World altered the significance of women's reproductive labour within industrialized countries. Employers no longer needed to be bound by pro-natalist restrictions on female labour within a particular nation state in order to secure an adequate labour supply. The preferred option of the third and subsequent periods involved the movement of capital to the most abundant and least costly sources of labour (Cox 1987). This led to a kind of global division of reproductive labour. Women in industrialized nations produce low-quantity, high cost, highly skilled labour, while Third World women living within a familial patriarchal mode of reproduction produce high-quantity, low-cost, unskilled, labour (Meillasoux 1981, 138). The cost of labour is still effected by supply; however, supply is now measured globally and no longer domestically.

From a state perspective, capital's labour supply strategies outgrew the boundaries of state control. While the state still played an important role in controlling the supply of labour within the nation state, through immigration policies and labour law, the largest labour supply issues were resolved outside of state control, through multinational corporations' pursuit of lower-waged Third World labour. Within the industrialized nation state, previous strategies of promoting domestic labour supplies (through the allocation of women's labour to reproduction) became untenable. In the face of this reality, the state abandoned its regulatory function. The social patriarchal function of controlling women's labour devolved, in large part, from the state to the market place.

Questions concerning the continued connection between the state and patriarchy centre around the outcomes of the devolution of control over women's labour from the state to the market place. I have documented the manner in which this process served to erode the support-service family structure. Women's employment erodes male-female economic interdependency and, in keeping with Levi Strauss's (1971) analysis, one would expect it to erode the material imperative to heterosexuality, marriage and procreation. Procreation, the primary product of patriarchal families, becomes increasingly optional in industrialized nations as major labour supply issues are resolved globally. If the primary mechanism of maintaining control of reproduction is eroded and the primary product of that control becomes replaceable by Third World labour, wherein lies the state's interest in patriarchy?

Evidence of the state's changing commitment to patriarchy begins in the third period, as the state abandoned legislation restricting the use of female labour in production. As the state lost control over the allocation of women's labour, it abandoned many of its former pro-natalist statutes. By the end of the third period, a further dismantling of patriarchal legislation occured with the liberalization of divorce and abortion statutes and the legalization of birth control.

The restructuring of production required the state to abandon its control of women's labour. This, however, did not result in an abandonment of patriarchy, for employers greatly benefited from the conscious patriarchal structuring of the labour market (Armstrong and Armstrong 1984a). The review of labour legislation in the third period suggests that the state was complicit in the perpetuation of discriminatory hiring and remuneration policies. While patriarchal practices proliferated in the market place, during the third period, the Royal Commission on the Status of Women signalled the fact that state complicity would not continue to go unchallenged. Thus, further evidence of the state's ambiguous commitment to patriarchy is seen in its response to the emergence of the women's movement as a major political force in the fourth period (1969–92).

During the 1970s and 1980s the state was subject to pressure from national women's organizations to dismantle discriminatory laws, policies and practices and to develop programs to compensate for structurally entrenched gender biases in a broad range of public institutions. The invocation of the state's legal apparatus to undo gender injustices it previously reinforced and sanctioned was dramatic evidence of the changing relation of the state to patriarchy. Changes in labour, criminal, constitutional and family law in the 1970s and 1980s has repositioned the state from the role of benevolent patriarch in the 1950s to the self-professed champion of sexual equality in the 1980s. This new social expectation is thorough-going. Not only does recent legislation provide for monitoring and prosecution in cases of sexual discrimination, it also requires the implementation of compensatory programs. Affirmative action programs, pay equity and employment equity legislation are the most recent examples of this direction (Findley 1990).

The turnabout of the state on gender equality issues was neither automatic nor easy. Each area of legislative change, from family law reform to the inclusion of gender equality in the charter of rights, was hard fought for by women's groups across the country. While I do not claim that these changes have been completely successful in achieving the goals intended, they exist as compelling evidence that the state has been subject to mounting political pressure to undo and reverse its relation to a broad range of social patriarchal operations.

However, in the face of these dramatic changes, there exists some equally compelling evidence of a continued interest of the state in patriarchal relations. This lies in the fact that the patriarchal family remains the sole means of keeping the costs of reproduction largely privatized. Familial patriarchy ensures that the primary costs of generationally reproducing the labour force lie within the family. At the same time that the patriarchal family is dependent upon state subsidization, it also defines the limits to which reproductive costs are socialized by supplying free reproductive (female) labour (Finch and Groves 1983). As the fiscal consequences of the welfare state became apparent and overwhelming during the economic recession of the 1970s, the state attempted to reduce its commitment to subsidizing the reproductive unit. In the 1980s we witnessed a reversal of the process documented in the first three periods. The pressure to displace the costs of reproduction onto ever larger resource bases met its limit in the economic recession and political reaction of the late 1970s. The state now seeks to off-load its increasingly weighty responsibilities for reproductive costs (Moscovitch and Albert 1987, 40).

The contraction of state responsibility for subsidizing reproduction is synonymous with privatization and correlates with expansions in regulatory legislation. During the 1970s, we saw significant expansion of family legislation, a key feature of which is the reassertion of the principle of the primacy of familial obligation. The erosion of the support-service marriage structure resulted in increasing divorce rates, while the disadvantaged position of women in the labour force led to increased numbers of women living in poverty. Family law reforms, fought for by women's organizations, aimed at increasing women's claim to family assets and improving the procedures for maintenance enforcement. These feminist goals dovetailed with the state's growing concern over rising social expenditures and its interest in reasserting the principle of privatizing reproductive costs.

The recent aggressive pursuit of maintenance enforcement has been a major privatizing strategy of the state in the face of the increasing number of women living in poverty. It is unambiguously a process of state policing of family obligations for reproductive costs. While its individual impact is undeniably beneficial for women and children who are economically dependent, the social impact harkens back to the state use of family law in the 1920s. While it seems just that husbands and fathers should behave in an economically responsible way to their family after separation and that, if necessary, the power of the state be invoked to ensure that they do, there is a concern that within a privatizing strategy individual males will be held responsible to compensate for the consequences of a structurally biased social system (Foote 1989). The problem with this possibility is less moral than practical — few men are in a position to be able to maintain a former family unit in a manner that corrects and compensates for the structured economic barriers to women's economic independence. Thus, in light of intensified state interest in reprivatization, there is the concern that maintenance enforcement not be used to permit or justify cutbacks in social expenditures. In addition, there is the concern that maintenance enforcement not be pursued against the wishes of the dependants as a precondition to access to social benefits. These are not outlandish scenarios; these were the consequences of regulatory family law focussed on privatization as in the second period.

Further privatizing strategies are evident in recent federal and provincial initiatives, invariably couched in progressive rhetoric but consistently adopted as cost-cutting measures. De-institutionalization initiatives move toward the reprivatization of the care of persons with disabilities and infirmities, displacing the costs of their care from the state to the family. Similarly, other cost cutting measures, reducing hospital stays, slowing the growth rate of personal care homes, cutting back on homemaker services and meals on wheels, all result in returning the care of the sick and elderly to private family income or labour resources (Aronson 1986). Attempts at de-indexing the pension and the recent elimination of universal Family Allowance have the unabashed goal of reducing state responsibility for reproductive costs. The success of all of these privatizing strategies is dependent upon the continued functioning of a patriarchal family, in which free reproductive labour is an accepted and enforced social convention.

The restructuring of state fiscal and jurisdictional relations, particularly as it was proposed in the Meech Lake Accord, serves to cap federal responsibility and revisit health and welfare costs upon the provinces. The provinces, caught as usual in the fiscal-jurisdictional squeeze, seek to reprivatize reproductive costs wherever possible. This contraction of state support points to its sustained interest in and support of the patriarchal family structure. Where else and how else will it succeed, even in part, in the reprivatization of reproductive costs, unless there is a family structure in which free reproductive labour is an accepted and enforced social convention?

The evidence on the nature of the state's relation to patriarchy is mixed, to say the least. Conditions have changed dramatically since 1884. The one factor that does, however, remain unchanged is the contradictory structuring of production and reproduction and the continued necessity of state mediation. I suspect that the current confused pattern of state policies on family and patriarchy reflects the consequences of earlier mediation strategies. As the state attempted to contain the contradiction between production and reproduction by absorbing their costs and consequences, the state also absorbed the contradictions. Thus, while the productive-reproductive dynamic has become globally polarized, the costs and consequences of this polarization remain and reverberate within our nation. As a result the relations between the family and the state, familial and social patriarchy, become increasingly contradictory.

These contradictions provide some scope for further dismantling patriarchal structures, as well as some disturbing possibilities for reprivatization. The theoretical and empirical questions generated by this study centre around these dual possibilities. What are the limits to which the state can be pushed to dismantle gender discrimination within the system? What are the limits to which the state can pursue a policy of reprivatizing reproductive costs, and how will this interact with the state's public stance as champion of gender equality?

As the contradiction between production and reproduction now becomes manifest in negative population growth, dependency ratio problems (on a national, rather than familial scale) and state fiscal crises, how will patriarchy and the family fit into state mediating strategies? Given the combined problems of a shrinking adult productive population and the high cost of producing them domestically, I anticipate a two-pronged response on the part of the state: first, the immigration of adult productive labour and, second, the reprivatization of a significant portion of the costs of domestically produced labour. In short, state mediation strategy of the fourth period amounts to a displacement of the costs of reproduction, a process we have traced for the past one hundred years. The federal state, like families and provinces before them, seeks to off-load its responsibility for reproductive costs. However, displacement of the costs of reproduction from the vantage point of the nation state moves in two directions. In the first instance, the case of immigration, reproductive costs are displaced onto the donor state, whose social investment in the production of labour is exploited by the recipient state. In the second instance, the case of reprivatization, reproductive costs are simply revisited upon the Canadian family. Both options seem to imply a continued role for patriarchy, to produce the large quantities of Third World labour and provide the family ideology and structure necessary for the reprivatization of reproductive costs and services in Canada.

The countervailing pressures at work in Canada today — the demand for women in production and the reprivatization of reproductive costs — are bringing the contradiction between production and reproduction to the forefront of contemporary political and social debates. The oblique language of the past — the social reformers preoccupation with "race suicide," organized labour's demand for a fair wage, welfare advocates' talk of universal risk — was a discourse of symptoms of the contradiction between production and reproduction. The women's movement, a product of the collision of the competing demands of production and reproduction in women's every day lives, is articulating this conflict more directly. A more accurate "naming of the problem" enhances our ability to develop more effective strategies for change.

Strategies for Change

This book is about the control of reproduction because the manner in which a society manages and controls reproduction determines women's status and choices in life. Consequently, feminist strategies for change must develop from an analysis of this process of control. This history of the transition from familial to social patriarchy is the history of changing patterns of control of reproduction in Canada. However, it is also a history of resistance to the commodification of human life intrinsic to the wage-labour system. It is the history of constructing conditions and allocating resources necessary for reproduction in an economic order that makes no such accommodation. This study documents how the state has responded to successive waves of social reform/resistance to the commodification of human life. It also documents how this was accomplished through the construction of social patriarchy. It is a history of progress and repression.

The double-edged sword of state intervention is located in its mandate to mediate the contradiction between the demands of production and the requirements of reproduction. This mandate implicates the state in complex and contradictory dynamics that contain the dual possibilities of progress (resisting the commodification of human life) and exploitation (shoring up patriarchy to do so). In the context of these dual possibilities, the state is a contested terrain. I understand the women's movement both as part of the tradition of resistance to the commodification of human life and as a radical departure from this tradition in its refusal to tolerate "reforms" constructed as the expense of women, for example, the support-service marriage "solution" of the past.

Feminism is fundamentally a struggle against the commodification of human life, particularly as it is made possible on the backs of and from the wombs of women. Feminism is also, at its core, a struggle over who controls reproduction. Even feminists most sceptical of the state, call for legislative control of reproductive technology rather than permit the control of human life to rest in the hands of a medical-industrial complex. This call for legislative control of reproductive technology has a common thread with the call of nineteenth-century feminists for legislative restrictions on the employment of women and children and a common thread with the labour movement's struggle for a fair wage. All are defenses against the encroachment of the market place upon reproduction.

The contradiction between production and reproduction has been politically manifest throughout the twentieth century as successive waves of public pressure to socialize the costs of reproduction, culminating in the modern welfare state. The women's movement sustains this tradition in its struggles to resist the dismantling of the welfare state. In addressing the strategic debates within feminism — how we approach, use and resist the state — it is important to understand what feminism has in common with reform movements of the past, what is distinctive about feminists struggles today, and how the changing dynamics between production-reproduction and the state raise questions about the location of our struggles and the need for new strategies.

The feminist debate on the state, as it is currently framed, presents two views of state intervention. Some feminists emphasize the co-optive consequences of state intervention, while others suggest that state intervention can, under certain circumstances, contribute to progressive reform and favour women's interests. My analysis suggests a dual potential in state intervention. I have documented circumstances in which legislation has benefited women and circumstances in which legislation has limited and restricted women. Sometimes the interests of women and the state converge, sometimes not.

In this analysis I have documented the state's active involvement in dismantling old familial patriarchal rights and practices to facilitate a better fit between production and reproduction. Old rules of patriarchal domination, which were necessary or tolerable under the old pro-natalist familial patriarchal system, became obsolete and/or impediments to the new social order. In these cases the state did act to undo the old relations, because it had become in the interests of state (as well as women) to do so. In short, the perpetuation of the old relations had become costly to the state (as well as to women). Under these circumstances, history has indicated that it is possible to introduce reforms in the interests of women and to use the power of the state to do so. Some of the better known examples are the Married Women's Property Act, the Dower Act and the Maintenance Enforcement Act, to name a few. In these cases, the state is primarily motivated by the need to minimize the number of dependants upon the public purse. However, this motivation coincided with women's desire to own their own property, keep their own wage and, in the case of Maintenance Enforcement, have the father of their children contribute to the costs of raising their children. One need not argue that the state and women have the same interest (since this is extremely unlikely) but only that they have a shared interest in dismantling laws, practices and conventions of an old patriarchal order that have always been costly to women and, over time, became costly to the state.

While I have equated the ascendance of social patriarchy with the construction of the welfare state, this does not indicate that the dismantling of old (familial) patriarchal structures had been completed by the end of the third period. In fact, I would argue that many of the state-focussed struggles women are engaged in today involve the dismantling of old rules of familial patriarchal dominance. For example, the criminalization of abortion has its roots and logic in the old pro-natalist patriarchal system. It makes less sense in contemporary society, in which women's productive labour is more highly valued than her reproductive labour. Nevertheless, it took years of sustained political struggle by women to remove this legal vestige of an old patriarchal order. The decriminalization of abortion in 1990 is understandable in terms of the mounting political pressure created by the women's movement to make it too costly (politically) for the state to attempt to retain a pro-natalist policy in an anti-natalist period. In the absence of any structural imperative to maintain the old law, women were able strategically to structure a convergence of the interests of the state and their own. Women clearly are the agents of change, but the determination of the progressive or co-optive impact of state intervention lies in the structural possibility for a convergence of interests.

Recent state involvement in the wife abuse issue is another example of women strategically structuring a convergence of interests. The social tolerance of wife abuse is also a vestige of the old familial patriarchal system, in which the patriarch had ultimate control over the lives and well being of his wife and family. However, as a result of the active and aggressive lobbying of women across Canada for over a decade, it has now become evident to the state that the perpetuation of wife abuse is costly, both in terms of the social costs of the sustained victimization of large segments of the population and in terms of the political costs (legitimacy of the state). If this has, once again, structured a convergence of women's interests with the interests of the state, then it is a reasonable, indeed, preferred strategy for the women's movement to use the full force of the state, its money, its legal apparatus, its political legitimacy to provide more support and more options to battered women and women at risk.

The state's mandate to co-ordinate the competing pressures from production and reproduction is what creates the possibility of converging interests. Within each strategy of accommodation, there are progressive and regressive elements. The state has participated in the construction of progressive reforms, including the dismantling of laws and conventions of the old patriarchal order, the socialization of the costs of reproduction and the facilitation of women's entry into the labour force. These situations capture the more progressive or supportive aspects of state mediation and suggest that the use of the state as a force for change is a reasonable and progressive strategy in such cases. To cite such instances and pursue such reforms does not, however, deny that there are other circumstances in which state interventions are clearly at the expense of women. The contraction of the welfare state and the move to reprivatize the costs of reproduction exists today as one of the most serious threats to the interests of women.

This book traces the transition from familial to social patriarchy in the centralization of authority and support for reproduction within the state. As the state evolves, in its relation to women and children as provider and patriarch, one can understand why it has become the terrain of feminist struggles in the twentieth century. Over the last two decades, feminists in Canada have developed strong national organizations to defend their interests at the level of the nation state. While women continue to struggle at all levels — in the home, at work, in civic and provincial arenas — the existence of organizations like the National Action Committee on the Status of Women (NAC), the Legal Education and Action Fund (LEAF) or the Coalition on Reproductive Choice (CORC) attest to the growing focus of attention on the nation state. However, just as we are getting good at it, we must confront dramatic structural changes in the organization of production and reproduction that may shift the terrain of struggle away from the nation state in the twenty-first century.

The global division of reproductive labour and the global organization of production are manifest in the concurrent dynamics of economic continentalization and political decentralization. The dismantling of the modern welfare state is a symptom of these more fundamental shifts in the organization of production and reproduction. Events in Europe and to a lesser extent in North America attest to the fact that economic continentalism presumes or provokes political decentralization. A dilution of the powers of the nation state seems essential to continental economic strategies. On the other hand, history indicates that the development and operation of a welfare state is premised on a centralization of powers at the federal level. As the two processes proceed in opposite directions, we understand that the global pursuit of lower-waged labour and the continental organization of production is the latest strategy for capital's flight from the costs of reproducing labour. The alienation of production from reproduction on a global scale.

Once capital has outstripped the nation state, the compelling question becomes locating the effective terrain for resistance to this global commodification of human life. It is questionable whether the nation state will continue to be the critical site of resistance to this commodification and women's struggle for equality when the organization of production outstrips the boundaries of its jurisdictional control. And if responsibility for welfare is devolved to the provinces, will this shift some of women's organizing strategies to a more local base? Won't it also be necessary to pursue strategies to link us to women in other nations? With the contradictory structuring of production and reproduction on a global scale, women will face a new set of strategic challenges in the twenty-first century. The new terrains of women's struggle may well be the local as well as supra-national organizations from which women can confront and contest the global division of reproductive labour that keeps all women subject to different aspects of patriarchal control.

APPENDICES

Appendix 1: A Note on the Research Process

This study grew out of my interest in the fact that the state, its legal system and its bureaucracy has become the critical terrain on which women's rights are contested. The location of feminist struggle suggested a strong connection between the state and patriarchy. The variable outcomes of these struggles suggested a complex, perhaps contradictory, relation between the state and patriarchy. My motivation in undertaking this study was political, as well as scholarly. I wanted to understand the nature of the state's connection to patriarchy in order to develop strategies that would maximize women's gains and minimize women's losses in their struggle with the state. From the beginning my approach was shaped by the important linkage I perceive between theory — research-policy — and practice. I wanted to inform my practice through a better theoretical understanding of the connection between the state and patriarchy and with evidence on how that connection operated over time. Therefore, I undertook to study the relation between the institution structured by patriarchy, the family and the institution that has become the terrain of struggle over patriarchy, the state.

The immediate problem I faced was the selection of a theory that would provide the focus I needed to address my concerns. In making my choice, I was led by two very specific concerns: the necessity of maintaining a central focus on reproduction and the necessity of the model to speak to the linkages between theory-research-policy-practice, since my motive was grounded in the intersection of my political and my academic interests. I required a theory sufficiently grounded in material reality to make explicit the political interests and policy implications of the processes I studied.

I was aware of the need to break out of old problematics. I wanted strong theoretical direction in order to resist the tendency to economic reductionism endemic to historical materialist analyses. I selected a dual-systems theory because it met my requirements of being materially grounded and maintaining a central focus on reproduction. It also met my requirement of keeping policy issues at the forefront of analysis, because it is a theory that identifies a very specific reproductive mandate for the state. While the basic premise of a dual-systems theory is simple and straightforward, its focus on production and reproduction as the base of society, the application of dual systems, is not simple.

Dual systems is a demanding model, not only because it introduces many more variables and indicators to be considered, but because it draws our attention to new relationships and dynamics. Dual systems provides a critical focus (reproduction) for breaking out of old problematics. Every draft analysis that did succumb to economic reductionism, which lost sight of reproduction, was so obviously short of the mark that it stood out, much as a wrong note in a melody cannot be missed. The outcome was a searching reconsideration of the historical materials, innumerable rewrites and re-analyses of each period. This project proceeded as a series of successive approximations until reproduction came into focus. I was conscious at all stages of the interplay between theory, research and analysis.

Given the dual focus on production and reproduction, my first step was to read the separate histories of these two processes in Canada. I read the history of production in studies of Canadian industrialization, labour force formation, unionization, monopolization and class struggle. I read the more fragmented history of reproduction in demographic studies, histories of the women's movement and the reform movement, analyses of family law and the formation of the welfare state. Through these sources I was able to map out parallel histories, key events in each sphere and key indicators of change within each sphere. Through this process I was able to identify the key structural and social indicators of change necessary for my analysis. I was also able to identify time frames in which enough changes were occurring within each sphere to provide some evidence of impact or intersection between the two spheres.

With a rough idea of time frame and critical indicators, I began a review of state activities that spoke to or were seen to speak to these changes. I began with the broadest possible search, looking at house debates, a wide range of legislation, all available inquiries, government departmental reports and private papers. From this very wide search, which I conducted at the national archives in order to have access to federal and provincial papers, I began to narrow the search using three criteria: What could be done in a reasonable period of time? Which government activities best captured the intersection between production and reproduction? Which government activities had a sufficient frequency of occurrence and/or change to provide an adequate number of observations?

The first criterion directed me to select specific jurisdictions rather than attempt to do a study of all of Canada. My selection was informed by both practical and academic considerations. The three jurisdictions I chose made practical sense because they were accessible in language and location and had good records throughout the eighty-four years under review. The specific selection of Ontario and Manitoba was made with the idea that I might capture some interesting information about the flow of legislative influence between a more- and a less-developed industrialized province. The inclusion of the federal government was necessary because of the location of welfare legislation during the third period.

The second criterion, derived from my theoretical perspective, led me to select state activities that dealt most directly with intersections between production and reproduction, specifically with regard to the regulation of labour and resource flows within and between the two spheres. As a result, a large number of statutes included in my preliminary investigation, such as legislation concerning education, immigration and juvenile delinquency were not included for more detailed analysis. While all of these statutes had some impact on reproduction or production, they did not meet the criteria of being good measures of the intersection between the two spheres.

The third criterion led me to select areas in which there was enough state activity to provide a sufficient number of observations. My decision not to focus on federal legislation regulating marriage, divorce, birth control and abortion was made largely because activity in these areas was sporadic — often fifty or sixty years would pass without any new legislation or any significant amendments. Thus, while I began with a large collection of statutes, I was able to focus in on three areas — family, labour and welfare law — that best measured the intersection between production and reproduction and were characterized by fairly continuous activity over the eighty-four years studied.

Having decided on the legislative focus of my study, the next task was to add this information to the parallel histories of production and reproduction. At this stage I was still working with the larger events rather than the details of changes within the three entities — production, reproduction and the state. For example, I had collected all new statutes in the three legislative areas, but I had yet to research amendments, inquiries and bureaucracies. Putting the history of production, reproduction and legislation side by side, I traced the sequence of major events in all three spheres. Through this process patterns began to emerge. These patterns suggested to me that the ongoing "misfit" between production and reproduction was manifest in quite different ways over the eighty-four years I reviewed. From these observations I decided to divide my analysis into periods to provide a better focus on the key events occurring over the large, initially undifferentiated time frame under consideration.

The periods gave form to the task as well as order to the content. I proceeded to structure my research by period. Because each period appeared to deal with a different manifest problem and a different intervention strategy, this knowledge helped to guide me to the most relevant primary materials I would need. I began my research of a period by immersing myself in all secondary sources that dealt with the major events of the period. I felt it was necessary to have a good grounding in the history of each period. Because the history of reproduction is often buried in unlikely places and because the idea of intersections between production and reproduction is often unfamiliar, I began with the assumption that useful data could be found almost anywhere.

After a broad general reading of the history of the period, I began a process of researching primary materials to flesh out the details of events mentioned in passing in the secondary sources. At this stage I was seeking more information on the structural and social indicators of change within production and reproduction. For example, I spent time researching labour newspapers to get further information on labour's attitude to women's employment. The labour newspaper *The Voice* was a valuable source of information on this topic during the first women's strike called in Winnipeg at the turn of the century. Other important primary sources were the reports of charitable organizations that housed destitute women and abandoned children in the first two periods.

From this detailed reading of the primary and secondary materials, I identified indicators of the manifest tension between production and reproduction and the social or political articulation of these tensions within each period. Against this political-economic-demographic backdrop, I then began to collect evidence of state intervention. The major sources of information were inquiries, statutes and departmental reports. While I presented these events in the chronological order of their occurrence in my analysis, I began the research with the statutes. The statutes are the best starting point because they identify what the government did in fact do, saving me from the distraction of researching a whole variety of policies and plans that never reached fruition. I began with *what* the government did, then went backward to the inquiries and commissions to research *why* the government acted on these issues, then forward again to the departmental reports to research *how*, the government enforced the legislation.

Once I began the exhaustive search of enactments and amendments, it became evident that the sheer volume of activity was prohibitive. Labour and child-welfare legislation, which began as a few acts with a few sections and perhaps half a dozen clauses, became ever more complex over time, filling fifty pages of the statute book, involving dozens of sections and hundreds of clauses. It became clear that my goal of following the sequence of change over time could only be achieved through further selection within each legislative field.

In narrowing my focus to specific sections and clauses of family, labour and welfare law, two criteria were used. First, I wanted to focus on those acts or clauses that captured the process of centralizing authority and responsibility (for production and/or reproduction) within the state. Second, I also wanted to focus on those acts or clauses that identified the state's role in mediating labour and resource allocations between production and reproduction. In the case of family law, the first criterion was most relevant and directed my attention to the acts or clauses that dealt with the disposition of property and children. In the case of labour law, I selected statutes that specified distinctions between male and female labour or protected labour's wage rights (minimum wage) as good measures of the state's mediation of labour and resource allocations between the two spheres. Later, in the third period the Labour Relations Act served as a good indicator of centralizing responsibility within the state. Finally, in the case of welfare law, I selected two types of acts or clauses because of their relevance to the two criteria. Child-welfare law provided a good measure of centralizing authority over the family and within the state, while redistributive statutes (e.g., Old Age Pension Act or the Mothers' Allowances Act) spoke both to the issues of centralized responsibility and the reallocation of resources.

While I undertook the research of each period as a discrete project, and I researched each period in roughly the same sequence (a general search of secondary materials, followed by a search of primary materials, concluding with a search of government documents), there was, nevertheless, much back and forth between the periods and research stages as the analysis proceeded. The analysis process, which I described as a series of successive approximations, meant frequent returns to primary and secondary materials for more information on the reproductive issues/dynamic of a period. The appearance of major anomalies or big gaps in information as I researched the statutes led me back to primary and secondary sources for further clues or led me to broaden my search to include a wide range of seemingly unrelated government activities. Thus, while I organized myself with a specific research schedule, there was in fact a great deal of fluidity between the periods and stages of collecting and interpreting the information because of the challenges presented by the data.

Two particular problems I encountered — the suspension of dower in western Canada and the introduction of family allowances — illustrate the actual fluidity in the research process. The case of the suspension of dower claims in western Canada presented an anomaly that demanded explanation. While most of eastern Canada was systematically strengthening women's dower rights, all of the western Canada was suspending them. The explanation lay in the interest of government and large landholders in eliminating any encumbrances on land-claims when a new land claim system (the Torrens system) was being introduced. However, discovering the connection between a land-claim system and dower rights was truly a challenge because their connection was legislatively obscure.

At the time of its repeal, 1885, dower did not exist as a specific act, but rather as a number of clauses reflecting British common law and was found in various acts regarding inheritance. The reason for its sudden repeal from all acts concerning inheritance was not at all evident in any developments in the areas of family, labour or welfare law. Having exhausted all sources of information in these three legislative fields, I began a detailed review of primary and secondary sources to see if there were any clues to this development. Having come up empty handed, I then undertook a complete reading of the *Hansard Report* for the years 1884 and 1885. I discovered one sentence by one member of the House that alluded to a connection between Torrens and dower. This was the first good lead I had.

With the suggestion of a link between Torrens and dower,

I returned to secondary sources to discover that the Torrens land-claim system was found only in western Canada and not in eastern Canada. With further digging through land-registry reports, I discovered that the Torrens system guaranteed, upon issue of land titles, uncontestable ownership of property. The new system required the government registry department to settle all claims before issue of title. Thus, anticipating and following the Real Property Act (SM 1885), which established the Torrens system, a whole series of enactments and repeals of legislation occurred to clarify and often eliminate claims based on old laws and agreements. Dower rights, which constituted a major encumbrance upon clarifying land claims, were, therefore, repealed.

This research experience reinforced my notion that you may find important pieces of the history of reproduction in the most unlikely places — land registry departments had not been at the top of my research list. It also illustrates how much work was sometimes required for a very few facts. Explaining the anomaly of dower suspension in western Canada took two months of intensive research to produce what appears here simply as a two paragraph explanation.

Another research puzzle was presented by the unusual history of Family Allowance legislation in Canada. The statute books indicated that the statute was enacted in 1944; however, when I went to the national archives to research its development, there was no evidence of it in the records of the Department of Health and Welfare. After reading all of their official documents from 1942 to 1944 and coming up empty handed, I began a search of materials relating to labour or family law. Within the labour materials, it appeared again as a suggestion contained within the majority report of the Inquiry into the War Labour Board. However, there was no recorded discussion of the issue arising in the public hearings, nor any explanation offered about why it would become the subject matter of the Labour Board Review. Having no success with these documents, I then turned to the private papers of the Minister of the Department of Health and Welfare Ian Mackenzie and the diary of Prime Minister King.

Most of the papers in Ian Mackenzie's file revealed his intense interest in a National Health Plan; only one small note had any reference to Family Allowances. The Minister had made a note (undated) to remind himself to talk to the Deputy Minister of Finance about "all this talk about family allowances." This reference to the Department of Finance led me to their files as well as to the files of the Economic Advisory Council of which the Deputy Minister of Finance was a member. It was in these, somewhat unlikely sources, that the history of the design and planning of the Family Allowances Act as well as the political motivations for implementing it were to be found. The King diaries provided further information on the political process of convincing cabinet of the necessity of family allowances and the strategy for presenting the legislation to the public.

These two examples, dower and family allowances, illustrate the necessity of undertaking a broad search of materials and the importance of using multiple sources of information. The latent functions of certain legislation are not usually identified in official inquiries or government reports. The more sensitive the material the more likely its history is sealed in confidential government documents. The history of the Family Allowances Act is an excellent case in point.

While collecting the data presented some special problems, analyzing the data was often the more difficult task. It was at this point that theoretical direction was essential and cross-period comparisons helpful in maintaining a focus on reproduction. Some periods were much easier to analyze than others. For example, in the first period it was easier to focus on reproductive issues because the Social

Reform Movement was preoccupied with birth rates and infant mortality, and government documents were filled with long commentaries on the negative impact of industrialization and women's employment on birth rates. Reproductive concerns dominated public discourse and public documents. In fact, as long as the state was involved in supporting the support-service marriage structure, it was fairly easy to discern the reproductive component in state activities.

In contrast the third period, particularly the post-war years, involved a real struggle to keep my focus on reproduction. During this period reproduction disappeared from public discourse, the state abandoned its support of the support-service marriage structure, and the usual sequence of state intervention changed. Ironically, at the point in time in which the Canadian state was launching its largest schemes to socialize the costs of reproduction, the issue of reproduction was disappearing from public documents and public discourse. While the Social Reform Movement of the first period was unambiguously oriented to reproduction, the welfare philosophy of the third period was not consciously familistic. The pervasive demand for state intervention to provide income security and social services in the post-war years was not expressed or experienced as a specifically reproductive or familial issue. The demands for social reform in this period were expressed in general humanitarian terms that obscured the reproductive origins of those demands.

Throughout the history I reviewed, it appears that public consciousness about reproduction is directly related to the degree to which it is embattled or in crisis. The concurrence of the post-war baby boom and the economic boom obscured any awareness of conflict between production and reproduction. In addition, people tended to define matters that are private and familial as reproductive. Thus, as the costs and some of the functions of reproduction became socialized, public awareness of these costs or functions as reproductive tended to diminish. The language of reform in the post-war period was that of "universal risk" and "income security," a language remote from the day-to-day experience of family life.

In addition to the fact that the language and consciousness of social reformers obscured the issue of reproduction, the actual processes of state intervention were opaque. The withdrawal of state support for the support-service marriage structure required the state to cease to intervene, to let the market process proceed without interruption. This became a much more difficult measurement problem than documenting intervention. The state's prior involvement in supporting the old marriage structure generated a large paper trail of documentation, inquiries, legislation and bureaucratic reports, all of which identified the nature of the state's concerns and the anticipated effect of intervention. To identify what the state ceased to do left no paper trail at all. Thus, the dismantling of the support-service marriage structure appears to occur independent of state activity or interest.

Finally, in the post-war period the actual sequence of state intervention changed. In each previous period my analysis began with the documentation of a rising tension or crisis between production and reproduction and the identification of the options pursued by the state to ameliorate the crisis. The post-war period began with fifteen years of uninterrupted growth in production, reproduction and state development. However, in the absence of all the usual measures of crisis, the state was on a course of increasing intervention, particularly through the Labour Relations Act and welfare legislation. It was difficult to explain galloping state intervention without a crisis and with a booming economy and rising birth rates.

This was the period in which I most thoroughly succumbed to economic reductionism. Over and over, I produced draft analyses that did not get beyond the economics of the welfare state. At this point my theoretical perspective was most valuable and most frustrating, as it revealed each draft as so evidently inadequate. Through a labourious process of rereading primary and secondary sources, through lining up and comparing the events of the first and second period with the third and through rethinking the implications of the erosion of the support-service marriage structure, I began to locate the reproductive issues. Perhaps the single most useful document in this process was the *Report of the Royal Commission on the Status of Women* (1968), which brought me back in touch with the contradictions between production and reproduction.

Focussing on the consequences of the state's new mediating strategy, I began to work backward, tracing the origins of the mid 1960s crisis, which provoked the Royal Commission on the Status of Women, back to the legislation and activities of the state in the 1950s and early 1960s. The contradictions between production and reproduction were still there — covered by economic prosperity and buried beneath layers of bureaucratic management. The manifestation of the contradiction had changed; its new expression was to be found in the cross-sphere intensification of women's labour. I began to reread the post-war period as a crisis forestalled by the incredible economic growth and vast reallocations of income (welfare), a crisis emerging in the increased intensification of women's labour and a crisis expressed in the pages of the *Report of the Royal Commission on the Status of Women*. The commission's report documented declining birth rates, rising demands for abortion, a rising cost of living and increasing numbers of women living in poverty. From the collision of work and family responsibilities in the lives of women in the late 1960s, I was able to reconstruct the reproductive issues of the third period, as well as the processes and pressures that contributed to its obscurity.

In outlining the process of my research it is apparent that it was a lengthy and time-consuming project. However, in concluding I would like to suggest that it was a good process for learning about the nature of the relationship between the family and the state and more specifically about the operation of patriarchy in the state. Since my initial interest in the study was political as well as academic, the critical test for me was how well this research informed my practice. Having worked for five years within the state, I had to put my knowledge to work in very pragmatic ways, largely working in the area of wife abuse. My seemingly remote historical studies became a very practical source of information as I undertook my struggles within and with the state. Identifying the different dynamics of patriarchy made me aware of the contradictions in the operation of patriarchy in the state. Seeing social patriarchy as complex and contradictory, rather than undifferentiated and monolithic, has permitted me to identify where contradictions can be located and/or cultivated in order to promote women's interests. I can refer to a past in which the state actively participated in dismantling particular familial patriarchal practices as a guide to determining where such dismantling might occur again.

Appendix 2: Tables

Table A2.1

Protective Labour Legislation in Ontario and Manitoba, Period I

	Ontario		Manitoba	
1884	SO c.39	Factories Act—provides for health and safety regulations and restrictions on female and child labour		
1885	SO c.29	Wages Act—regulates wages, profit sharing and "truck system" in certain cases		
1886	SO c.28	Workmen's Compensation Act—provides some compensation to workers in case of injury		
1888	SO c.33	Shops Act—standards for women and children, hours, safety and sanitation	SM c.32	Shops Act—standards for women and children, hours, safety and sanitation
1889	SO c.45	Steam Threshing Engines Act—provides some safety regulations		
1890	SO c.10	Mines Act—provides safety regulations and restrictions on youth labour and exclusion of female and child labour		
1891	SO c.22	Woodmen's Lien for Wages Act—first restrictions on "truck" in logging		
	SO c.31	Stationery Engineers Act—provides some safety regulations		

Year		
1893	SM c.39	Workmen's Compensation Act—provides some compensation to workers in case of injury
1894	SO c.42	Trades Disputes Arbitration Act—disputes to be referred to arbitration board (purely voluntary)
1897	SM c.17	Mines Act—provides safety regulations
1900	SM c.13	Factories Act—provides for health and safety regulations and restrictions on female and child labour
1909	SM c.2	Act Respecting Wages and Salaries—limits conditions for garnishing wages
1910	SO c.98	Steam Boilers Act—provides safety regulations
1911	SO c.71	Building Trades Protection Act—some safety regulations.
1913	SM c.19	Act to Prevent Employment of Female Labour in Certain Capacities—prohibition of oriental's employment of white women
1913	SO c.37	Railway and Municipal Board Act—provides for compulsory investigation and conciliation in rail and street rail disputes

Table A2.2

Ontario Legislation: Changes in the Regulation of Female and Child Wage Labour, Period I

Year	Legislation	Exclusions	Restrictions	Protections
Prior to 1884	None	None	None	None
1884	Factories Act SO c.39	Boys 12 yrs. and girls 14 yrs. cannot be employed in factories	Boys 12–14 yrs. and girls 14–18 yrs. need parental approval for employment in factories operation Children and women may work no more than 10 hrs./day or 60 hrs./week	Women cannot clean machinery with moving parts during machine operation Children and women must have 1 hr./day for meals
1888	Shops Act SO c.33		Boys 14 yrs. and girls 16 yrs. may work no more than 74 hrs./week: 12 hrs./day: 14 hrs./Saturday	Women must be provided with seats or chairs
1889	Factories Act SO c.43		Women and children may work no more than 36 days of overtime/yr.	
1890	Mines Act SO c.10	All women and boys less than 15 yrs. cannot be employed in mines	Males 15–17 yrs. cannot be below ground more than 8 hrs./day, 48 hrs./week Males under 20 yrs. cannot be in charge of transportation machinery in mine, restriction is 16 yrs. of age if machinery is animal driven	
1895	Factories Act SO c.50	Government may exclude boys 16 yrs. and girls 18 yrs. from dangerous or unwholesome employment		

Year	Act		
1897	Shops Act RSO c.257	Children under 10 yrs. cannot be employed in shops. Women and children employed full-time in factories cannot be employed in shops	Children and women cannot be employed before 7 a.m. or after 6 p.m.
	Mines Act 50 c.36		Males 15–17 yrs. cannot be employed underground on Sundays
1908	Shops Act 50 c.58	Children 12 yrs. and under cannot be employed in shops	No children of school age or attending school may work during school hours without a certificate of permission
	Factories Act 50 C.57		Youth category of males 14–16 yrs. introduced. All restrictions and protections for women and children apply to youths
	Mines Act 50 c.21	Exclusions of women and girls waived for mica-trimming operations	
1912	Mines Act 50 c.8	Boys less than 14 yrs. cannot be employed in mines. Girls and women can be employed as stenographers and bookkeepers for mining companies	Males less than 17 yrs. cannot be employed underground. Males less than 18 yrs. cannot be in charge of hoisting apparatus in mines

Table A2.3

Disposition of Marital Property, Period I: in Ontario and Manitoba

Year	Ontario	Year	Manitoba
1859 SUC	c.73 Married Women's Property Act (MWPA) — married woman capable of *holding property* as "femme sole"	1871 SM	c.8 Act Relating to Deeds by Married Women — entitles married women to *convey real estate* with husbands concurrence
SUC	c.84 Dower Act — reaffirms women's dower rights	1875 SM	c.25 MWPA — married woman capable of holding property as "femme sole" — right to own wages available only through an order of protection
1871 SO	c.24 Act Respecting Conveyance of Real Estate by Married Woman — entitles married woman to *convey real estate*; provides for court examination of woman to insure she does so of her own will	1885 SM	c.28 Real Property Act — *Dower rights abolished Curtsey abolished*
1872 SO	c.16 MWPA — married woman capable of holding property as "femme sole" including *wages and earnings*; husbands claim to *curtsey abolished*	1891 RSM	c.95 MWPA — married woman capable of holding property including *wages and earnings* as "femme sole"
1877 RSO	c.125 MWPA — right to obtain order of protection to secure *children's earnings*	1900 SM	c.27 MWPA — women now liable for maintenance of child
1888 SO	c.23 Maintenance of Deserted Wives — *husbands liable for support of deserted wife* (Adultery clause)		SM c.28 Married Women's Protection Act — husband liable to maintain estranged wife; husband liable to maintain child in custody of the wife; subject to adultery clause
		1902 RSM	c. 106 MWPA — under order of protection right to secure *children's earnings*

Table A2.4

Legislation of Parental Custody Rights and Responsibilities in Ontario and Manitoba, Period I

Year	Ontario		Year	Manitoba	
1855	SUC	c.126 Custody of Infants Act — mothers married but separately domiciled may petition court for custody of child less than 12 yrs; subject to adultery clause	1878	SM	c.7 Infants Act — mother may petition court for custody of child under 12 yrs; mother may petition court to appoint a guardian other than one appointed by father's will
1859	SUC	c.77 Support of Illegitimate Children Act — woman may sue father of illegitimate child for financial support	1900	SM	c.27 MWPA — mother now liable for maintenance of child
1877	RSO	c.125 MWPA — mother may file for order of protection to secure children's earnings		SM	c.28 Married Women's Protection Act — under order of protection mother can petition court for custody of children under 16 yrs; subject to adultery clause
	RSO	c.130 Custody of Infants Act — mother can be appointed guardian of child less than 12 yrs. contrary to father's will; subject to adultery clause	1902	RSM	c.106 MWPA — under order of protection mother can petition court to secure children's earnings
1887	RSO	c.137 Custody of Infants Act — mother may petition court for guardianship of child older than 12 yrs; mother acquired equal right with father to appoint guardians in case of death; subject to adultery clause	1912	SM	c.29 Illegitimate Children's Act — woman may sue father illegitimate child for financial support

Table A2.5

Ontario Family Legislation, Period I: Reductions in Patriarchal Authority over Family Property and Guardianship and Increased Responsibility for Maintenance

Year	Legislation	Property	Guardianship of Children	Maintenance
Prior to		Dower right and Curtsey		
1867	Custody of Infants SUC 1855 c.126 Support of Illegitimate Children SUC 1859 c.77		Mothers (married, separately domiciled) may petition court for guardianship of child less than 12 yrs.	Father may be sued for the maintenance of his children in mother's custody Woman may sue father of illegitimate child for financial support
1872	Married Women's Property SOC 16	Married women have rights to ownership of property, wages and inheritances, just as if unmarried; curtsey revoked		
1873	Married Women's Real Estate Act SOC 18	Married women can convey real estate with husband's consent		
1877	Married Women's Property Act RSO c.125	Married women may get an order of protection to secure children's earnings		
1887	Infants RSO c.137		Mother may petition for guardianship of child less than 12 yrs Mother can appoint guardians for her children via wills	
1888	Married Women's Real Estate Act SOC 21	Married women can convey real estate without husband's consent if husband is insane, imprisoned or separated		
	Maintenance of Deserted Wives SO c.23			Husband must support wife living apart for just cause

Table A2.6

Welfare Legislation in Ontario and Manitoba, Period I

Year	Ontario	Year	Manitoba
1874	SO c.19 Apprentices and Minors Act—provides for indentures of orphaned or abandoned child	1877	SM c.26 Apprentices and Minors Act — similar to Ontario Act
	SO c.29 Industrial Schools Act—stipulates conditions for apprehension and institutionalization	1883	SM c.16 Charity Aid Act — empowers the treasurer of the province to pay aid periodically, no formula stipulated
	SO c.33 Charity Aid Act—provides a formula for provincial support of hospitals and institutes for the destitute	1897	SM c.60 Child Immigration Act—similar to Ontario Act
1887	RSO c.234 Industrial Schools Act—amends empowered charitable agencies to set up schools	1898	SM c.6 Child Protection Act—similar to Ontario Act
	SO c.36 Protection of Infants Act—regulates private maternity homes	1899	SM c.21 Maternity Boarding Homes Act—same as Ontario Protection of Infants
1888	SO c.40 Child Protection Act—stipulates conditions for apprehension of neglected children and their disposition	1900	SM c.6 An Act respecting the Children's Aid Society of Winnipeg—clarify Society's legal authority
1890	SO c.78 Houses of Refuge Act—provides government aid to county poor houses	1910	SM c.29 Industrial Schools Act—similar to Ontario act
1891	SO c.56 School Attendance Act—school attendance made compulsory, provides truant officers		
1893	SO c.56 Female Refuges Act—provides government aid to poor houses for women		
1897	RSO c.262 Child Immigration Act—regulates child being admitted as immigrants and monitors their disposition		
1912	SO c.60 Maternity Board Homes Act—repeals infants protection act; renames it and extends regulations		

		Criteria for Apprehension of Children	
Year	Legislation	Family Status	Actions of Parents or Child
Prior to 1884	Apprentice and Minors Act 1874 SO c.19 Industrial Schools Act (not in force) 1874 SO c.29	Abandoned, orphaned fatherless boys <21 yrs., girls <18 yrs.	-
1877	Industrial Schools Act RSO c.213	Destitute or homeless child <14 yrs.	Child: Begging, petty crime Parents: imprisoned, drunken, neglectful, cannot control child
1887	Protection of Infants Act SO c.36	Born in private maternity home	-
1888	Child Protection Act SO c40	Neglected children: boys <14 yrs., girls <16 yrs. Child <14 yrs. brought to court	
1897	Protection of Infants Act RSO 258	Child <1 yr. born in maternity homes	-
-	Industrial Reffuse for Girls Act RSO c.310	-	Child 8-14 yrs. expelled for vicious or immoral acts
-	Child Protection Act RSO c.259	-	Curfew violation
1910	Child Immigration Act RSO c.262	Immigrant child with unsuccessful placement	-
1910	Industrial Schools Act SO c.105	Children 14 – 16 yrs.	-
1912	Maternity Board Homes Act SO c.60	Child <3 yrs. born in public institution or private maternity	-
1913	Child Protection Act SO c.62	Neglected child: boys <14 yrs. girls <16 yrs.	

Table A2.7 reads across these facing pages.

Extension of State Authority Over Children

State Agents	Possible Dispositions			
-	Indentured Apprentice	Institutions	Adoption	Other
Mayors, Magistrates and Charitable Institutions	Yes			
Magistrates and Schools		Industrial Schools		
Charitable Institutions Dept.				Records must be kept on children
Superintendent of Neglected Children		Refuge and Industrial Schools		Foster homes Towns 10,000 must have refuges
Children's Aid Society			Supervision of adoption of children 1 year	Physician must attend birth
Towns				Towns may enact curfew bylaws
Children's Aid Society and Department of Public Health			Supervision of all adoptions	

Table A2.8

New Labour Laws in Ontario and Manitoba, Period II

Year	Ontario	Manitoba
1914	SO c.38 Employment Agencies Act—requires licensing of employment agencies and empowers Lieutenant Governor to make regulations.	SM c.12 Building Trades Protection Act—outlines safety regulations for building trades.
1915	SO c.24 Workmen's Compensation Insurance Act—rewritten on the basis of collective liability and establishes administrative board.	SM c.6 The Bureau of Labour Act—establishes a bureau attached to Dept. of Public Works to collect statistics on employment and wages.
1916	SO c.13 Trades and Labour Branch Act—responsible for collecting statistics and administering labour legislation.	SM c.121 Fair Wages Act—establishes board to determine min. wages and max. hrs. for workmen employed on Public Works.
		SM c.125 Workmen's Compensation Act—same as Ontario (SO 1915 c.25)
1918		SM c.38 Minimum Wage Act—establishes a board to determine min. wages, standards of hrs. and working conditions for women and youth.
		SM c.25 Employment Bureau Act—establishes bureaus throughout province.
1919		SM c.43 Industrial Conditions Act—establishes joint council of industry to investigate conditions of industry and labour.
1920	SO c.87 Minimum Wage Act—same as Manitoba (SM 1918 c.38)	
1922	SO c.93 One Day's Rest in Seven—requires one day's rest for all full-time employees.	SM c.45 One Day's Rest in Seven—same as Ontario (SO 1922 c.93)
1927	SO c.27 Labour Dept. Act—establishes dept. of labour with same mandate as labour branch.	
1928	SO c.25 Apprenticeship Act—provides an inspector to inspect and regulate conditions and contracts for apprentices.	

1929   SO c.71 Silicosis Act—requires medical certificate for employees in high-risk areas and protective equipment and appliances for workers.

1931   SO c.38 Blind Workmen's Compensation—insures coverage under Workmen's Comp. Act and empowers CNIB to determine proper placement of blind workers.

1932   SO c.20 Industrial Disputes Investigation Act—adopts federal IDIA to apply to province.
        SO c.23 Operating Engineers Act—safety requirements for engineers.
        SO c.27 Ontario Municipal Board Act—empowers board to mediate in strikes and walkouts.

1934   SO c.66 Woodmen's Employment Act—regulation of wages, hrs. and conditions of labour in forestry industry.

1935   SO c.28 Industrial Standards Act—provides for appointment of officers to establish industrial codes and min. wages.

1936   SO c.26 Government Contracts Hours and Wages Act—provides regulation of min. wages and max. hrs. for workers in public works.

1937   SM c.50 Wages Recovery Act—replaces Master and Servant act; provides for enforcing payment of wages due.
        SM c.40 Strikes and Lockouts Prevention Act—Minister of Labour to appoint board to arbitrate industrial disputes within the provincial jurisdiction.

1938   SO c.42 Teacher's Boards of Reference Act—appointment of board to handle disputes between teachers and school boards, esp. cases of dismissal.

Table A2.9
Ontario Labour Legislation: Changes in the Regulation of Female and Child Labour, Period II

Year	Legislation	Exclusions	Restrictions	Protection
1914	c.229 Factories, Shops and Office Bldg.	s.6 Persons under 18 yrs. cannot operate or control elevators.	s.3 8 hrs. max. employment for child in canning factory (formerly 10 hrs.) s.2 Chinese cannot employ or supervise white women.	
1918	c.44 Factories, Shops and Office Bldg.	s.9 No child to be employed in any factory (including canning factories).	s.10 No woman to be employed in any factory later than 6:30 p.m.	s.12 When 35 women employed, employer must provide dressing and eating rooms; matron must attend rooms.
1919	c.12 Mines Act	s.157 Males less than 16 yrs. not to be employed in or about mines (formerly 14 yrs.) s.158 Males less than 18 yrs. not to be employed underground (formerly 17 yrs.)		
1919	c.64 Factories Shops and Office Bldg.			s.2 Extends provisions of this act to camp employment of women. Minister can regulate seasons and hrs. of women's employment and supervise physical and social protection of women.

Year	Act		
1920	c. 87 Minimum Wage Act		s.3 Establishes a board of 5 persons and minimum of 2 women to determine minimum wages for girls, women and youths by trade and locality. s.4 Seats must be provided for all employed women if work can be done seated.
1921	c.76 Factories, Shops and Office Bldg.	s.3 No persons under 14 yrs. to be employed in shops (formerly 12 yrs.) s.5 No employment of youths in contravention of Adolescent School Attendance Act.	
1922	c.91 Minimum Wage Act		s.2 Board empowered to investigate wages for women and youths and set penalties for violations. s.41 One closet for each 15 (formerly 25) female employees
1932	c.35 Factories, Shops and Office Bldg.	s.27 No person under 16 yrs. to be employed without certificate from school permitting absence.	
1937	c.43 Minimum Wage Act (Volume I)		s.2 Minimum wage extended to men; board stipulated higher minimum wage for men than for women.
1939	c.47 Factories, Shops and Office Bldg.		s.10 Protections and restrictions provided by this act extend to include small shops.

Table A2.10

New Family Legislation in Ontario and Manitoba, Period II

Year	Ontario	Manitoba
1919		SM c.26 Dower Act—entrenches women's dower rights
1920		SM c.72 Legitimation Act—asserts right of child born out of wedlock, whose parents have subsequently married to be deemed legitimate with all the rights of a child born in lawful wedlock.
1922	SO c.52 Parents' Maintenance Act — asserts legal obligation of adult children to support their elderly dependent parents. SO c.53 Legitimation Act — same as Manitoba. SO c.54 Child of Unmarried Parents Act — provides for the position of "Provincial Officer" to keep record of children born out of wedlock, oversee their family situation and enforce the act dealing with filiation orders, maintenance, etc. SO c.55 Adoption Act — outlines the necessary conditions and procedures for legal adoptions.	
1922	SO c.57 Deserted Wives and Children's Maintenance Act — repealed and superceded the Maintenance of Deserted Wives Act and added children's maintenance claims.	
1929	SO c.47 Dependants Relief Fund—empowers judge to alter provisions of parents' will when child deemed inadequately provided for.	
1931	SO c.34 Children's Maintenance Act—asserts obligation of every parent for maintenance and education of child under 16 yrs.; provides penalty of 3 months imprisonment for parent in default.	
1933		SM c.31 Parents' Maintenance Act — same as Ontario.

Table A2.11

Family Law: Clarification of Familial Rights and Obligations in Ontario and Manitoba, Period II

Year	Ontario	Manitoba
1921	SO c.52 Parents' Maintenance Act—asserts legal *obligation that children* support their elderly dependent parents. SO c.53 Legitimation Act—asserts *right of child* born out of wedlock, whose parents have subsequently married, to be deemed legitimate with all the rights of a child born in lawful wedlock. SO c.54 Child of Unmarried Parents Act—provides for the position(s) of "Provincial Officer" to keep record of children born out of wedlock, oversee their family situation and otherwise enforce the act which stipulates (s.9) mother of such child has the *right* to apply to "Provincial Officer" for advice and protection. *Officer* has the *right* to be appointed guardian either alone or jointly with the mother (s.10); negates common-law assumption of mother's legal guardianship of child born out of wedlock. *Father liable* for support of child (s.18). *Mother liable* for support of child even if deemed not worthy of custody. *Note:* s.18.2 establishes principle of equity of parental liability in cases of child born out of wedlock.	SM c.31 Parents' Maintenance Act (1933) SM c.72 Legitimation Act (1920). SM c.2 Child Welfare Act (1922): Part IV Children Whose Parents Have Not Been Legally Married to Each Other (s.28–71) SM c.4 Child Welfare Act (1926 Amend.) s.12 — where mother does not attempt to get maintenance from putative father, state can take custody and require maintenance from mother.

1922	SO c.55 Adoption Act—outlines necessary conditions and procedures for adoption, which must be adhered to, in order to be recognized as a legal adoption bestowing all the rights and obligations of a legitimate parent-child relation. *Note:* asserts state authority over parental wish or community tradition.	SM c.2 Child Welfare Act (1922): Part IX Adoption, s.113–121.
1922	SO c.57 Deserted Wives and Children's Maintenance Act — repealed and superceded the Maintenance of Deserted Wives Act. Elaborated *husband/father's liability* and added *children's right* to maintenance.	RSM c.206 Wives and Children's Maintenance and Protection Act (1913).
1923	SO c.33 Infants Act (Amend.)—asserts *mother's right* to be equally entitled to the custody, control and education of children. *Note:* the *adultery clause* previously used to disqualify mother petitioning for custody *dropped* as principle of equity established. *Father* still only parent stipulated by law as liable for maintenance.	SM c.2 Child Welfare Act (1922): Part X Guardianship of Children, s. 122–147.
1929	SO c.47 Dependants Relief Fund—asserts *child's right* to adequate maintenance and empowers judge to alter provisions of parents' will.	SM c.2 Child Welfare Act (1924 Amend.): Part III Bereaved and Dependent Children: s. 19–28.
1931	SO c.34 Children's Maintenance Act—asserts obligation of every parent for maintenance and education of child under 16 yrs.; provides penalty of 3 months imprisonment for parents in default. *Note:* established principle of equity; *mothers* equally *liable* for maintenance.	SM c.27 Married Women's Property Act (1900) — mother equally liable for maintenance of child. *Note:* Manitoba has no directly equivalent law for imprisoning parents in default.

Table A2.12

Welfare Legislation Enacted in Ontario and Manitoba, Period II

Year	Manitoba	Year	Ontario
1916	SM c.69 Mother's Allowance — provides monthly allowances for mothers without economic support due to death or permanent incapacitation of their husbands; establishes a board to process claims and administer funds.	1919	SO c.54 Ontario Housing Act — permits utilization of federal funding for provincial housing.
1916	SM c.81 Old-Folk's Home Act — provides some provincial funds and regulations for homes for the elderly.	1920	SO c.89 Mother's Allowance — same as Manitoba except it stipulates only mothers of 2 or more dependent children can qualify.
1917	SM c.69 Public and Other Institutions Act— provides for a commission to investigate and report on institutions and systematize provincial expenditures on public institutions.	1927	SO c.92 Boy's Welfare Act — establises a board to establish homes for dependent and neglected boys.
1918	SM c.6 Blind Persons, Support and Maintenance Act — provides routines for provincial support and education of blind persons and their transportation to out-of-province schools or institutions.	1929	SO c.73 Old Age Pension Act— same as Manitoba except it provides for separate commission to administer act. (1928 SM c.44)
1919	SM c.42 Manitoba Housing Act — permits utilization of federal funding for provincial housing projects.	1931	SO c.5 Department of Public Welfare — establishes a separate dept. to execute the provisions of all acts dealing with public welfare.
			SO c.60 Industrial Training School Act — establishes an advisory board to take place of inspector; repeals and supersedes Boy's Welfare Act (1927 c.92).

1922   SM c.112 Act Respecting Welfare Supervision — appoints a board to investigate existing programs and recommend new programs.

SM c.2 Child Welfare Act — a major consolidation of old welfare and family laws into a new and comprehensive statute concerning all matter of state involvement in child welfare.

1924   SM c.27 Home for the Aged and Infirm Act — consolidation of existing acts concerning both aged and infirm.

1928   SM c.21 Health and Public Welfare Act — establishes a Dept. of Health and Welfare responsible for administering all health and welfare statutes.

SM c.44 Old Age Pension Act — includes Manitoba in federal Old Age Pension Program & provides for Workmen's Comp. Board. to process claims and administer funds.

1931   SM c.53 Unemployment Relief Act (re-enacted every year until 1940; in force until 1942) authorizes the implementation of Fed. Relief Act (1931 SC c.58)

1932   SM c.41 St. Boniface Home for Aged and Infirm Act — brings St. Boniface home under the terms of the Aged and Infirm Act.

1935   SM c.33 Pensions for Blind Persons Act — extends Old Age Pension provisions to certain blind persons.

1931   SO c.80 Inspector of Public Institutions Act — appoints inspector(s) to oversee management and operation of Penal and Reformative Institutions.

1939   SO c.51 Industrial Training Schools Act — consolidates industrial training schools act and provides for one administration board.

Table A2.13
New Federal Welfare Legislation, Period II

Year		Legislation
1914	c.8	(2nd sess.) Canadian Fund Act—establishes a corporation to collect and administer funds for assistance of wives and dependants of men in active service during the war.
1917	c.38	War Charities Act—sets out regulations for and requires registration of any nonreligious fundraising association for the relief of soldiers or their families.
1917	c.21	The Soldier Settlement Act—provides crown land and loans for returning soldiers, establishes the soldier settlement board to administer act. (advanced 25 million dollars to soldiers in 1919 Appropriation Act #3 c.35)
1918	c.42	Dept. of Soldiers Civil Re-establishment Act—creates a federal dept. to provide necessary and economic services for returning soldiers and/or their dependants.
1919	c.43	The Pension Act—establishes the Board of Pension Commissioners of Canada to provide pensions to war disabled or their dependants (3.5 million dollars disbursed in first year of operation in 1919 Appropriation Act #2 c.34)
1919	c.24	The Department of Health Act—establishes a separate dept. of health to administer all federal public health acts.
1920	c.54	The Returned Soldiers Insurance Act—empowers the Minister of Finance to set up special insurance programs for returned soldiers.
1927	c.35	Old Age Pension Act—provides means-tested pensions for Canadian citizens over seventy years of age in conjunction with provinces who enter in agreement; provides for federal funding of 50% of the program.
1928	c.39	Department of Pensions and National Health Act—repeals and supersedes the Department of Health Act and the Department of Soldiers Civil Re-establishment Act.
1930	c.48	War Veterans' Allowances Act — establishes a committee to hear claims and grant allowances to veterans sixty years of age or more, who by virtue of physical and/or mental disability are unemployable.

Continued on next page

Year		Legislation
1931	c.58	The Unemployment and Farm Relief Act — empowers the Governor General to pay out of consolidated revenue monies for unemployment and farm relief.
1932	c.36	The Relief Act — empowers the Governor General to enter in agreements with the provinces respecting relief measures and financial assistance to provinces with relief debts in order to protect the credit and financial position of the Dominion or any province. (Renewed annually until 1939.)
1935	c.58	Dominion Housing Act — provides low-interest loans for house building.
1935	c.38	Employment and Social Insurance Act — establishes an Employment and Social Insurance Commission to provide for a national employment service, for insurance against unemployment, for aid to the unemployed and for other forms of social insurance and security. (Ruled *Ultra Vires* 1935, i.e., not within federal jurisdiction.)
1936	c.47	The Veterans Assistance Commission Act — establishes a commission to assist towards the employment of former members of the forces.
1936	c.7	National Employment Commission Act — establishes a commission to conduct national registration and classification of persons on relief, mobilize agencies for relief, develop public works and supervise relief expenditures.
1937	c.13	Old Age Pension Act — amended to include blind persons over forty years of age with income less than 640 dollars per annum.
1938	c.49	National Housing Act — repeals and supersedes Dominion Housing Act — provides federal funds for local low-rental housing projects (up to 30 million dollars).

Table A2.14
Privy Council Orders Pertaining to Labour
During World War II, Period III

Date	Order	Content
19 June 1940	P.C.2685	War Labour Policy — declares right to form unions and bargain collectively; bans strikes /lockouts
16 Dec. 1940	P.C.7440	Wage freeze in war industries
24 January 1941	P.C.552	Establishes National Labour Supply Council (advisory only)
10 March 1941	P.C.1708	Extend Industrial Disputes Investigation Act (SC 1907) to war industries
6 June 1941	P.C.4020	Establishes 2-stage conciliation, Industrial Disputes Investigation Commission IDI to report on anti-union discrimination
27 June 1941	P.C.4643	Restrict cost-of-living bonus
2 July 1941	P.C.4844	Strike ban, reinstatement orders by federal Labour Minister
16 Sept. 1941	P.C.7307	Compulsory strike vote
24 Oct. 1941	P.C.8253	2nd wage freeze — establishes National and Regional War Labour Board (WLB)
13 Nov. 1941	P.C.8821	Representation vote by all employees affected
5 Dec. 1941	P.C.9514	Establishes 9 regional WLB subject to 12-man national WLB
27 May 1942	P.C.26/4430	Provides consultation with Labour on wage policy
10 July 1942	P.C.5963	Relaxes wage freeze slightly
1 Dec. 1942	P.C.10802	Esablishes right to organize in Crown corporations, excluded CBC and National Labours Board
19 Jan. 1943	P.C.496	IDI Commission may be established in "any threat to war effort"
11 Feb. 1943	P.C.1141	National War Labour Board NWLB disbanned, replaced by McTague Commission
20 May 1943	P.C.4175	Criminal offence to disobey Ministers Order
9 Dec. 1943	P.C.9384	3rd wage order includes cost-of-living bonus in basic wage.
13 Mar. 1944	P.C.1727	Re-establish NWLB — lifts restrictions of cost-of-living bonus.
17 Feb. 1944	P.C.1003	Establishes Wartime Labour Relations Regulations, collective bargaining and "unfair" practices law.

Table A2.15
Federal Welfare Legislation, Period III, 1940–1947

1940   SC c.44 Unemployment Insurance Act — provides for a compulsory contributory unemployment-insurance program at the national level and for the establishment of a national employment service to function in conjunction with the unemployment-insurance operation

1942   SC c.33 Veterans' Land Act — provides for provisions of lands and financial support to encourage veterans to see rehabilitation in agricultural industry

1944   SC c.22 The Department of National Health and Welfare Act — establishes a national Department of Health and Welfare and repeals the Department of Pensions and National Health Act.

1944   SC c.19 — *The Department of Veterans' Affairs* — establishes a separate Dept. of Veteran's Affairs and repeals Part 1 of the Dept. of Pensions and National Health Act.

1944   SC c.40 The Family Allowances Act — provides for the payment by the federal government of allowances in respect of every child under 16 yrs. born in Canada or resident for three years.

1944   SC c.46 The National Housing Act — provides funds for persons wishing to build or repair their own funds to aid slum-clearance projects and funds to stimulate building of low-rent housing units.

1944   SC c.49 Veterans' Insurance Act — provides for a federal government life-insurance program for Veterans of World War II.

1945   SC c.35 The Veterans' Rehabilitation Act — provides allowances for veterans who are temporarily incapacitated, out of work, awaiting returns from a business or pursuing courses of training.

1946   SC c.43 The Civilian War Pensions and Allowances Act — provides for pensions and allowances to Canadian nationals serving in specified essential occupations and who suffered disability as a result of World War II.

1946   SC c.52 The Fire Fighters War Service Benefits Act — extends all veterans' benefits to Canadian fire fighters in the United Kingdom and entitles them to a gratuity.

1946   SC c.36 Allied Veterans' Benefits Act — extends veterans' benefits to individuals in service with allied armies who within 2 yrs. of discharge come to be a resident in Canada.

1946   SC c.66 Supervisors War Service Benefits Act — extends all veterans' benefits to representatives from religious and social organizations who were attached to Canadian Armed forces.

1946   SC c.75 War Veterans' Allowance Act — repeals and replaces the War Veterans' Allowance Act 1930.

Table A2.16
New Labour Laws in Ontario and Manitoba, Period III, 1940–1968

Year	Ontario	Year	Manitoba
1943	SO c.4 Collective Bargaining Act—establishes a labour court to adjudicate collective bargaining agreements, appeals, etc. (repealed 1944 c.29).	1944	SM c.48 Manitoba Wartime Labour Relations Act—establishes a provincial board to enforce Federal Wartime Labour Regulations.
1944	SO c.29 Labour Relations Act—establishes a provincial board to enforce Federal Wartime Labour Regulations.		SM c.1 The Apprenticeship Act—creates a provincial board to regulate training and use of apprentices in trades.
	SO c.26 Hours of Work and Vacations with Pay Act—empowers labour board to enforce 8 hr. day, 48 hr. week and 1 week paid vacation for every working year.	1947	SM c.62 Vacations with Pay Act—legally requires employers to provide annual vacation with pay.
	SO c.54 Rights of Labour Act—exempts unions from restraint of trade charges.		
1948	SO c.51 Labour Relations Act—adopts a labour-relations code modeled on PC 1003.	1948	SM c.27 Manitoba Labour Relations Act—adopts a labour-relations code modeled on PC 1003.
1950	SO c.34 Labour Relations Amendment Act—a completely new provincial act provides for 2-stage conciliation under ministers control; Labour board restricted to certificates and rulings on "illegal" strikes or lockouts.	1949	SM c.58 Stream Pressure Plants Act—provides safety regulations and calls for regular inspections.
1951	SO c.24 Fair Employment Practices Act—prohibits discrimination against men and women in employment because of race, creed or colour; does not stipulate discrimination by sex. Applied to all employers with 5 or more employees and to trade unions.	1950	SM c.15 Employment Services Act—an act to regulate license employment agencies; prohibits them supply-labour under conditions of strike (1st session).
	SO c.26 Fair Remuneration to Female Employees Act—prohibits pay discrimination on basis of sex; establishes Fair Employment Practices Branch of the Dept. of Labour.	1953	SM c.18 Fair Employment Practices Act—very similar to Ontario's act SO 1951 c.24.
1953	SO c.33 Elevators and Lifts Act—safety regulations for operation of elevators and lifts provoked by Lakehead grain explosion.	1956	SM c.18 Equal Pay Act—prohibits pay discrimination on the basis of sex.
1954	SO c.99 Trench Excavators Protection Act—provides safety regulations (following subway cave in).		

1958   SO c.70 Anti-Discrimination Commission Act—establishes Ontario Anti-discrimination Commission in the Dept. of Labour to administer Fair Employment Practices Act (1951 c.26) and the Fair Accommodation Act (1954).

1960–61   SO c.11 Construction Hoists Act—provides safety regulations.
1961–62   SO c.18 Construction Safety Act—provides safety regulations for construction workers; provides inspectors from Dept. of Labour.
1962–63   SO c.103 Pension Benefits Act—establishes Pension Commission of Ontario to regulate private pensions plans.
   SO c.121 Public Works Creditors Payments Act—repeals and supercedes Public and Other Works Wages Act; provides procedures for workers to claim wages from contractors.
   SO c.83 An Act to Amend the Minimum Wage Act — sets a single provincial minimum wage for men and women workers.
1964   SO c.45 Industrial Safety Act—consolidation of Factory and Shop and Office Building Acts.
1965   SO c.48 Hospital Labour Dispute Arbitration Act—granted collective bargaining rights but refused right to strike.
1965   SO c.131 Toronto Hydro Electric Employees' Union Dispute Act—back-to-work law and compulsory arbitration.
1966   SO c.3 Age Discrimination Act—prohibits employers' trade unions from refusing to hire or discriminate against persons between ages 40–65.
1968   SO c.86 Labour Management Arbitration Commission establishes commission of full and part-time paid arbitrators to handle dispute cases.

1957   SM c.20 Employment Standards Act—a major consolidation of labour law; provides regulations on hours, wages and conditions of work. Repealed Factories Act, Hours and Conditions of Work Act and Minimum Wage Act.
1964   SM c.9 Construction Industry Wages Act—provides wages and hours of work regulations; repeals Fair Wages.
1965   SM c.24 Employment Safety Act—provides safety rules for employees especially in construction.

Labour Legislation and Statutory Orders Facilitating
the Employment of Women, Period III, 1940–1968

Year	Jurisdiction	Statute, Amendment or Order
1951	Ontario	SO c.26 Fair Remuneration to Female Employees Act —prohibits pay discrimination on basis of sex; establishes Fair Employment Practices Branch of the Dept. of labour. *Exclusion*: civil servants not covered by the provisions of this act.
1955	Federal	SOR 55/406 Public Service Act Regulations — removes regulations against employment of married women in federal civil service.
1956	Federal	SC c.38 Female Employees Equal Pay Act— calls for equal pay for identical work for employees in crown corporations and other undertakings under federal jurisdiction. *Exclusion*: employees of Public Service of Canada not covered.
	Manitoba	SM c.18 Equal Pay Act—prohibits pay discrimination on the basis of sex. *Exclusion*: provincial civil servants.
1958	Federal	SOR 58/232 Public Service Act Regulations — provided maternity leave clause for federal civil servants. *Exclusion*: unmarried women would not be covered.
1960	Manitoba	MR 30/60 Minimum Wage Regulation — establishes single minimum wage for men and women workers.
1962	Federal	SOR 62/121 Public Service Act Regulations—extends maternity leave to all women regardless of marital status.
1963	Ontario	SO c.83 An Act to Amend the Minimum Wage Act —sets a single minimum wage for men and women workers.
1964–65	Federal	SC c.38 Canada Labour (Standards) Code, Part II section II—sets a single min. wage for men and women and single max. work hrs. (40) per week for men and women.

Continued on next page

Year	Jurisdiction	Statute, Amendment or Order
1965	Ontario	SO c.85 .3 Human Rights Code—amendment stipulates that all crown employees (including civil servants) are covered under the provisions of this Act.
1967	Federal	SOR 67/78 Public Service Pension Regulation—removes clause requiring women to retire from the federal civil service upon marriage.
1970	Ontario	SO c.33 Women's Equal Employment Opportunity Act—prohibits discrimination on basis of sex or marital status; establishes Ontario Women's Bureau and provides for maternity leave.
	Manitoba	SM c.H175 Human Rights Act—includes prohibition of discrimination on the basis of sex or marital status.
1971	Federal	SC c.48 Unemployment Insurance Act Amendment, part VII s.140—prohibits discrimination on basis of sex or marital status for job referrals.
1972	Manitoba	SM c.E110 Employment Standards Act—amendment provides maternity leave.
1973	Federal	SOR 73/278 Fair Wages and Hours of Labour Regulations—all government contracts must include clause prohibiting discrimination including sex and marital status.
1973	Ontario	SO c.112 Employment Standards Act—amendment extends equal pay and maternity provisions to civil servants.
1976	Manitoba	SM cE65 Employment Standards Act—amendment extends all provisions of this act to civil servants.
	Federal	SC c.33 Human Rights Act—amendment extends all provisions of this act to civil servants.

Table A2.18

New Provincial Welfare Legislation in Ontario and Manitoba,
Period III, 1940–1968

Year	Ontario	Manitoba
1946	SO c.17 Day Nurseries Act — empowers municipalities to pass by-laws to establish daycare centres; establishes *regulations* and provides 50% provincial funding for such centre.	SM c.2 Blind Person's and Deaf Person's Maintenance Act — extends the same benefits to the deaf as were available to the blind (1918 SM c.6).
1947	SO c.31 District Homes for the Aged Act — repeals and supercedes Houses of Refuge Act and District Houses of Refuge Act (1937 c385–c386) SO c.46 Homes for the Aged Act.	
1948	SO c.98 Welfare Units Act — provides for the establishment of municipal and district administrative units; the province through the Department of Public Welfare will provide the personnel and *regulations* for such units.	
1949	SO c.41 Homes for the Aged Act — consolidation of c.46 and c.31 above; provides *regulations* and provincial funding for the construction and maintenance of homes for the elderly; requires every municipality to provide for a home for the aged.	SM c. 55 Social Assistance Act — provides for provincial granting of aid to municipalities for social assistance; *outlines regulations* and procedures for such grants.

1954	SO c.8 Child Welfare Act — a consolidation and revision of the Children's Protection Act, the Children of Unmarried Parents Act and the Adoption Act. SO c.50 Mental Health Act — provides for a director and staff of mental health in the Department of Health to *regulate* and inspect facilities and programs for the mentally ill.	SM c.23 Old Age Pension Debt Cancellation Act — cancels all debts owed to the crown resulting from pensions improperly paid due to nondisclosure of facts or false representation.
1955	SO c.33 Indian Welfare Services Act —provides for provincial delivery of general welfare services to Native Canadians covered by the Indian Act upon reaching cost-sharing agreements with relevant federal agency.	
1956	SO c.31 Hospital Services Commission Act — establishes a commission to *inspect, supervise* and approve hospital services in the province.	RSM c.5 Charities Endorsement Act — requires *provincial authorization of all public and private* charities involved in fund-raising activities.
1957	SO c.11 Children's Boarding Homes Act — provides for *provincial regulations and inspection of homes* containing five or more children under 16 yrs. of age who are not related to caretakers.	RSM c.14 Elderly Persons Housing Act — provides provincial funding for housing developments for the elderly.

Table A2.19
**Federal Social Welfare Legislation by Taxation Agreement
and Election Cycles, Period III, 1940–1968**

Taxation Agreement Cycle	Election Cycle	Federal Response
1947–52 TAX RENTAL Federal Government maintained exclusive occupancy of personal tax; Ontario and Quebec occupied 9% corporate and 50% excise tax field.	**1949** Liberal majority	**1951** SC c.18 Old-Age Security Act (2nd session) SC c.55 Old-Age Assistance Act SC c.38 Blind Persons Act **1952** SC c.54 War Veterans' Allowance Act
1953–57 TAX RENTAL Federal Government maintained exclusive occupancy of personal tax; Ontario and Quebec occupied 9% corporate and 50% excise tax field.	**1953** Liberal majority	**1953** SC c.27 Children of the War Dead Act **1954** SC c.55 Disabled Persons Act SC c.23 National Housing Act **1956** SC c.26 Unemployment Assistance Act **1957** SC c.28 Hospital Insurance Act
1957–62 TAX SHARING Federal Government offered a 10-9-50 formula* for personal-corporate-excise taxes; Quebec occupied all 3 fields; Ontario occupied corporate and excise taxes; other 8 provinces opted to rent their fields to Ottawa.	**1957** Conservative minority **1958** Conservative majority	**1961** SC c.26 Vocational Rehabilitation Act Royal Commission on Health
1962-1967 TAX SHARING Federal Government offered a 20-9-50 formula. Quebec, Ontario, Manitoba and Saskatchewan chose occupancy; other provinces chose rental.	**1963** Liberal minority **1965** Liberal minority **1968** Liberal majority	**1964–65** SC c.54 Established Program Financing Act SC c.23 Youth Allowance Act SC c.24 Canada Students Loans Act SC c.51 Canada Pension Plan **1966–67** SC c.64 Medical Care Act SC c.42 Health Resources Fund Act SC c.27 Training Allowance Act SC c.36 Company of Young Canadians SC c. 65 Guaranteed Income Supplement SC c.45 Canada Assistance Plan Royal Commission on the Status of Women

The formula 10-9-50 provided provinces with a direct return of 10% of personal income tax, 9% of corporate tax and 50% of excise tax collected within their jurisdiction.

Table A2.20

Joint Federal-Provincial Welfare Legislation, Period III, 1940–1968

Year	Federal Initiative	Year	Provincial Response
1944	SC c.46 The National Housing Act — provides funds to build low-rent housing, slum clearance and household repair (superceded by The National Housing Act 1954 c.23).	1946 1948 1952 1956	SM c.23 The Housing Act SO c.44 The Housing Development Act SO c.27 Elderly Persons Housing Aid Act SO c.92 Rural Housing Assistance Act RSM c.14 Elderly Persons Housing Act
1951	SC c.38 The Blind Persons Act — provides federal aid to the provinces of 75% of the cost of allowances for the blind, aged 21 yrs. and over; repealed s.8A of the Old Age Pension Act, 1927, which previously provided pensions for needy blind.	1951 1952	SO c.1 Blind Persons Act (2nd session) SM c.5 Blind Persons Act
1951	SC c.55 The Old Age Assistance Act —provides federal aid to the provinces of 50% for assistance to persons aged 65–69 yrs., subject to means test.	1951 1952	SO c.2 The Old Age Assistance Act (2nd session) SM c.46 The Old Age Assistance Act
1954	SC c.55 The Disable Persons Act — provides federal aid to the provinces of 50% of the cost of allowances to permanently disabled persons over 18 yrs., subject to a means test.	1955	SO c.13 The Disabled Persons Act SM c.17 The Disabled Persons Act
1956	SC c.26 The Unemployment Assistance Act — provides federal reimbursement to any province entering into an agreement of 50% of amount spent by provinces/municipalities on needy unemployed.	1958 1959	SO c.33 General Welfare Assistance Act SM c.57 Social Allowance Act, s. 12 — provides for Minister to enter into agreements with the federal government for cost-sharing arrangement

1957	SC c.28 The Hospital Insurance and Diagnostic Services Act — authorizes contributions by federal government for programs administered by the provinces, providing hospital insurance and diagnostic services.	1957	SO c.46 Hospital Services Commission Act — amendments act (1955 c .46) to include a hospital-care insurance plan in cooperation with the federal legislation
		1958	SM c.24 Hospital Services Insurance Act
1961	SC c.26 The Vocational Rehabilitation of Disabled Persons Act — provides federal sharing of costs incurred by the provinces in programs of vocational rehabilitation for disabled persons.	1966	SO c.159 The Vocational Rehabilitation of Disabled Persons Act
		1967	SM c.58 Social Allowances Act — amended to include rehabilitation services
1966–67	SC c.45 The Canada Assistance Plan — provides federal aid to provinces of 50% of amount spent on assistance to persons in need; effective July 1966 consolidated all previous cost-shared social-assistance programs.	1966	SO c.54 Family Benefits Act — consolidates all provincial social-assistance programs
1966–67	SC c.64 The Medical Care Insurance Act — provides aid to provinces of 50% of costs of insured medical-care services, which must be comprehensive, nonprofit plans; effective July 1968.	1967	SM c.36 Manitoba Medical Services Insurance Act
1966–67	SC c.42 Health Resource Act — establishes a federal fund to assist provinces in the acquisition, construction and renovation of health-training facilities and research institutions.	1968–69	SO c.43 Health Services Insurance Act

Notes

PART 1: *Towards a Theory of Reproduction*

1   For examples of radical feminist writings see Daly (1978), Firestone (1970) and MacKinnon (1982).

2   For examples of Marxist-feminist writings see Humphries (1977), Quick (1977) and Seccombe (1986a).

3   For specificity of the components and dynamics of production, I rely on the writings for political economists and political historians such as Pentland (1981), Clement (1984), Cross and G. Kealey (1984) and Armstrong and Armstrong, (1984a, 1984b and 1985).

4   Anthropological literature indicates there were societies in which communal patriarchy was associated with the oppression of women, such as the Mundugumor of New Guinea (Harris 1975) or the Mundurucu (Murphy 1959). However, other ethnographic studies record societies in which communal patriarchy was *not* associated with the oppression of women, such as the Arapesh and the Tchaombuli of New Guinea (Mead 1935).

5   "The first separation of productive functions from the reproduction of the kin group occurs in capturing members of other social groups, divorcing these people from their kin groups, i.e., it occurs through alienating members of the group for production outside the group..." Another form of exploitation is labour service, that is, alienation of labour power from the group — as distinct from the whole person. — Later, in the state formation process it occurs by alienating the means of production from the kin group (e.g., land)." Muller (1977: 13).

6   High birth rates in the industrial cities reflected the composition of the population. Cities that attracted large numbers of young women because of employment opportunities (usually textile industries) tended to have higher birth rates (Tilly and Scott 1978, 100).

7   For a discussion of the Social Reform Movement and its composition in Canada see L. Kealey (1979), Mitchinson (1977) and Allen (1971).

8   The first legislation banning abortion altogether did not originate in Catholic canon law, as is widely believed, but in the secular law of England in 1803. The Catholic Church only legislated similarly in 1869, and in the United States most states had outlawed all abortions during the Civil War period (L. Gordon 1977).

9   Lasch (1979) and Donzelot (1979) have argued that social patriarchy is the only mechanism of reproductive control operative and that its

predominance was, in fact, based on the deliberate destruction of familial patriarchy.

10 For an excellent discussion of the psychological impact of current familial structures, see Chodorow (1978).

11 While this is generally the case there are some notable exceptions. In Eastern European nations (until 1989) France and Quebec, there is public concern and public policy designed to deal with the declining birth rate. What all of these states have in common is an inability to rely upon immigration to provide labour. For political, language, or cultural reasons immigration either does not occur or is too disruptive to the host state. Thus they must fall back upon their indigenous population to maintain their labour supplies and this in turn focuses public concern and political attention to the issue of birth rates.

PART 2: Historical Background:
The Impact of Industrialization in Canada

1 In 1910 the Ontario legislature commissioned a special report on Infant Mortality conducted by Dr. Helen MacMurchy, which included studies from other industrializing countries as well as data on Ontario. These reports unambiguously linked the changing nature of work to changing family patterns and the consequent problem of infant mortality. Much attention was given to four themes: poverty, women's employment, illegitimacy and institutionalization, all of which were believed to be critical contributing factors. Subtitles within the report such as "The mother works and the baby dies" leave little doubt as to what was presumed to be women's proper sphere. The data indicating dramatically higher mortality rates among illegitimate and institutionalized children further suggested the dire consequences of a break down in traditional family patterns. Section 6 of the recommendations suggests a strong suspicion on the part of the investigators that some infant mortality was purposeful. They recommend that doctors "report, or notify all cases of abortion or miscarriage. There are grave reasons for this. It is only too well known that in this Province we have disgraceful instances of criminal abortion..."(*Special Report on Infant Mortality, Ontario, 1911* Sessional Papers 9 Sec. 6: 12).

2 For a discussion of historians' attempts to identify the common denominator among diverse reform groups see Bacchi (1978, 468).

3 While a 21% increase in women's employment looks alarming, national employment rates appear to belie the mounting concern of reformers that women had abandoned the home. Only 11% of Canadian women ten years of age and over were employed in 1891. Prior to 1891 the Census did not record employment by sex. Despite

the small percentage of women employed, their concentration in industrial centres made them more visible. Furthermore, the clear pattern of Canadian development in the direction of industrialization and urbanization raised the spectre that nineteenth-century employment rates of women and children were but a harbinger of their eventual complete absorption in the labour force. Employment figures are cited in Mitchinson (1979, 376). Her source is recorded as the *Sixth Census of Canada 1921*, vol. 4, xi–xiv.

4   The extent of the co-operation and sense of shared values between reformers and government is perhaps best illustrated by the following interchange between Prime Minister Borden and three leading women's organizations. While this incident falls outside of our period by a couple of years, it assumes a long history of trust and co-operation, which undoubtedly built up during the first period. In 1916, Borden sent a telegram to the presidents of the NCW, the WCTU and the IODE (Imperial Order of the Daughters of the Empire) requesting that the various organizations across the country take a straw-vote to estimate the effect of full enfranchisement on the conscription issue. Although the NCW and the WCTU were public advocates of women's suffrage all three organizations reported back that there were dangers in full enfranchisement because of the vote among the foreign women (Bacchi 1978, 117).

5   In discussing the "labour" position we are referring to organized labour, which generated newspapers, lobbying groups and organization, providing us with a well-recorded history.

6   For a history of the transition of the early feminist movement to a "maternal" feminist position in Canada, see Bacchi (1976) and Kealey (1979). For the United States, see O'Neill (1971).

7   For a discussion of Canadian feminists like Flora MacDonald Denison, who resisted the appeal of "maternal feminism," see Gorham (1979).

Period I: 1884–1913

1   For a discussion of a similar pattern of labour legislation in Britain, see Lewis (1983). For discussion of American and French labour legislation, see Jensen (1989). Jane Jensen contrasts American legislation (also very similar to Canadian) with French labour laws, which were much more accommodating to the concept of women's dual roles in production and reproduction.

2   The following table taken from McKie et al. (1983) indicates how inaccessible divorces were during this period. While there is an in-

Table 5
Number and Rates of Divorce, 1871–1900

Quinquennial Periods	Numbers of Decrees Granted: Annual Averages	Decrees per 100,000 Population
1871–1875	3	0.08
1876–1880	6	0.1
1881–1885	10	0.2
1886–1890	11	0.2
1891–1895	12	0.2
1896–1900	11	0.2

SOURCE:Pike, Robert 1975, 125; taken from the *Canada Year Book* 1921, 825.

crease in the number of divorces from 3 to 11, the rate remains fairly constant at about 0.2 per 100,000 population.

3   While ownership once certified within the Torrens system was uncontestable, defects in claims were judicable. The real Property Act of 1885 establishing the Torrens system included the development of an assurance fund, whereby a claimant upon proof of a defect in a claim would receive compensation from the fund, but would not have the right to the property. The old registry system issued titles, but conflicting claims could be taken to court, and title holders could lose claim to the land.

4   Of the 3,154 river lots that were sought after in Manitoba, approximately 10% were covered by claims of women enforcing dower rights, in the sense that this portion emerged as patentees. What percentage of women had dower rights that were lost in the shuffle of lots from their occupancy in 1870 to speculators in the 1870s–80s only a lot by lot scrutiny of titles in the Winnipeg land titles office could tell. Information taken from table 5: Recognition of River Lot Occupants by Government of Canada (Sprague 1983).

5   Authors such as Christopher Lasch (1979) and Jacques Donzelot (1979) equate patriarchy with male privilege and on the basis of this falsely conclude that the growth of the welfare state and the reforms in family law indicate that patriarchy is dead.

6   By disposition of children we refer to conditions in which children become wards of the state with parental loss of custody and control of their children. Thus, we are not including institutions (education) that play an important role in sharing the socializing role with

parents, but only those situations in which the parents' role is usurped altogether.

7 The record of this case and subsequent investigation can be found in Lieutenant Governor J.C. Patterson's correspondence (1899) Manitoba Archives, M G 12F1 Box 4.

Period II: 1914–1939

1 During the second period, Canada passed the half-way mark in the urban-rural distribution of the population. By 1931 53.7% population lived in urban settings. By 1909 every province in Canada had Public Health Acts, and most municipalities had public health inspectors and bylaws (Sutherland 1976, 40). This combination of greater population density and greater regulation of urban living conditions reduced the extra-market options available to women and children for subsidizing family livelihoods. The maintenance of gardens was more difficult in dense population areas (typically poorer urban neighbourhoods), and public health rules prohibited the keeping of small livestock in urban areas.

2 We use the term reform parties as a short-hand term for a larger number of populist parties during this period who were supported by the working class: for example, Progressives, Canadian Commonwealth Federation, Reconstruction, as well as Labour.

3 "The trades, labour, and industrial unions of the early part of the twentieth century represented only a small part (between 10% and 15%) of Canada's wage earners and a still smaller proportion (6% to 7%) of the "gainfully employed" (Pentland 1968, 109). This pattern prevailed throughout the second period.

4 Based on his research on trade-union history in British Columbia, Paul Phillips suggests that the increase in claims correlates with the increase in unionization in Canada. Membership in a union would provide union lawyers to workers who previously could not afford legal representation (Phillips 1967).

5 Canada Year Book 1978–79 gives provincial population figures for two census years during this period:

6 The Canadian Patriotic Fund Act SC 1914 c.8 (2nd sess.) established a charitable corporation to collect and administer funds for assistance for wives and dependants of men in active service during the war.

Year	Province	Population
1921	Ontario	2,933,700
	Manitoba	610,100
1931	Ontario	3,431,700
	Manitoba	700,100

7 State attempts to reduce this effect by passing the Parents Maintenance Act, legally requiring children to support their elderly dependent parents, merely served to prove the old adage, "you can't get
blood from a stone." Attempts to enforce the act, according to testimony before the Old Age Pension Commission (1933), would in
most cases simply drive the whole family into destitution (Bryden
1974, 100).

8 While the introduction of a federal-provincial cost-shared Old Age
Pension was initially resisted by some provinces because of the added
expenditure, it relieved the long-term expenditures by providing
federal funding for the support of elderly who would otherwise be
dependent upon municipal welfare roles or the more costly provincial
program of old-folk's homes.

9 The one exception was the enactment of a statute to provide public
pensions for coal miners in Nova Scotia in 1908. However, it was
never proclaimed and was dropped from the statutes in 1923 (Bryden
1974, 51).

10 The federal government's response to the crises of the Depression was
to priorize getting the resources, leaving the provinces largely responsible for their dispersal. "Getting the resources" involved a new
revenue policy heavily dependent upon personal income tax.

Period III: 1940–1968
Patriarchy and Patriotism: The War and
Reconstruction Years 1940–1947

1 The Excess Profits Act was accompanied by eight remarkably
generous "relief measures." Four of these relief measures took the
form of accelerated depreciation allowances that were granted on
expenditures of well over $500 million. One company alone, the
Aluminum Company of Canada, was granted a depreciation allowance of about $180 million dollars (Perry 1955, 355). In addition
to taxes not paid, there was a substantial return to corporations
through government investment in private corporations and post-war
refund policies. Despite substantial revenue from excess profit tax,
$787 million or 44% was returned to corporations: $220 million in
post-war tax refunds, $402 million in direct government investment
in private corporations and $165 million in direct government invest-
ments in alterations and expansions to private corporations. While
workers and corporations provided comparable levels of revenue, for
example, $698 million from wage earners in 1943 and $740 million
from corporations, wage earners did not benefit from post-war tax
returns as did the corporations (Perry 1955).

2 Until the summer of 1943, the whole history of family allowances in

Canada was contained in four isolated events. Family allowances were discussed by a Parliamentary Committee on Industrial and International Relations in 1929, by a Quebec provincial commission in 1932, were approved in principle at the CCF convention in 1942 and advocated in the Marsh report in the spring of 1943. To interpret these events as a growing political pressure for family allowances would, however, misrepresent their significance. No reference to any of the four events appears in the planning documents prepared by the department of finance, although the recommendations of Marsh and Beveridge were invoked in the later stages of Cabinet approval to encourage the support of recalcitrant ministers. Reports of the War Information Board indicate that the CCF convention and the Marsh report had no measurable impact upon the press or the public's interest in family allowances (*War Information Board Reports* Jan. 1942 – Aug. 1943). For a detailed summary of discussions of Family Allowances in Canada, see Kitchen (1987).

3 *Labour Relations Law*, Industrial Relations Centre, Queen's U, 1981.

4 While labour's position on the development of welfare has been consistently supportive, there is a debate in the literature concerning capital's position. Finkel (1979) maintains that the Depression resulted in the conversion of a significant number of Canadian capitalists to the idea that state intervention and welfare was an essential balance wheel for modern capitalism. Cuneo (1979), on the other hand, argues that the converted were few in number and the conversion limited to the grim years of the Depression. He maintains that post-Depression Canadian capitalists were consistently antagonistic to state welfare measures. Both theorists, however, concentrate upon the productive sphere, largely ignoring the reproductive sphere. But more important than capital's ritualistic denunciations of proposed welfare measures is the fact that those proposals were legislated and that the key to understanding why lies in the state's mandate to co-ordinate production and reproduction. While we could not expect capital to be enthusiastic about the welfare state, we must consider whether they could afford (politically and economically) to do without it.

5 For an excellent summary of the Marsh, Whitton and Cassidy reports, see Guest (1980).

Period III: 1940–1968
Post-War Canada 1948–1968

1 Because the Depression had so dramatically reduced the rate of reproduction, the return to pre-Depression birth rates had the effect of creating a baby boom. The average crude birth rate prior to the Depression (1921–26) was 27.4. The average crude birth rate in the

immediate post-war years (1951–56) was very similar at 27.9. The combined effect of the end of the war, high employment and more income resulted in an increase in the marriage rate, especially early marriages. Early marriages led to childbearing at increasingly younger ages at the same time that older couples were making up for delays in childbearing caused by the Depression and the war (Romaniuc 1984, 13). Between 1952 and 1965 close to half a million children were born annually. The rate of natural increase went from 9.7 in 1937 to 20.0 in 1957, with an average crude birth rate of 27.9, and the Canadian population doubled — from ten million in 1930 to over twenty million by 1970 (Leacy 1983, Series B1–14).

2   Post-war Europe was a source of a large and desperate labour pool of war refugees and displaced persons. In April of 1947 the Canadian government repealed an order-in-council of the previous a generation that had prevented contract labour being brought into this country. A special committee of government and industrialists was struck and empowered by Privy Council Orders to recruit and contract labour from displaced persons' camps in Europe. Between 1947 and 1951, 100,000 war refugees were recruited by this committee for Canadian employers experiencing labour shortages (Dirks 1977, 151–52). While this special recruitment program ended in 1951, large numbers of immigrants continued to be a source of cheap labour throughout the post-war period. Over a million and a half immigrants entered Canada between 1951 and 1960, and another 900,000 entered between 1964 and 1968 (Dirks 1977, 260). As the demand for labour continued, immigration increased accounting for 26% of the population growth in the 1950s and 22% in the 1960s. (Clement 1984, 83).

3   A particularly thorough review of this process in the United States is found Gordon, Edwards and Reich (1982). For Canada, see Kumar (1975), Aw (1980), Armstrong and Armstrong (1984a), Fox and Fox (1986).

4   Armstrong and Armstrong (1984a), Phillips and Phillips (1983), White (1980).

5   Workmen's Compensation had become a major program for transferring income into the family, insuring workers and their families from economic crisis due to injury or work-related illness. The extension of coverage and the massive growth in the labour force throughout the third period resulted in dramatic increases in compensation payouts. In 1940 Workmen's Compensation payments amounted to $5 million in Ontario, less than a million in Manitoba, and $17 million in the whole of Canada. By the end of the third period payments had increased to $68 million in Ontario, $5 million in Manitoba, and close to $200 million was paid out to workers and their dependants throughout Canada (Leacy 1983, Series C274–286).

6   The appearance of greater legislative activity on the part of Ontario is merely a reflection of their later move to consolidation. Manitoba was every bit as active in extending protective legislation. However, much of this activity is contained within the large, consolidated Employment Standards Act.

7   Ontario's leadership on this issue is puzzling as it preceded the adoption of equal-pay resolutions by any of the Canadian Labour unions by a year or two. The question that arises is where did the demand come from? The answer lies in the composition of the legislature at the time. In 1950 the CCF held twenty-two seats and was the official opposition in Ontario. At the beginning of the session four CCF members and one labour Progressive introduced seven private-members bills dealing with labour reforms including Equal Pay, Fair Employment, Hours of Work and Vacations with Pay bills. In this manner the CCF used their status as official opposition to keep labour reform a high profile issue in the house. Of the four proposed bills, the Hours of Work and Vacations with Pay bills would be most costly to employers and hence were much more contentious. The Fair Employment and Equal Pay bills, however, amounted to asserting a principle rather than implementing a policy with clear calculable costs. The compromise was obvious.

8   The Labour Relations Board had some real discretionary power in the determination of employees eligible for certification. According to the Labour Relations Acts, individuals categorized as managerial or confidential could be excluded from the bargaining unit. Bairstow's study (1968) reveals that, in all jurisdictions across Canada, labour boards made little distinction between managerial and supervisory staff and that white-collar workers were subject to large-scale exclusion due to dubious categorization. Bairstow recounts the experience of Ontario Hydro's union drive in the late 1950s in which nine hundred white-collar workers were excluded due to managerial or confidential categorization. Another instance of large-scale exclusions involved Quebec Hydro. Five thousand white-collar workers were employed by Hydro, and only 2,800 were permitted to become members of the bargaining unit. All senior clerks were excluded, thus eliminating promotion possibilities within the bargaining unit (Bairstow 1968, 55).

9   All of the social-welfare commissions and inquiries in this period were health inquiries. Because of the limited number of commissions and their very specific focus, I will discuss them in the context of the legislation they addressed or contributed to.

10 The Ontario clause was removed in 1950 (SO c.66 s.4), and the Manitoba clause was removed in 1954 (SM c.7 s.35).

11 Mothers' Allowances payments were less regularly reported as separate from over-all assistance payments in Manitoba. By the early

1960s, Mothers' Allowances became incorporated in the revised Social Assistance Acts of both provinces, no longer existing as a separate, calculable expenditure.

12 In his analysis of Old Age Pensions, Bryden points out that throughout Canadian history the provinces attitude to federal involvement was always co-operative. "The provinces' response was not to try to reclaim their jurisdiction but to encourage more complete federal involvement.... Provincial participation in policy making was confined to some supplementation of the benefits paid under federal law and to occasional attempts to persuade the federal government to improve benefits" (Bryden 1974, 202). This approach was characteristic of Quebec as well until the 1960s.

13 In the third period the relative importance of conditional grants rose from 19% of total federal payments to the provinces in 1955 to 72% a decade later. As their proportional importance grew, provinces chaffed against the "conditional" nature of the grants. As a result the mid 1960s saw a move away from conditional granting. Two acts were implemented to consolidate and routinize these payments. The first was the Established Programs Financing Act in 1964, which largely covered education and health, and later the Canada Assistance Plan Act, which largely covered social-welfare payments and services. The former was calculated on a per capita formula basis and the latter on a fifty percent reimbursement basis (Moore, Milton, Perry, and Beach 1966, 112).

14 The guaranteed income supplement was deliberately designed as a transitional measure that would ultimately phase itself out when full benefits would become payable under the contributory scheme. No one who had been born after 1910 and, thus, would reach sixty-five after 1975 was to be eligible for the GIS. However, the continued need to supplement pensioners' incomes resulted in the removal of this limitation by an amending act in 1970. GIS is still in place today (Bryden 1974, 131).

15 The Commission on Health was referred to as the Hall Commission after Chief Justice Emmet Hall, Chairperson of the Royal Commission.

Bibliography

Abramowitz, M. 1988. *Regulating the lives of women: Social welfare policy from colonial times to the present.* Boston: South End.

Acton, J., P. Goldsmith, and B. Shepard, eds. 1974. *Women at Work: Ontario, 1850–1930.* Toronto: Women's.

Allen, Richard. 1971. *The social passion: Religion and social reform in Canada.* Toronto: U of Toronto P.

Althusser, Louis. 1971. *Lenin and philosophy.* Trans. Ben Brewster. New York: Monthly Review.

Ambert, Anne-Marie. 1976. *Sex structure.* 2nd ed. Toronto: Longmans.

———. 1980. *Divorce in Canada.* Don Mills: Academic.

Ames, Herbert Brown. 1972. *The city below the hill.* Toronto: U of Toronto P.

Anderson, Michael. 1971. *Family structure in nineteeth century Lancashire.* Cambridge: Urizen.

Andrew, Caroline. 1984. Women and the welfare state. *Canadian Journal of Political Science* 17 667–83.

Arensberg, C.M., and S.T. Kimball. 1968. *Family and community in Ireland.* 2nd ed. Cambridge: Harvard UP.

Armitage, Andrew. 1975. *Social welfare in Canada: Ideals and realities.* Toronto: McClelland.

Armstrong, Hugh, and Pat Armstrong. 1975. The segregated participation of women in the Canadian labour force 1941–71. *The Canadian Review of Sociology and Anthropology* 12: 370–84.

Armstrong, Pat. 1984. *Labour pains: Women's work in crisis.* Toronto: Women's.

Armstrong, Pat, and Hugh Armstrong. 1978. *The double ghetto: Canadian women and their segregated work.* Toronto: McClelland.

———. 1983. Beyond sexless class and classless sex: Towards feminist marxism. *Studies in Political Economy* 10: 7–43.———. 1984a. *The double ghetto: Canadian women and their segregated work.* Rev. ed. Toronto: McClelland.

———. 1984b. More on Marxism and feminism: A response to Patricia Connelley. *Studies in Political Economy* 15: 179–84.

———. 1985. Political economy and the household: Rejecting separate spheres. *Studies in Political Economy* 17: 167–77.

Armstrong, Pat, Hugh Armstrong, Pat Connelly, and A. Miles. 1985. *Feminist Marxism or Marxist feminism.* Toronto: Garamond.

Aronson, Jane. 1986. Care of the frail elderly: Whose crisis? Whose responsibility? *Canadian Social Work Review [1]:* 45–58.

373

Artibise, Alan F. 1975. *Winnipeg: A social history of urban growth, 1874–1914.* Montreal: McGill-Queen's UP.

Aw, Chan F. 1980. A dual labour market analysis: A study of Canadian manufacturing industries. Ottawa: Economic Analysis Branch, Central Analytical Services, Labour Canada, Queen's Printer.

Bacchi, Carol. 1976. Liberation deferred: The ideas of the English Canadian suffragists, 1877–1918. MA Thesis McGill.

———. 1978. Race regeneration and social purity. *Social History* 11 [22]: 468.

Bairstow, Frances. 1968. *White collar workers and collective bargaining.* Task Force on Labour Relations, Project No. 43. Draft Study. Queen's UP.

Barnsley, Jan. 1988. Feminist action, institutional reaction. *Resources for Feminist Research* 17.3: 18–30.

Barrett, Michelle. 1980. *Women's oppression today.* London: New Left Review.

Barrett, Michelle, and Mary McIntosh. 1982. *The anti-social family.* London: Verso.

Benston, Margaret. 1969. The political economy of women's liberation. *Monthly Review* Sep.: 13–27.

Berle, A.A., and G.C. Means. 1932. *The modern corporation and private property.* New York: Macmillan.

Binney, Elizabeth, and Carroll Estes. 1988. The retreat of the state and its transfer of responsibility: The intergenerational war. *International Journal of Health Services* 18.1: 83–96.

Bird, Richard. 1970. *The growth of government spending in Canada.* Toronto: Canadian Tax Foundation.

Bliss, Michael. 1974. *A living profit.* Toronto: McClelland.

Borchorst, Annette, and Berte Siim. 1987. Women and the advanced welfare state — A new kind of patriarchal power? Sassoon 128–57.

Boulet, Jac-Andre, and Laval Lavallee. 1984. *The changing economic status of women.* Ottawa: Canadian Government Publishing Centre.

Boyd, Monica, and Elizabeth Humphreys. 1979. Labour markets and sex differences in Canadian incomes. Economic Council of Canada, Discussion Paper No. 143. Ottawa: Economic Council of Canada.

Bradbury, Bettina. 1979. The family economy and work in an industrializing city: Montreal in the 1870s. *Canadian Historical Papers:* 71–96.

———. 1984. Pigs, cows and boarders: Non-wage forms of survival among Montreal families, 1861–91. *Labour/Le Travail* 14: 9–46.

Brenner, Johanna, and Maria Ramas. 1984. Rethinking women's oppression. *New Left Review* 144: 33–71.

Bridenthal, R., C. Koonz, and S. Stuard. 1987. *Becoming visible: Women in European history.* Boston: Houghton.

Bronfenbrenner, V. 1958. Socialization and social class through time and space. *Readings in social psychology.* 3rd ed. Ed. E.E. Maccoby, T.M. Newcomb, and E.L. Hartley. New York: Holt.

Brown, J. 1975. Iroquois women: An ethnohistoric note. Reiter 235–51.

Bryden, Kenneth. 1974. *Old age pensions and policy-making in Canada.* Montreal: McGill-Queen's UP.

Burke, Mary Anne. 1990. Urban Canada. Mckie and Thompson 35–43.

Burstyn, Varda. 1983. Masculine dominance and the state. *The socialist register 1983.* Ed. Ralph Miliband and John Daville. London: Merlin.

Burstyn, Varda, and D. Smith. 1985 *Women, class, family and the state.* Toronto: Garamond.

Burton, Clare. 1988. *Subordination: Feminism and social theory.* London: Allen.

1890. *Canadian Practitioner and Review* 33: 253.

Caporaso, James A., ed. 1987. *A changing international division of labour.* Bolder, CO.: Lynn Rienner.

Chodorow, Nancy. 1987. *The reproduction of mothering: Psychoanalysis and the sociology of gender.* Berkeley: U of California P.

Clark, Samuel D., J. Paul Grayson, and Linda M. Grayson. 1975. *Prophecy and protest: Social movements in twentieth-century Canada.* Toronto: Gage.

Clarke, Simon. 1977. Marxism, sociology and Poulantzas' theory of the state. *Capital and Class* 2: 1–31.

Clement, Wallace. 1984. Canada's social structure: Capital, Labour, and the State, 1930–1980. Cross and Kealey 81–101.

Comack, Elizabeth and Steve Brickey, eds. 1991. *The social basis of law: Critical readings in the sociology of law.* Toronto: Garamond.

Connelly, M. Patricia. 1978. *Last hired: First fired.* Toronto: Women's.

———. 1983. On Marxism and feminism. *Studies in Political Economy* 12: 153–61.

1961. Consideration of Health and Health Insurance. *Canadian Medical Association Journal.* 14 Jan: 116–17.

Cook, Gail C.A., ed. 1976. *Opportunity for choice: A goal for women in Canada.* Ottawa: Information Canada.

Cox, Robert. 1987. *Production, power and world order.* New York: Columbia UP.

Cross, Michael S., and Gregory S. Kealey, eds. 1984. *Modern Canada, 1930–1980s.* Toronto: McClelland.

Cuneo, Carl J. 1979. State, class, and reserve labour: The case of the 1941 Canadian Unemployment Insurance Act. *Canadian Review of Sociology and Anthropology* 16.2: 147–70.

———. 1980. The Canadian state and unemployment insurance. *Studies in Political Economy: A Socialist Review* 3: 37–65.

Currie, Dawn. 1990. Battered women and the state: From the failure of theory to a theory of failure. *Journal of Human Justice* 1.2: 77–96.

Dahl, Robert. 1961. *Who governs? Democracy and power in an American city.* New Haven: Yale UP.

——. 1967. *Pluralist democracy in the United States: Conflict and consent.* Chicago: Rand.

Dahlerup, Drude. 1987. Confusing concepts — confusing reality: A theoretical discussion of the patriarchal state. Sassoon 93–127.

dalla Costa, Maria. 1972. *The power of women and the subversion of the community.* Bristol, Eng: Falling Wall.

Daly, Mary. 1978. *Gyn/ecology: The metaethics of radical feminism.* Boston: Houghton.

Delphy, Christine. 1984. *Close to home: A materialist analysis of women's oppression.* Amherst: U of Massachusett P.

Denton, Margaret, and Alfred Hunter. 1984. *Equality in the workplace. Economic sectors and gender discrimination in Canada: A critique and test of Block and Walker ... and some new evidence.* Ottawa: Supply and Services Canada for Women's Bureau, Labour Canada.

Diamond, I. 1983. *Families, politics and public policy: A feminist dialogue on women and the state.* New York: Longmans.

Dickinson, James, and Bob Russell, eds. 1986. *Family, economy and state.* London: Croom.

Dirks, G.E. 1977. *Canada's refugee policy.* Montreal: McGill-Queen's UP.

Donzelot, Jacques. 1979. *The policing of families.* New York: Basic.

Eichler, Margrit. 1973. Women as personal dependants. *Women in Canada.* Ed. Marylee Stephenson. Toronto: New. 36–55.

——. 1983. *Families in Canada today: Recent changes and their policy consequences.* Toronto: Gage.

Eisenstein, Zillah. 1979. *Capitalist patriarchy and the case for socialist feminism.* New York: Monthly Review.

——. 1980. The State, the patriarchal family and working mothers. *Kapitalistate* 8: 43–66.

——. 1984. The patriarchal relations of the Reagan state. *Signs: Journal of Women in Culture and Society,* 10.21: 329–37.

——. 1988. *The female body and the law.* Berkeley: U of California P.

Engels, Frederick. 1968a. *The condition of the working class in England.* Stanford: Stanford UP.

——. 1968b. *Origin of the family, private property, and the state.* Moscow: Progress.

——. 1968c. Preface to the first edition of *The origin of the family, private property and the state. Selected works.* By Karl Marx and Frederick Engels. New York: International. 5–7.

Esping-Andersen, Gosta. 1989. The three political economics of the welfare state. *Canadian Review of Sociology and Anthropology* 26.1: 10–36.

Esquiros, A. 1846. Les enfants trouves. *Revue de Deux Mondes* 13: 211–42, 1007–44.

Evan, W. 1962. *Law and sociology: Exploratory essays.* New York: Fress.

Finch, Janet, and Dulcie Groves. 1983. *A Labour of love: Women, work and caring*. London: Routledge.

Findlay, Sue. 1990. Making sense of pay equity: Issues for feminist political practice. Pay Equity Conference: Theory and Practice, Centre for Research on Public Law and Public Policy and Osgoode Hall, Toronto, 10–12 May.

Finkel, Alvin. 1979. *Business and social reform in the thirties*. Toronto: Lorimer.

Finn, Geraldine. 1982. On the oppression of women in philosophy. *Feminism in Canada*. Ed. Angela Miles and Geraldine Finn. Montreal: Black Rose. 145–74.

Firestone, Shulamith. 1970. *The dialectic of sex: The case for feminist revolution*. New York: Bantam.

Foot, David. 1982. *Population in Canada*. Ottawa: Queen's Printer.

Foote, Catherine. 1989. A feminist response to "Nabbing divorce cheats": Critique of recent developments in spousal and child support enforcement. Canadian Law and Society Association, Learned Societies Conference, Quebec City, June.

Forebel, F., J. Heinrichs, and O. Kreye. 1980. *The new international division of labour*. Cambridge: Cambridge UP.

Foster, John. 1974. *Class struggle and the industrial revolution: Early industrial capitalism in three English towns*. London: Weidenfeld.

Foucault, Michel. 1980. *The history of sexuality*. Trans. Robert Hurley. New York: Vintage.

Fox, Bonnie, ed. 1980. *Hidden in the household: Women's domestic labour under capitalism*. Toronto: Women's.

Fox, Bonnie. 1988. Conceptualizing patriarchy. *Canadian Review of Sociology and Anthropology*, 25.2: 161–82.

Fox, Bonnie, and John Fox. 1986. Women in the labour market 1931–1981: Exclusion and competition. *Canadian Review of Sociology and Anthropology* 23: 1–22.

Fox, Paul, ed. 1970. *Politics Canada*. 3rd ed. Toronto: McGraw.

Franzway, S., D. Court, and R.W. Connell. 1989. *Staking a claim: Feminism, bureaucracy and the state*. London: Polity.

Fryer, P. 1965. *The birth controllers*. New York: Stein.

Gee, Ellen M. 1988. The life course of Canadian women: An historical and demographical analysis. McLaren 187–204.

George, Vic, and Paul Wilding. 1976. *Ideology and social welfare*. London: Routledge.

Gillespie, Irwin. 1980. On the redistribution of income in Canada. *Structural inequality in Canada*. Ed. J. Harp and J. Hofley. Toronto: Prentice. 22–53.

Glendon, Mary Ann. 1981. *The new family and the new property*. Toronto: Butterworth's.

Gold, David Clarence Lo, and Erik Wright. 1975. Recent developments in Marxist theories of the capitalist state. *Monthly Review* Oct.: 29–43.

Gordon, David M., Richard Edwards, and Michael Reich. 1982. *Segmented work, divided workers*. Cambridge: Cambridge UP.

Gordon, Linda. 1977. *Woman's body, woman's right: Birth control in America*. New York: Penguin.

Gorham, Deborah. 1979. Flora MacDonald Denison: Canadian feminist, L. Kealey 47–70.

Gough, Ian. 1979. *The political economy of the welfare state*. London: Macmillan.

Graham, Elizabeth. 1974. School marms and early teaching in Ontario. Acton, Goldsmith, and Shepard 165–209.

Guest, Dennis. 1980. *The emergence of social security in Canada*. Vancouver: U of British Columbia P.

Hamilton, Roberta. 1978. *The liberation of women: A study of patriarchy and capitalism*. London: Allen.

Hamilton, Roberta, and Michelle Barrett. 1986. *The politics of diversity*. Montreal: Book Centre.

Harris, Marvin. 1975. *Cows, pigs, wars and witches: The riddles of culture*. New York: Vintage.

——. 1980. *Cultural materialism*. New York: Vintage.

Hartman, Heidi. 1979. The unhappy marriage of Marxism and feminism: Towards a progressive union. *Women and Revolution*. Ed. L. Sargent. Boston: South End. 1–43.

Hernes, Helga M. 1987. Women and the welfare state: The transition from private to public dependence. Sassoon 72–92.

The history of federal electoral ridings, 1867–1980. Information and Reference Branch of the Library of Parliament, Vol. 1. Ottawa. Queen's Printer.

Hofstadter, Richard. 1955. *The age of reform: From Bryan to F.D.R.* New York: Knopf.

Holloway, John, and Sol Picciotto. 1978. Introduction: Towards a materialist theory of the state. *State and capital: A Marxist debate*. Ed. J. Holloway and S. Picciotto. London: Edward Arnold. 1–31.

Homans, George C. 1941. *English villagers of the thirteenth century*. Cambridge: Harvard UP.

Hood, William C., and Anthony Scott. 1957. *Output, labour and capital in the Canadian economy*. Ottawa: Royal Commission on Canada's Economic Prospects, Queen's Printer.

Hougham, George M. 1962. *The relationship between unemployment insurance and Canada's other income maintenance programs*. Ottawa: Royal Commission of Inquiry into the Unemployment Insurance Act, Queen's Printer.

Hum, Derek P.J. 1983. *Federalism and the poor: A review of the Canada Assistance Plan*. Toronto: Ontario Economic Council.

Humphries, Jane. 1977. The working-class family, women's liberation, and class struggle: The case of nineteenth-century British history. *Review of Radical Political Economics* 9.3: 25–41.

Jamieson, Stuart M. 1962. *Report of the Committee of Inquiry into the Unemployment Insurance Act*. Ottawa: Queen's Printer.

———. 1968. *Times of trouble: Labour unrest and industrial conflict in Canada 1900–66*. Task Force of Labour Relations Study 22. Ottawa: Queen's Printer.

Jennissen, Theresa. 1981. The development of the Workmen's Compensation Act of Ontario, 1914. *Canadian Journal of Social Work Education*. 7.1: 55–71.

Jenson, Jane. 1986a. Gender and reproduction: Or babies and the state. *Studies in Political Economy*, 20: 9–46.

———. 1986b. Paradigms and political discourse: Protective legislation in France and the United States before 1914. *Canadian Journal of Political Science* 22: 2.

———. 1989. "Different" but not "Exceptional": Canada's permeable Fordism." *Canadian Review of Sociology and Anthropology* 26.1: 69–94.

Johnson, Laura C., and Robert E. Johnson. 1982 *The seam allowance: Industrial home sewing in Canada*. Toronto: Women's.

Johnson, Leo. 1974. The political economy of Ontario women in the nineteenth century. Action, Goldsmith, and Shepard 13–32.

Kealey, Gregory S., ed. 1973. *Canada investigates industrialism*. Toronto: U of Toronto P.

———. 1974. *Hogtown: Working class Toronto at the turn of the century*. Toronto: New Hogtown.

———. 1980. *Toronto worker's respond to industrial capitalism, 1867–1892*. Toronto: U of Toronto P.

Kealey, Gregory S., and Peter Warrian, eds. 1976. *Essays in Canadian working-class history*. Toronto: McClelland.

Kealey, Linda, ed. 1979. *A not unreasonable claim: Women and reform in Canada, 1880–1920*. Toronto: Women's.

Keniston, Kenneth. 1977. *All our children: The American family under pressure*. New York: Harcourt.

Kinear, Mary, and Greg Mason, eds. *Women and Work*. Winnipeg: Institute for Social and Economic Research, U of Manitoba.

King, William Lyon Mackenzie. *Industry and humanity*. Toronto: U of Toronto P.

1898. *Kingston Medical Quarterly*, 3: 165.

Kitchen, Brigitte. 1981. Wartime social reform: The introduction of family allowances. *Canadian Journal of Social Work Education* 7.1: 29–54.

———. 1987. The introduction of family allowances in Canada. Moscovitch and Albert 222–41.

Klein, Alice, and Wayne Roberts. 1974. Besieged innocence: The problem and problems of working women — Toronto, 1896–1914. Acton, Goldsmith, and Shepard 211–59.

Kohn, Melvin. 1959. Social class and parental values. *American Journal of Sociology*, 65: 337–351.

———. 1963. Social class and parent-child relationships. *American Journal of Sociology* 68: 471–80.

Kolko, Joyce. 1988. *Restructuring the world economy*. New York: Pantheon.

Komarovsky, M. 1962. *Blue collar marriage*. New York: Vintage.

Kovacs, Aranka E. 1961. *Readings in Canadian labour economics*. Toronto: McGraw.

Kubat, D., and D. Thornton. 1974. *A statistical profile of Canadian society*. Toronto: McGraw.

Kuhn, Annette. 1978. Structures of patriarchy and capital in the family. Kuhn and Wolpe 42–67.

Kuhn, Annette, and Ann Marie Wolpe, eds. 1978. *Feminism and materialism: Women and modes of production*. London: Routledge.

Kumar, Pradeep. 1975. *Relative wage differentials in Canadian industries*. Kingston: Industrial Relations Centre, Queen's U.

The Labour Relations Law Casebook Group. 1981. *Labour Relations Law*. Kingston: Industrial Relations Centre, Queen's U.

Laclau, Ernesto. 1975. The specificity of the political: Around the Poulantzas-Miliband debate. *Economy and Society* 4.1: 87–110.

Land, Brian. 1970. A description and guide to the use of Canadian government publications. P. Fox #501–12.

Langer, William. 1963. Europe's initial population explosion. *American Historical Review* 69: 1–17.

Lasch, Christopher. 1979. *Haven in a heartless world: The family besieged*. New York: Basic.

Laslett, Barbara, and Johanna Brenner. 1989. Gender and social reproduction: Historical perspectives. *Annual Review of Sociology* 15: 381–404.

Lazonick, William. 1978. The subjugation of labour to capital: The rise of the capitalist system. *Review of Radical Political Economics* 10.1: 1–31.

Leacock, Eleanor. 1978. Women's status in egalitarian societies: Implications for social evolution. *Current Anthropology* 19.2: 247–75.

Leacy, F.H., ed. 1983. *Historical statistics of Canada*. 2nd ed. Ottawa: Statistics Canada in joint sponsorship with the Social Science Foundation of Canada.

Leman, Christopher. 1980. *The collapse of welfare reform: Political institutions, policy, and the poor in Canada and the United States*. Massachusetts: MIT P.

Leslie, Genevieve. 1974. Domestic service in Canada, 1880–1920. Acton, Goldsmith, and Shepard 71–125.

Levi-Strauss, Claude. 1969. *The elementary structures of kinship*. Trans. J.H. Bell, J.R. Sturmer, and R. Needham. Boston: Beacon.

——. 1971. The family. *Man, culture and society.* Ed. H. Shapiro. London: Oxford UP. 333–57.

Lewis, Jane. 1983. *Women's welfare — Women's right.* London: Croom.

——. 1984. *Women in England 1870–1950: Structural divisions and social change.* Bloomington: Indiana UP.

——. 1986. *Labor and love: Women's experience of home and family 1850–1940.* Oxford: Blackwell.

Linton, Ralph. 1936. *The study of man.* New York: Appleton.

Lipton, Charles. 1973. *The trade union movement of Canada, 1827–1959.* 3rd ed. Toronto: NC.

Lowe, Graham S. 1980. *Bank unionization in Canada: A preliminary analysis.* Toronto: Centre for Industrial Relations, U of Toronto.

Luxton, Meg. 1980. *More than a labour of love: Three generations of women's work in the home.* Toronto: Women's.

McIntosh, Mary. 1978. The state and the oppression of women. Kuhn and Wolpe 254–89.

McKie, Craig, and Keith Thompson, eds. 1990. *Canadian social trends.* Toronto: Thompson.

McKie, D.C., B. Prentice, and P. Reed. 1983. *Divorce: Law and the family in Canada.* Ottawa: Statistics Canada.

MacKinnon, Catherine. 1982. Feminism, Marxism, method, and the state: An agenda for theory. *Signs: Journal of Women in Culture and Society* 7.3: 515–45.

——. 1983. Feminism, Marxism, method, and the state: Toward feminist jurisprudence. *Signs: Journal of Women in Culture and Society* 8.4: 635–58.

——. 1989. *Towards a feminist theory of the state.* Cambridge: Harvard UP.

McLaren, A. 1978a. Birth control and aborton in Canada, 1870–1920. *Canadian Historical Review* 59: 319–39.

——. 1978b. *Birth control in nineteenth-century England.* London: Croom.

——. ed. 1988. *Gender and society.* Toronto: Copp.

McLaren, Angus, and Arlene Tigar McLaren. 1986. *The bedroom and the state. The changing practices and policies of contraception and abortion in Canada, 1880–1980.* Toronto: McClelland.

McLellan, David. 1971. *The thought of Karl Marx.* London: Macmillan.

Mandell, Betty Reid. 1975. *Welfare in America: Controlling the dangerous classes.* Englewood Cliffs: Prentice.

Marchak, Patricia. 1991. *The integrated circus: The new right and the restructuring of global markets.* Montreal: McGill-Queen's UP.

Maroney, H.J. 1986. Embracing motherhood: New feminist theory. Hamilton and Barrett 398–423.

Marsh, Leonard. 1975. *Report on social security for Canada.* Toronto: U of Toronto P.

Marx, Karl, and Frederick Engels. 1947. *The German ideology.* New York: International.

———. 1968. *Selected works.* New York: International.

Masters, D.C. 1947. *The rise of Toronto, 1850–1890.* Toronto: U of Toronto P.

Mead, Margaret. 1935. *Sex and temperament in three primitive societies.* New York: Morrow.

Meillassoux, Claude. 1981. *Maidens, meal and money.* New York: Cambridge UP.

Meissner, Martin, Elizabeth W. Humphreys, Scott M. Meis, and William J. Scheu. 1975. No exit for wives: Sexual division of labour and the culmination of household demands. *Canadian Review of Sociology and Anthropology* 12.4, Pt. 1: 424–39.

Miles, Angela. 1985. Economism and feminism: Hidden in the household a comment on the domestic labour debate. Armstrong, Armstrong, Connelly, and Miles 39–52.

Miliband, Ralph. 1969. *The state in capitalist society.* London: Weidenfeld.

———. 1970. Reply to Nicos Poulantzas. *New Left Review* 59: 53–60.

———. 1973. Poulantzas and the Capitalist State. *New Left Review* 82: 83–92.

———. 1977. *Marxism and Politics.* Oxford: Oxford UP.

Mitchell, Juliet. 1971. *Woman's estate.* Harmondsworth, Eng.: Penguin.

———. 1975. *Psychoanalysis and feminism: Freud, Reich, Laing, and women.* New York: Vintage.

Mitchinson, Wendy. 1977. Aspects of reform: Four women's organizations in nineteenth-century Canada. Diss. York U.

———. 1979. The YWCA and reform in the nineteenth century. *Social History* 12 [24]: 376.

Moore, A., J. Milton, Harvey Perry, and D.I. Beach. 1966. *The financing of Canadian Federation: The first hundred years.* Toronto: Canadian Tax Foundation.

Morgan, Robin. 1970. *Sisterhood is powerful.* New York: Vintage.

———. 1977. *Going too far: The personal chronicle of a feminist.* New York: Bantam.

Morton, Desmond, and Terry Copp. 1980. *Working people.* Ottawa: Deneau.

Morton, W.L. 1967. *Manitoba: A history.* 2nd ed. Toronto: U of Toronto P.

Moscovitch, Allen, and Jim Albert. 1987. *The benevolent state: The growth of welfare in Canada.* Toronto: Garamond.

Mosley, H. 1978. Is there a fiscal crisis of the state? *Monthly Review* 30.1: 34–35.

Muller, Viana. 1977. The formation of the state and the oppression of women: Some theoretical considerations and a case study in England and Wales. *Review of Radical Political Economics* 9.3: 7–21.

Murphy, Robert. 1959. Social structure and sex antagonism. *South Western Journal of Anthropology* 15.1: 89–98.

Myles, John F. 1980. The aged, the state, and the structure of inequality.

Structured inequality in Canada. Ed. John Harp and John R. Hofley. Scarborough, ON: Prentice. 317–42.

National Bureau of Economic Research and the Brookings Institute. 1964. *The role of direct and indirect taxes in the federal revenue system*. Princeton: Princeton UP.

O'Brien, Mary. 1981. *The politics of reproduction*. London: Routledge.

——. 1986a. Feminism and revolution. Hamilton and Barrett 424–31.

——. 1986b. Hegemony and superstructure: A feminist critique of neo-morphism. Hamilton and Barrett 255–65.

O'Conner, James. 1973. *The fiscal crisis of the state*. New York: St. Martin's.

O'Connor, Julia. 1989. Welfare expenditure and policy orientation in Canada in comparative perspective. *Canadian Review of Sociology and Anthropology* 26.1: 127–50.

O'Neill, William. 1971. *Everyone was brave*. Chicago: Avadrangle.

Oddson, A. 1938. *Employment of women in Manitoba*. Winnipeg: Manitoba Economic Survey Board, King's Printer.

Ogburn, William F. 1929. The changing family. *Publications of the American Sociological Society* 23: 124–33.

Organization for Economic Co-operation and Development. 1985. *Social expenditure 1960–1990*. Paris: OECD.

Palmer, Brian. 1979. *A culture of conflict*. Montreal: McGill-Queen's UP.

Panitch, Leo, ed. 1977. *The Canadian state: Political economy and political power*. Toronto: U of Toronto P.

Parr, Joy. 1990. *The gender of breadwinners*. Toronto: U of Toronto P.

Parsons, Talcott. 1957. The distribution of power in American society. *World Politics* 10.1: 123–43.

——. 1969. *Sociological theory and modern society*. New York: Free.

Parsons, Talcott, and Robert F. Bales. 1955. *Family, socialization and interaction process*. New York: Free.

Pentland, H. Clare. 1968. *A study of the changing social, economic and political background of the Canadian system of industrial relations*. Task Force on Labour Relations. Ottawa.

——. 1981. *Labour and capital in Canada*. Toronto: Lorimer.

Perry, J. Harvey. 1955. *Taxes, tariffs, and subsidies*. Vol. 1. Toronto: U of Toronto P.

——. 1982. *Background of current fiscal problems*. Toronto: Canadian Tax Foundation.

Phillips, Paul. 1967. *No power greater*. Vancouver: British Columbia Federation of Labour, Bogg Foundation.

Phillips, Paul, and Erin Phillips. 1983. *Women and work: Inequality in the labour market*. Toronto: Lorimer.

Phillips, Paul, and Stephen Watson. 1984. From mobilization to continentalism: The Canadian economy in the post-Depression period. Cross and Kealey 20–45.

Pickersgill, Jack W. 1960. *The Mackenzie King record*. Toronto: U of Toronto P.

Pierson, Ruth Roach, and Marjorie Cohen. 1984. Educating women for work: Government training programs for women before, during, and after World War II. Cross and Kealey 208–43.

Pike, Robert. 1975. Legal access and the incidents of divorce in Canada: A socio-historical analysis. *Canadian Review of Sociological Anthropology* V 12.2: 115–33.

Pleck, Joseph H., and Jack Sawyer. 1974. *Men and masculinity*. Englewood Cliffs: Prentice.

Poulantzas, Nicos. 1969. The problem of the capitalist state. *New Left Review* 58: 67–78.

——. 1975. *Classes in contemporary capitalism*. London: New Left.

Prentice, Alison. 1977. The feminization of teaching. Trofimenkoff and Prentice.

Quick, Paddy. 1977. The class nature of women's oppression. *Review of Radical Political Economics* 9.3: 42–53.

Rainwater, Lee. 1959. *Workingman's wife*. New York: Oceana.

——. 1960. *And the poor get children*. Chicago: Quadrangle.

Ramkhalawansingh, Ceta. 1974. Women during the great war. Acton, Goldsmith, and Shepard 261–307.

Randall, Melanie. 1988. Feminism and the state: Questions for theory and practice. *Resources for Feminist Research* 17.3: 10–15.

Reich, Wilhelm. 1970. *The mass psychology of fascism*. New York: Farrar.

——. 1972. *Sex-pol: Essays, 1929–1934*. New York: Vintage.

Reiter, Rayna R., ed. 1975. *Toward an anthropology of women*. New York: Monthly Review.

Reynolds, Morgan, and Eugene Smolensky. 1977. Public budgets and the US distribution of income: 1950, 1961, and 1970. *American society incorporated*. 2nd ed. Ed. Maurice Zeitlin. Chicago: Rand.

Rich, Adrienne. 1976. *Of woman born*. New York: Bantam.

Roberts, Wayne. 1976. *Honest womanhood: Feminism, femininity and class consciousness among Toronto working women, 1893–1914*. Toronto: New Hogtown.

Roberts, Wayne, and John Bullen. 1984. A heritage of hope and struggle: Workers, unions, and politics in Canada, 1930–1982. Cross and Kealey 105–40.

Robin, Martin. 1971. *Radical politics and Canadian Labour, 1880–1930*. Kingston: Industrial Relations Centre, Queen's U.

Romaniuc, A. 1984. *Fertility in Canada: From baby-boom to baby-bust*. Ottawa: Supply and Services Canada.

Rose, Arnold. 1967. *The power structure: Political process in American society*. New York: Oxford UP.

Rotenberg, Lori. 1974. The wayward worker: Toronto's prostitute at the turn of the century. Acton, Goldsmith, and Shepard 33–69.

Rubin, Gayle. 1975. The traffic in women: Notes on the "Political economy" of sex. Reiter 157–210.

Russel, Bob. 1984. The politics of labour force reproduction: Funding Canada's social wage, 1917–1946. *Studies in Political Economy: A Socialist Review* 14: 43–73.

Sangster, J. 1978. The 1907 Bell telephone strike: Organizing women workers. *Journal of Canadian Labour Studies.*

Sapiro, V. 1986. The gender basis of American social policy. *Political Science Quarterly* 101: 221–38.

Sassoon, Anne S., ed. 1987. *Women and the state.* London: Hutchinson.

Schur, Edwin. 1968. *Law and society: A sociological view.* New York: Random.

Seccombe, Wally. 1980. Domestic labour and the working-class household. B. Fox 25–99.

———. 1986a. Patriarchy stabilized: The construction of the male breadwinner wage norm in nineteenth-century Britian. *Social History* 11: 43–76.

———. 1986b. Reflections on the domestic labour debate and prospects for Marxist-feminist synthesis. Hamilton and Barrett 190–209.

Shorter, Edward. 1977. *The making of the modern family.* New York: Basic.

Smucker, Joseph. 1980. *Industrialization in Canada.* Scarborough: Prentice.

Snider, Laureen. 1990. The potential of the criminal justice system to promote feminist concerns. *Studies in Law, Politics, and Society* 10: 141–69.

Splane, Richard. 1965. *Social welfare in Ontario, 1791–1898.* Toronto: McClelland.

Sprague, D.N., ed. 1988. *The geneology of the first Metis nation: The development and dispersal of the Red River Settlement, 1820–1900.* Winnipeg: Pemmican.

Strong-Boag, Veronica. 1981. Working women and the state 1889–1945. *Atlantis* 6.2: 1–9.

Struthers, James. 1983. *No fault of their own: Unemployment and the Canadian welfare state 1914–1941.* Toronto: U of Toronto P.

Sufrin, Eileen. 1982. *The Eaton Drive.* Toronto: Fitzhenry.

Sutherland, Neil. 1976. *Children in English Canadian society.* Toronto: U of Toronto P.

Taylor, Malcolm G. 1978. *Health insurance and Canadian public policy.* Montreal: McGill-Queen's UP.

Teeple, Gary, ed. 1972. *Capitalism and the national question in Canada.* Toronto: U of Toronto P.

Thompson, E.P. 1979. *The poverty of theory.* New York: Monthly Review.

Tilly, Louise, and Joan Scott. 1978 *Women, work, and family.* New York: Holt.

Trofimenkoff, Susan, and Allison Prentice, ed. 1977. *The neglected majority.* Toronto: McClelland.

Urquhart, M.C., and K.A.H. Buckley. 1965. *Historical statistics of Canada.*

Ottawa: Statistics Canada, in joint sponsorship with the Social Science Foundation of Canada.

Ursel, Jane. 1977. The nature and origin of women's oppression: Marxism and feminism. *Contemporary Crises* 1: 23–36.

——. 1986. The state and the maintenance of patriarchy. Dickinson and Russell 150–91.

——. 1991. Considering the impact of the battered womens movement on the state: The example of Manitoba. Comack and Brickey 261–288.

——. 1991. Reproducing Canada: A feminist analysis of family state dyanmics. Diss. McMaster U.

Vanderkamp, John. 1968. *The time pattern of industrial conflict in Canada, 1901–1966.* Task Force on Labour Relations, Project No. 52(a). Draft Study. Ottawa: Queen's Printer.

Vanderpol, A. 1982. Dependent children, child custody, and the mothers' pensions. *Social Problems* 29: 223–34.

Walters, Vivienne. 1980. *Class inequality and health care.* London: Croom.

——. 1982. State, capital, and labour: The introduction of federal-provincial insurance for physican care. *Canadian Review of Sociology and Anthropology* 19.2: 157–72.

Westergaard, J., and H. Resler. 1975. *Class in a capitalist society.* London: Heinemann.

White, Julie. 1980. *Women and unions.* Ottawa: Supply and Services Canada for the Canadian Advisory Council on the Status of Women.

Wilensky, Harold L. 1975. *The welfare state and equality: Structural and ideological roots of public expenditures.* Berkeley: U of California P.

William, Raymond. 1978. Base and superstructure. *New Left Review* 109: 3–17.

Wilson, Elizabeth. 1977. *Women and the welfare state.* London: Tavistock.

——. 1980. Marxism and the welfare state. *New Left Review* 122: 79–89.

Wirth, Louis. 1938. Urbanism as a way of life. *American Journal of Sociology* 44: 1–24.

Wolfe, David. 1977. The state and economic policy in Canada, 1968–1975. *The Canadian state: Political economy and political power.* Ed. Leo Ponitch. Toronto: U of Toronto P.

Wright, Erik O. 1979. *Class structure and income determination.* New York: Academic.

Zaretsky, Eli. 1974. *Capitalism, the family, and personal life.* Winnipeg: *Canadian Dimension* Pamphlet.

——. 1982. The place of the family in the origin of the welfare state. *Rethinking the family: Some feminist questions.* Ed. B. Thorne. New York: Longman's.

Zimmerman, Carle C. 1947. *Family and civilization.* New York: Harper.

Government Documents

Advisory Committee on Reconstruction. 1944. *Post-war problems of women: Final report of the subcommitte.* Ottawa: King's Printer.

Annual Report of the Bureau of Industries for the Province of Ontario, Pt. 4, 1889 Sessional Papers 22.7.

Beveridge Report. 1942. Social Insurance and Allied Services. New York, MacMillan.

Canada Year Book 1978-79. 1979. Ottawa: Queen's Printer.

Canadian Federal Law Reform Commission. 1976. *Family law.* Vol. 47. Ottawa: : Queen's Printer.

Cost of Living Inquiry. 1915. Report of the Royal Commission to Investigate the Increase in the Cost of Living in Canada, Ottawa.

Curtis Report. 1944. Housing and Planning Report, Ottawa, National Archives.

Dominion-Provincial Commission Report. 1937. Ch. 2. See Royal Commission on Dominion-Provincial Relations.

Green Book Proposals. 1945. Dominion-Provincial Conference. Federal Submission, Ottawa, National Archives.

Hall Commission Report. 1965. Report of the Royal Commission on Health, Ottawa, National Archives.

Labour Relations Law Casebook. 1981.

McTague Report. 1943. Majority Report of the Commission to Inquire into the War Labour Board, Ottawa, National Archives.

Mather's Commission. 1919. Report of the Royal Commission to Inquire into Industrial Relations in Canada, Ottawa, National Archives.

Manitoba Dept. of Health and Welfare Annual Report. 1946.

Manitoba and Ontario Dept. of Public Welfare Annual Reports. 1948-68.

Manitoba Public Accounts. 1940-68.

Marsh Report. 1943. Report on Social Security for Canada, Reprint. Toronto, University of Toronto Press, 1975.

Ontario, Dept. of Family Services Annual Report. 1968.

Ontario Dept. of Labour Annual Reports. 1951.

Ontario Dept. of Public Welfare Annual Reports. 1948-62.

Ontario Dept. of Welfare Annual Report. 1951-69.

Ontario Public Accounts. 1940-68.

Price Spreads Inquiry. 1937 c.9. Report of the Royal Commission on Price Spreads, Ottawa, National Archives.

R.G.R. ... Ontario (see *Registrar General's Report for the Province of Ontario*).

R.I.P.I. ... Manitoba (see *Report of the Inspector of Public Institutions. Department of Public Works for the Province of Manitoba*).

R.I.F. ... Ontario (see *Reports of the Inspectors of Factories for the Province of Ontario*).

R.M.P.W. ... Ontario (see *Report of the Minister of Public Welfare for the Province of Ontario*).

R.S.N.C. ... Ontario (see *Report of the Superintendent of Neglected Children for the Province of Ontario*).

Rand Report. 1966. Report of the Inquiry into Industrial Disputes: Province of Ontario, Toronto, Queen's Printer.

Registrar General's Report for the Province of Ontario, 1888 Sessional Papers 3.

Registrar General's Report for the Province of Ontario, 1895 Sessional Papers 30.

Registrar General's Report for the Province of Ontario, 1896 Sessional Papers 30.

Registrar General's Report for the Province of Ontario, 1901 Sessional Papers 9.

Registrar General's Report for the Province of Ontario, 1905 Sessional Papers 9.

Report of the Department of Labour, Ontario, 1921 Sessional Papers 16.

Report of the Inspector of Public Institutions. Department of Public Works for the Province of Manitoba, 1890-1899 Sessional Papers.

Report of the Inspector of Public Institutions. Department of Public Works for the Province of Manitoba, 1905 Sessional Papers.

Reports of the Inspector of Charitable Institutions for the Province of Ontario, 1884-1912 Sessional Papers, 19, 40, 6, 35, 40, 43, 24.

Reports of the Inspectors of Factories for the Province of Ontario, 1905 Sessional Papers 37.

Report of the Inspectors of Factories for the Province of Ontario, 1908 Sessional Papers.

Report of the Minimum Wage Board, Ontario, 1922 Sessional Papers 73.

Report of the Minister of Welfare, Manitoba, 1918 Sessional Papers.

Report of the Minister of Public Welfare for the Provinces of Manitoba and Ontario, 1932-39 Sessional Papers.

Report of the Minister of Public Welfare, Ontario, 1922 Sessional Papers 89.

Report of the Minister of Public Welfare for the Province of Ontario, 1935 Sessional Papers 19.

Report of the Mothers' Allowance Commission of Manitoba, 1918 Sessional Papers.

Report of the Mothers' Allowance Commission, Ontario, 1922 Sessional Papers 89.

Report of the Public Welfare Commission, Manitoba, 1919 Sessional Papers 29.

Report of the Royal Commission on the Status of Women. 1970.

Report of the Royal Commission on Unemployment. 1914. Province of Ontario, Toronto.

Report of the Royal Commission to Inquire into the Cause of the Winnipeg General Strike. 1919. Manitoba Archives.

Report of the Superintendent of Neglected Children for the Province of Ontario, 1891 Sessional Papers 18.

Report of the Superintendent of Neglected Children for the Province of Ontario, 1894 Sessional Papers 47.

Report of the Superintendent of Neglected Children for the Province of Ontario, 1898 Sessional Papers 60.

Report of the Superintendent of Neglected Children for the Province of Ontario, 1902 Sessional Papers 43.

Report of the Superintendent of Neglected Children for the Province of Ontario, 1911 Sessional Papers 26.

Report of the Workmen's Compensation Board, Ontario, 1928 Sessional Papers 28.3.

Report of the Workmen's Compensation Board, Ontario, 1924 Sessional Papers 51.

Rowell-Sirois Report. 1940. See Royal Commission on Dominion-Provincial Relations.

Royal Commission on Canada's Economic Prospetcts. 1957. *Canada's economic future.* Toronto: Cockfield, Brown.

Royal Commission on Dominion-Provincial Relations Report Book II. 1940. Ottawa, National Archives.

Royal Commission on Equality in Employment. 1984. *Equality in employment.* Ottawa: Supply and Services Canada.

Royal Commission on the Status of Women. 1970. *Report.* Ottawa: Information Canada.

Sixth Census of Canada. 1921. Vol. 4.

Special Report on Infant Mortality, Ontario, 1910 Sessional Papers 9.

Taylor Report. 1954. Malcolm Taylor "Confidential Report on Health Insurance for the Ontario Government" 1954, Ontario Archives.

War Information Board Report 3 Dec. 1943.

Whitton Report. 1928. Inquiry into Child Welfare in Manitoba, Winnipeg, Manitoba Archives.

Newspapers

Canada Forward. Toronto: 1926–27. Connected with the central Toronto Labour Party.

Canadian Labour Defender. Toronto: 1930–1935. Published by Canadian Labour Defence League.

Canadian Labour World. Hamilton: 1923–1931.

Financial Post. 1957. Many more wives are working in Canadian industry. 4 May.

McArthur, Jack. 1955. The case against legislating equal pay for women. 26 Feb.

Schreiner, Jack. 1964. Sweet, lovely, and so plentiful — Women rushing into the labour force bringing some special problems. 12 Dec. 1958. Working women increase — Spell permanent problem? 31 May.

Grain Growers' Guide. Periodical of western farm women and men. 1908–28.

Hamilton Labour News. 1912–55.

Labour Gazette. Ottawa: 1900 to date. Journal of the Department of Labour. Particularly valuable from 1913 to 1918 when it contained a column from women correspondents composed of letters written from Montreal, Toronto, Winnipeg and Vancouver.

Toiler. Toronto: 1902–04. Toronto and District Labour Council.

Trades and Labour Congress Journal. Ottawa: 1922–56.

Tribune. Toronto: 1905–06. Toronto and District Labour Council.

Western Labour News. Winnipeg: 1918–23. (Also known as *The Voice* 1897–1918; *Peoples Voice* 1884–94.) Published by the Winnipeg Trades Labour Council.

Woman Worker. Toronto: 1926–29. Federation of Women's Labour Leagues. Workers Party.

Index

115, 115-116, 148-149; *Youth Allowances Act*, 273. *See also* Children's Aid Society; Infant mortality; Welfare bureaucracy

Children: abandoning of, 36, 66-67, 118; adoption of, 113, 117-118; destitute, 66-67, 155; foundlings, 65-67; illegitimate, 63, 66, 71, 104-105, 153, 162-163; immigrants, 109, 114; neglect of, 114, 118, 154; state control of, 111-116. *See also* Orphans and orphanages

Children's Aid Society, 109, 113-114, 116; and de-institutionalized care, 155-159, 259-261; in Manitoba, 117, 260; in Ontario, 116-117, 118-120, 150, 152, 260; and welfare bureaucracy, 161

Civil service. *See* Government, employees of

Clark, W.C., 191-196

Class, 9, 27-29; formation of, 25-27; and patriarchy, 29-34, 35, 39; and reproduction of labour, 48-54

Coalition on Reproductive Choice, 302

Cohen, J.L., 188-194

Cohen, Marjorie, 202

Coldwell, M.J., 184

Commissions, federal, 88-91, 96, 108, 124, 132, 166, 210-215, 238, 242-244, 272, 283-286

Commissions, provincial, 89, 96, 146, 243-244

Communal patriarchy, 6, 23, 23-25, 106

Conservative Party, 197, 218, 221, 271, 272

Cooperative Commonwealth Federation, 130, 184, 197, 207, 210-211, 221, 267, 268, 269, 271, 272

Corporations, 231-232; taxation of, 183. *See also* Business; Capital

Curtsey. *See* Property, laws of

D

Dandurand, Raoul, 131

Denison, Flora MacDonald, 73

Disabled persons, 269; *Blind Persons Act*, 268; *Vocational Rehabilitation Act*, 271-272

Divorce, 102, 238, 283, 291, 322n2

Domestic workers, 94

Dower, 300, 312; acts of, 103. *See also Married Women's Property Act*; Property, laws of

Drew, George, 197

E

Economic Advisory Committee, 191-194

Economic conditions: control of during World War II, 181-227; post-World War II, 208

Education, 171-172; *Canada Student Loan Act*, 273

Educational reform movement, 72-73

Eisenstein, Z., 18-19, 27, 28

Elders. *See* Older adults

Employment Equity, 292

Equal pay, 1, 241, 247-248, 250, 292; *Equal Pay Act*, 247, 248; *Fair Employment Practices Act*, 247; *Fair Remuneration for Female Employees Act*, 241, 247. *See also* Wages; Workers, female

Equal rights movement, 80-82

Eugenicism. *See* Race suicide

F

Factories Act, 83, 85, 86, 87, 92, 94; in Ontario and Manitoba, 92, 97-99; and wage disparity for women, 94-96

Familial patriarchy, 2, 6, 23, 27, 27-34, 39, 54-58, 120, 293; and sex-gender system, 43, 44-46; and social patriarchy, 41-46, 176; as support-service structure, 10, 84, 125, 164-165, 237-238, 289, 293, 315-316; transition to social patriarchy, 3-4, 7-11, 100-104, 106, 289, 300, 302

Family: with dependent children, 196; economic responsibilities of, 145; impact of industrialization on, 61-67; income, 128, 183, 189, 197, 231, 237; nuclear, 235, 238, 283; poverty of, 132, 212-213; as productive unit, 30-34; pro-family ideology, 261; social security for, 205; and social wage, 40, 281; state intervention in, 107-111; subsidization of incomes, 143-145, 226; under social patriarchy, 42-47; under wage-labour system, 10, 34-39, 62. *See also* Patriarchal family

Family allowance, 162, 190, 206, 218, 223, 295, 313-314; as economic management, 222-223; *Family Allowance Act,* 190-198, 217, 221

Family law, 8, 10, 11, 83, 100, 119; and family income allocation, 127, 143-145; integration with welfare law, 163-164; reform of, 101-106, 123, 173, 293-295

Fathers, 294; and child custody, 104-105; and paternity suits, 153-154; putative, 163-164, 257

Federation of Business and Professional Women, 241

Female labour force, 10, 37, 62, 70-71, 75-77, 87-88, 246; legislation for, 89, 89-91; in post-World War II economy, 204, 235-237; and telephone operators strike, 79-80; during World War II, 176, 202-204. See also Women's labour; Workers, female

Feminism: and equal rights, 81-82; Marxist, 17-18; maternal, 80; radical, 17-18; second wave of, 283-286; and state intervention, 298-304. *See also* Women's movement

Feudalism, 32-33, 34

Finch, J., 57

First World War, 168; economy of, 128, 180; post-war social assistance, 146-151, 165-166

Foster homes, 155

Foster, John, 35

French Canada, 71. *See also* Quebec

G

Gender, 21, 22; equality of, 292-293; stratification of labour, 239-242

Gough, Ian, 56

Government: employees of, 221, 243, 246, 249-251; and Social Reform Movement, 74; and welfare expenditures, 121-122, 169-172, 225-226

Great Depression, 19, 130-132, 141, 165, 209, 213-214; impact of on welfare state, 167-168

Green Book Proposals, 213, 214-216, 266, 276

Grove, D., 57

171-172, 258, 273; welfare law in, 255-263
Ontario Department of Labour, 141
Ontario Department of Public Welfare, 150, 161, 265, 273
Ontario Workmen's Compensation Board, 140
Organization for Economic Co-operation and Development, 44
Orphans and orphanages, 65-67, 118, 155

P

Parents: and child custody, 104, 114, 115; *Child of Unmarried Parents Act*, 153, 164, 256, 257; economic responsibilities of, 149; parental responsibilities of, 118, 119, 154; *Parents Maintenance Act*, 143, 256
Patriarchal authority, 45; decline of, 99-100, 101-106; and employment of women, 87; over household production, 30-31, 33, 34-35, 39
Patriarchal family, 100, 293, 295; and Social Reform Movement, 69-82. *See also* Familial patriarchy
Patriarchy, 5-7, 23, 28; and control of material reproduction, 17-18, 40; and control of women's reproductive work, 25, 102, 105, 124; feminist criticism of, 2-3, 283-286; ideology of, 75-77, 81; in class society, 53-54; and the state, 3-4; transformation of, 99-101, 122, 142; under wage-labour system, 6-7, 34-39. *See also* Communal patriarchy; Familial patriarchy; Social patriarchy

Pay equity. *See* Equal pay
Pedley, C.S., 119
Pensions. *See* Older adults
Pentland, H. Clare, 85, 128
Pierson, Ruth Roach, 202
Political economy: of reproduction, 47-54; of social patriarchy, 41
Population, 31-33, 61, 296
Procreation, 5, 65, 70, 289, 291; under capitalism, 35-39; under familial patriarchy, 29-31; under social patriarchy, 43. *See also* Birth control; Birth rates; Reproduction; Women's reproductive role
Production: erosion of, 51-52; global organization of, 230, 290, 303; and labour shortages, 48; socialization of, 40. *See also* Reproduction and production patterns
Property, laws of, 28, 31, 100; curtsey, 102; dower rights, 102, 103-104; in Feudal England, 32-33; for married women, 101-104, 105; Torrens System, 103, 312-313, 366n3
Prostitution, 71, 96

Q

Quebec, 62, 216; health insurance in, 275-278; and old age assistance, 175, 268; Quebec Pension Plan, 274-275

R

Race suicide, 36, 71, 76, 110, 114, 297
Racism, 114
Refuge homes: women and children in, 66, 155-156

Reproduction: and class formation, 25-27; definition of, 5; dual systems theory of, 17-20, 306; global division of, 290, 303-304; impact of industrialization on, 61-67; Marxian model of, 22, 53; political economy of, 47-54; privatization of, 105, 120, 163, 294; reconceptualization of, 20-23; reprivatization of, 295-297; restructuring of, 234-238; and Social Reform Movement, 67-75; socialization of, 11, 40, 49, 144, 163, 176, 206, 230, 253, 263, 267-278, 279-286; structural theories of, 17. *See also* Procreation; Women's reproductive role

Reproduction and production patterns, 19-20, 26-27; effects of capital and labour on, 48-54; under familial patriarchy, 29-34, 54-58; impact of Great Depression on, 130-132; impact of industrialization on, 61-67; impact of women's movement on, 298-304; and income allocation, 125-174, 281-282; and labour allocation, 83-106; Marxian model of, 22; mediation of, 197; in post-World War II era, 204, 229-252; realignment of, 282-286; and the welfare state, 169-172, 252-254; under wage-labour system, 35-39; during World War II, 175-227

Reproductive technology, 2, 299

Robertson, John, 73

Robertson, Norman, 191, 192

Royal Commission on Dominion-Provincial Relations (*Rowell-Sirois Report*), 210, 213, 219

Royal Commission on Labour and Capital, 89-90

Royal Commission on the Prison and Reformatory System, 108-109

Royal Commission on the Status of Women in Canada, 238, 283-286; *Report* of, 317

Royal Commission to Investigate the Increase in the Cost of Living in Canada, 124, 132

Rubin, Gayle, 20-21

Rural organizations, 73-74

S

Sangster, Joan, 79

Saskatchewan, 207, 250; health insurance in, 269, 271, 275-278

School: industrial, 109, 112-113, 150, 155-156; *Industrial School Act*, 111, 112-113, 114, 155; *School Attendance Act*, 154

Second World War 12; economic and labour policies during, 175-227; role of War Information Board, 207, 210; and wage controls during, 182-183, 185-187, 188-198

Sex-gender system, 20, 21, 22, 24-25, 25; and familial patriarchy, 43, 44-46

Sexual division of labour, 5, 11, 21, 22, 123, 157, 164, 236, 247, 289; legislation of, 87-88, 99-100

Shops Act, 87, 92, 97; in Ontario and Manitoba, 91-92

Smith, Goldwin, 73

Social patriarchy, 2-3, 6, 23, 27, 28, 32, 39-47, 61, 106, 176-177; business and labour relations of, 75-80; and Children's Aid Societies, 120; emergence of, 100; and income allocation, 142-174; and social reform movement, 69-75

market, 239-242; during World
War II, 182, 184-187. *See also*
Labour law; Labour, organized
United Grain Growers, 68, 73
Universal suffrage, 126, 128-129
Urbanization, 64-65, 121, 126

V

Veterans, 166, 269; Veterans Rental Housing, 222; *War Veterans'*
Allowance Act, 268

W

Wage-labour system, 12, 39-40,
42, 62, 122, 127, 169, 172, 172-
173, 196, 212; and anti-
natalism, 47, 51, 53; emergence
of, 34-39; and patriarchy, 6-7;
and pro-natalism, 22, 43, 77;
reform of, 84, 85-88; and
reproduction, 62-67, 198, 234-
235, 289
Wages, 9, 137, 208, 211-212, 297;
control of during World War II,
182-183, 185-187, 188-198; differentials in, 240, 241; and *Fami-*
ly Allowance Act, 190-198;
minimum wage, 138-140; *Mini-*
mum Wages Act, 137, 138, 141,
245; and price disparity, 132-
135; *Wages Act*, 86. *See also*
Equal pay; Workers, female
War economy. *See* First World
War; Second World War
Welfare bureaucracy: growth of,
116-120, 123-124, 160-165, 173,
221, 249; and the *National*
Health and Welfare Act, 217-221.
See also Child welfare law; Welfare law
Welfare law, 8, 11, 83, 100, 143,
151-154, 160; administrators of,

160-165; integration with family law, 163-164; post-World
War I statutes, 165; and provincial jurisdiction, 254-264; and
state authority over children,
107-111; during World War II,
216-223. *See also* Child welfare
law; Family allowance; Health
insurance; Housing; Mothers'
Allowance; Unemployment insurance
Welfare state, 40, 48; business support of, 131-132; Canada Assistance Plan, 272-273; and
capital, 49, 51; and child welfare, 106-111, 147-151; dismantling of, 1-3, 299-304; economic
and demographic problems of,
51; emergence of modern welfare state, 11, 176, 209; expenditures of, 55-57, 120-122,
169-172, 223-226, 231, 279-282;
and familial responsibilities, 42-
44; and *Family Allowance Act*,
190-198; federal-provincial
programming and cost sharing
of, 266-278; growth of federal
involvement in, 165-171, 179,
216-223, 224; and income allocation, 142, 169-172, 223-226;
during post-World War II era,
204, 252-266; reorganization of
programs in, 146-159; and social insurance security
programs, 135-136, 209-215.
See also Manitoba; Ontario; Social wage
Whitton, Charlotte, 148-149, 210
Wife abuse, 2, 301
Womanhood, 93; patriarchal
model of, 91
Women, destitute, 66, 113, 158
Women's Bureau of Ontario, 247

JANE URSEL was born and raised in Winnipeg where she now lives with her son. She studied Sociology at the University of Manitoba and McMaster University, and she is now teaching sociology at the University of Manitoba. She spent five years working for the Provincial Government in Manitoba where she worked on women's policy issues as the first Provincial Coordinator of Wife Abuse programs and later as an analyst in the Planning and priorities Committee of Cabinet and then in the Women's Directorate. Jane is now working on a two-year study of the first specialized Family Violence Court in North America. The specialized criminal court was begun in Winnipeg in September of 1990. It hears all cases of wife abuse, child abuse and elder abuse that proceed to court in Winnipeg.